SHAKESPEARE: THE TRAGEDIES

PATTERNS OF LITERARY CRITICISM

General Editors

MARSHALL McLUHAN
R. J. SCHOECK
ERNEST SIRLUCK

SHAKESPEARE: THE TRAGEDIES
A Collection of Critical Essays

Edited and with an Introduction by
CLIFFORD LEECH

The University of Chicago Press
Chicago & London

Library of Congress Catalog Card Number: 65-17295

THE UNIVERSITY OF CHICAGO PRESS, CHICAGO & LONDON
The University of Toronto Press, Toronto 5, Canada

CONTENTS

INTRODUCTION

The aim of this volume is to represent critical opinion on
Shakespeare's tragedies, with special reference to the writings
of recent years. Consequently, few essays are included written
earlier than Bradley's *Shakespearean Tragedy:* thereafter the
attempt has been to illustrate the remarkable variety of approach and manner which any student of the subject becomes
quickly aware of. Moreover, in addition to including discus-
sions of general topics—the special nature of Shakespeare's
tragic writing, the characteristic employment of imagery in his
tragedies—something of the wide diversity of opinion on, for
example, *Hamlet* and *Antony and Cleopatra* had to be represented. Little space was thus available for those plays commonly seen as below the rank of "major." Nevertheless, it is no
longer possible—as once it was—to discuss "Shakespearian tragedy" with exclusive reference to four or five or perhaps six
plays: the twentieth-century theater itself will rightly insist on
reminding us of *Timon* and *Titus.* In the result I hope that
reasonable justice has been done, and, except in the case of
Julius Caesar, I am fairly confident of this.[1]

During the past quarter of a century there has been a modest
but substantial market for books on Shakespeare's tragedies,
with the result that critical writing on this subject has, at least
in its final shape, more frequently appeared in volume form
than as articles in periodicals. Because the present collection
aims at being not only representatives of such writing but indicative of its most influential and authoritative trends, it has
been necessary to draw on material from books to a greater extent than will probably be the case with other volumes of the
"Gemini Books: Patterns of Literary Criticism" series. In most
instances the extracts given are self-contained, but there are a
few obvious instances of reference backward and forward:

[1] For the purposes of this volume, *Troilus and Cressida* is not regarded as a
tragedy, despite the original plan to include it in the tragedies section of the
1623 Folio and despite Dryden's unquestioning assumption that it belonged
there. See the Preface to his alteration (below, pp. 1–9).

I do not think that any troubling obscurity results from this. It is appropriate at this point to express gratitude to the authors and publishers concerned, without whose ready cooperation this volume could not have appeared. The first critic to write at some length on Shakespeare's tragedies was Dryden. The earliest critical comment was, of course, made much earlier—by Francis Meres in his *Palladis Tamia* of 1598, where Shakespeare was compared to Plautus in comedy and to Seneca in tragedy. And in his verses for the 1623 Folio, Ben Jonson similarly invoked the ancients in his search for a fit comparison. He would not, he said, be content with declaring how Shakespeare had outshone Lyly and Kyd and Marlowe, but would

> *call forth thund'ring* Æschilus,
> Euripides, *and* Sophocles *to vs,*
> Paccuuius, Accius, *him of* Cordoua *dead,*
> *To life againe, to heare thy Buskin tread,*
> *And shake a Stage: Or, when thy Sockes were on,*
> *Leaue thee alone, for the comparison*
> *Of all, that insolent* Greece, *or haughtie* Rome
> *sent forth, or since did from their ashes come.*

The terms of the comparison have been lasting: in the Preface to his version of Shakespeare's *Troilus and Cressida* (1679), Dryden begins by comparing Athenian veneration for Aeschylus with English veneration for Shakespeare.[2] But to assert Shakespeare's greatness was evaluation without criticism, and even Jonson's remarks in *Discoveries* (published 1641) are in general terms, drawing attention to an occasional extravagance in language but presenting no extended comment on an individual play or group of plays. Dryden in the *Essay of Dramatic Poesy* (1668) discussed Shakespeare at some length, along with Jonson and Fletcher, but it was Jonson's *Epicoene* that he chose as the subject of a detailed "examen." Nowhere does he give a similar treatment to a Shakespeare play, but his most sustained comment on Shakespearian tragic writing is in the *Troilus and Cressida* Preface.

It must be remembered that this Preface was written in peculiar circumstances. Shakespeare's play had attracted Dry-

---

[2] See p. 1.

den sufficiently for him to undertake its alteration, but he was manifestly puzzled by the conduct of the action, even where that action was in close agreement with the traditional story of Troilus, and embarrassed by the complexity and the harshness that are characteristic of the play's language. And his embarrassment was increased through the publication in 1678 of the first of Thomas Rymer's two critical volumes—*The Tragedies of the Last Age Considered and Examined by the Practice of the Ancients, and by the Common Sense of All Ages.* Here Rymer had begun by indicating that he was intent on exposing the weaknesses of Shakespeare and Fletcher, but his attention to certain Fletcher plays became so space-consuming that he postponed his full treatment of Shakespeare to a later volume. Rymer was learned, and had a keen eye for a superficial incongruity: the comments he made on Fletcher are commonly enough repeated today; on Shakespeare he could impress his contemporaries, including Dryden. In the *Troilus and Cressida* Preface the criticism of Shakespeare's and Fletcher's plotting is regarded as fully established;[3] Rymer is given the exclusive title "our English critic"; the Unities are accepted as unassailable, though Dryden often enough elsewhere viewed them lightly; and Dryden seems to follow Rymer's lead in laying stress on Shakespeare's extravagance of language. Not that this charge was new with Rymer: we have noted Jonson's reference to the matter in *Discoveries*, and one of the regular features of Restoration versions of Shakespeare's plays is their reduction of his figures in both number and range. Dryden chooses the Pyrrhus speech in *Hamlet* (believing, he says, that it came from another hand than Shakespeare's) as an apparently easy target for abuse, but shows how the poet can use figures in a restrained and open-textured way in the speech in *Richard II* where York describes the King's return to London.[4]

To indicate that Dryden is in conformity with his time here, and that Rymer differs only in degree of reprobation and in virulence of manner, we may look at some famous lines from *Macbeth* and see how they were treated by his admiring adapter and godson Davenant.[5] Here is Shakespeare:

---

[3] See p. 2.   [4] See pp. 6–7.
[5] The adaptation was first published in 1674, Davenant having died in 1668.

> Be innocent of the knowledge, dearest chuck,
> Till thou applaud the deed. Come, seeling night,
> Scarf up the tender eye of pitiful day,
> And with thy bloody and invisible hand
> Cancel and tear to pieces that great bond
> Which keeps me pale. Light thickens, and the crow
> Makes wing to th' rooky wood;
> Good things of day begin to droop and drowse,
> Whiles night's black agents to their preys do rouse.
>
> (III. ii. 45–52)

For the Restoration, "chuck" was too familiar; "seeling" and "Scarf" introduced a distracting image from falconry; "pitiful" complicated the picture by giving the day compassion in addition to sight; line 48 was metrically over-free; the canceling and tearing of the "great bond" introduced an idea not readily apprehensible in the Restoration playhouse; the thickening of light, suggestive of obstruction, of ominous pregnancy, was an impossibly violent image; a wood was unnecessarily "rooky" when the crow was on its way there; "droop" and "drowse," like "chuck" in the beginning, were words too everyday in their associations. So Davenant has it:

> Be innocent of knowing it, my dear,
> Till thou applaud the deed. Come, dismal night,
> Close up the eye of the quick-sighted day
> With thy invisible and bloody hand.
> The crow makes wing to the thick shady grove.
> Good things of day grow dark and overcast,
> Whilst night's black agents to their preys make haste.[6]

Thus we can understand Dryden's talking of Shakespeare's "bombast," and admire the independence with which he could praise without reserve the "passionate descriptions" which he found indeed more frequent than the passages irksome to a refined age.

Not only on Shakespeare but on Fletcher, too, was Dryden ready to disagree with Rymer. Dryden believed that Rymer had shown *A King and No King* to be defective in plot, but he declined to follow the "English critic" in his assertion that only the magic of the playhouse could give life to the text: if it was

---

[6] For the sake of comparison, I have modernized spelling and punctuation from the text given in Christopher Spencer's edition (*Davenant's Macbeth from the Yale Manuscript* [1961]).

moving when read—and Dryden found it was—then "the excellency of the action" (i.e., of the acting) could not be solely responsible for its popularity (its "taking").[7] And, though Dryden puts Fletcher firmly in a lower rank of excellence, he is not to be dissuaded from seeing him as a major writer for the English theater.

It was not, however, only Rymer who exercised an influence on Dryden in the writing of this Preface. He refers more than once to Rapin, whose *Réflexions sur la Poétique d'Aristote et sur les ouvrages des poëtes anciens et modernes* had appeared in 1674, and to Bossu for his *Du Poëme epique* of 1675. These French writers provided a fresh distillation from Aristotle, and Dryden's insistence on the need to fuse action with "manners" in the composition of a play (so that the event was always congruent with, if not consequent on, the dispositions of those taking part) is essentially Aristotelian in its suggestion of organic form.[8] But he is Neo-classic in his demand for a "moral" as the dominant structural principle in a tragedy or epic, and the examples he gives—from *The Iliad*, *Oedipus* and *The Conquest of Granada*—are not such as to inspire confidence in his ability to apply the notion to Shakespeare.[9] Pope and Johnson were to run into this same difficulty, and we shall meet it also in twentieth-century Shakespeare criticism. This apart, Dryden's picture of Shakespearian tragedy is judicious but over-generalized: the plotting may be defective, but it is well-linked to the "manners" depicted; the language may be extravagant, but not always; the thoughts expressed are to be admired. Shakespeare stands well above Fletcher, and apparently may dispute with Jonson for the English primacy. We are not given a hint of any peculiarity in Shakespeare's writing that may distinguish him, not in quality but in kind, from Aeschylus or Sophocles.

Rymer returned to the attack on Shakespeare in his *A Short View of Tragedy* (1693). By far the largest part of this book is given to the discussion of *Othello*, which is too long for complete quotation here and needs reading in full for its proper effect to be produced. But Rymer's position in the history of Shakespeare criticism must be recognized, and his brief account of *Julius Caesar* is therefore included. He anticipates Samuel Johnson in declaring that "Shakespeares genius lay for Comedy

---

[7] See pp. 2-3.   [8] See p. 4.   [9] See pp. 3-4.

and Humour,"[10] and castigates the vulgarity of his language in tragedy. He has a rigid notion of "decorum," finding it absurd that Brutus should speak nobly at one moment and luridly at another, or indeed that Romans should ever be shown as forgetting their dignity. He objects to the introduction of things of common life (a taper, a musical instrument in danger of breaking as the player falls asleep). He manifestly has no love for the theater, asserting that *Julius Caesar* might hold an audience through spectacle and noise[11] and failing to see the special tension given to the scene in Act II where Decius, Casca, and Cinna discuss the whereabouts of the east while Brutus and Cassius whisper together[12]—an effect indeed comparable in its complexity to that noted by Coleridge in the scene where Hamlet waits for the ghost.[13] Rymer's discussion of *Othello* drew attention to matters, such as the dramatist's handling of time, which have exercised critics of later years, and his attack on that play's morality has issued a challenge which has always to be taken up. On *Julius Caesar* he is hardly so rewarding, but the passage here chosen represents his critical manner and some of his basic assumptions.

There is a long gap between our first two selections and William Richardson's essay on *Hamlet,* and in that time important changes had taken place. We can say that in the Restoration Shakespeare still belonged primarily to the playhouse: editions before 1700, including the two Restoration folios, were not the fruits of scholarship, and Rymer's attacks on Fletcher and Shakespeare were directed at popular dramatists writing in a non-classic fashion which had scarcely as yet been formally defended. The situation changed through the long series of eighteenth-century collected editions, beginning with Rowe's in 1709 (2d ed. 1714) and quickly continuing with Pope's in 1725 and Theobald's in 1733. Men of learning, men with personal experience of writing poetry and plays, acquired a detailed knowledge of the text that went beyond even Dryden's. Through the prefaces to these editions, and perhaps more importantly through the notes on particular passages, the reading public came to have their minds directed to details they

[10] See p. 14. For Johnson's view, see the Preface to his edition of Shakespeare (1765) (*Johnson on Shakespeare*, ed. Walter Raleigh [1925], pp. 18–19).

[11] See p. 14.   [12] See pp. 12–13.   [13] See p. 30.

would certainly miss in the playhouse. Not that the theater paid the less attention to Shakespeare: although it continued to use altered versions for *Lear* and *Richard III*, and for some appreciable time for *Macbeth*, approximately one play out of every six acted in London in the eighteenth century was by Shakespeare.[14] Moreover, it was the tragedies that held first place in the actors' hearts. Of the twelve most frequently acted Shakespeare plays in the eighteenth century, the first six were tragedies (if we include *Richard III* in that group for the moment), the second six were comedies (if we include *1 Henry IV*). This provides its own comment on the assertion, shared by Rymer and Johnson, that Shakespeare was by nature a comic writer.

Meanwhile, with the coming of new trends in the writing of poetry and prose and drama, the critics grew ready to challenge received doctrine and to doubt whether a playwright's duty was to conform, as Dryden in the *Troilus and Cressida* Preface assumed, to an already established pattern of writing—departing from it only in so far as historical change in society compelled.[15] Addison in the *Spectator* rejected the notion of "poetical justice," as Rymer had called it in his attack on *Othello*, and argued that an exact proportioning of reward to desert had neither classical warrant nor truth to nature;[16] and on another occasion he discussed Shakespeare's use of purely imaginary characters—fairies, ghosts, witches—and urged that here we can make no reference to nature (for such beings are not part of our direct experience), but that Shakespeare's treatment of them convinces us that, if they did exist, they would act and speak as he has made them.[17] The appeal to nature was never abandoned in the eighteenth century, as indeed it never can be, but we see here the beginning of a realization that, in a piece of writing that explores remoter levels of experience, the nature that is appealed to includes the reader's intuition.

It was, however, in the later part of the eighteenth century

[14] Charles Beecher Hogan, *Shakespeare in the Theatre 1701–1800* (1952–57), II, 715.

[15] See p. 2.

[16] *Spectator*, No. 40, April 16, 1711.

[17] *Ibid.*, No. 419, July 1, 1712.

that what is called "character-criticism" came to establish itself firmly. We have come to associate this particularly with the nineteenth century, and in comparatively recent years it has fallen into some disrepute. The critic who approaches Shakespeare in this way applies the test of "nature" to an individual dramatic character and, if he has convinced himself that the figure is recognizable as a human being, considers how its actions are related to motive and to ideals of moral conduct. The common objection to this procedure is twofold: (1) this is to concern oneself with only one of a play's elements, which include plot structure and poetry and character-grouping and visual impact and the like; (2) it is to confuse dramatic characters with real people. We should, however, note that the best of the "character-critics," from Coleridge to Bradley, are by no means blind to other elements in the plays they examine: Hazlitt's *The Characters of Shakespeare's Plays* (1817) is, for example, unfortunately named.

Moreover, it is necessary to make a distinction between different types of dramatic character. The unnamed murderers and soldiers serve only as general voices in a play's composition, as unpersonalized as a Nuntius or Chorus. And there are many other figures which are given only that degree of "life" that is required for their function in the play: they cannot be imagined as existing outside the scenes in which they occur. We are never led to speculate about the private life of Osric. But there are characters whose whole lifetime is sketched for us, either directly or through reference and narration, and it is a special (though not exclusive) feature of Shakespearian tragedy that we are frequently impelled to imagine the sketch worked up into a total portrait. It is not unreasonable that we should consider Hamlet, outside the frame of the play, as a student at Wittenberg, as Ophelia's not yet too difficult suitor, as a son in his father's living presence. And we may even quite legitimately speculate on an unfulfilled condition: would he, we almost inevitably ask, have proved "most royal" if he had come to the throne in peaceful succession? The sense of a character of this sort and in this degree is not an invariable feature of a Shakespearian tragedy. We feel in this fashion in relation to Hamlet and Othello, but only to a much smaller extent in relation to Lear and Macbeth. We feel it in some measure in relation to non-central figures: to Desdemona, for example, but hardly at all to Cordelia. In the comedies such a response is much rarer, though it was appropriate that one of the earliest extended treatments of a Shakespeare character was Maurice Morgann's *Essay on the Dramatic Character of Sir John Falstaff* (written 1774, published 1777). Rosalind is a major figure in her play, but she does not exist outside it. Her words and actions convince us, within the hypothesis of an unlikely fable, that they belong to "nature"—in the sense that, for Addison, Shakespeare's fairies did—but it is only for the duration of a performance that we can accept her as a total human being. Character-criticism is a limited mode of inquiry into Shakespeare, and, like other approaches, it has had its gross excesses and absurdities. But to reject it is to run counter to an important part of every man's experience of some, at least, of the plays.[18] Even when a character does not give us that effect of total existence that Hamlet or Othello does, we need to recognize that the mode and the pattern of characterization in a play are important elements in its composition, important indications of the dramatic type the play belongs to.

Although there were earlier indications,[19] it is in Johnson's edition (1765) that we can recognize character-criticism as coming plainly into existence: in particular, the comment on Falstaff in the final note to *Henry IV* is a brief panegyric on, and a brief condemnation of, a real person. And along with Morgann we have William Richardson as the man who shows us the method in full development. Richardson's *A Philosophical Analysis and Illustration of Some of Shakespeare's Remarkable Characters* appeared in 1774, the year when Morgann's essay was written. The present volume includes his second and briefer essay on Hamlet, where he anticipates the "sensitive prince" interpretation of Goethe in *Wilhelm Meister* (1796) and the effect of moral shock that Bradley stressed in 1904. Richardson was Professor of Humanity at Glasgow, and was concerned to produce a moral defense of Hamlet's conduct. He freely admitted the character's irresolution, violence, unseasonable jocularity, employment of subterfuge, and occasional expression of inhuman sentiments. But, appealing to experience in the theater, he drew attention to the paradoxical

[18] See William Frost's comment, p. 193.

[19] See *Coleridge's Shakespearean Criticism*, ed. T. M. Raysor (1930), I, xxi, n. 2.

fact that an audience's attitude to Hamlet is one of esteem. The ghost's revelation, along with his mother's remarriage, had understandably induced a condition in which self-control was impaired. His words in the prayer scene were a convenient excuse to himself for a failure to act which, no longer explicable as uncertainty about the ghost, arises from "virtuous, or at least . . . amiable sensibility." The assumption of madness was a safety-measure, to disguise a real lack of control by a culti-vated extravagance. His jocularity was partly for concealment, partly the result of a wish to convince himself that he was unconcerned by the situation in which he was living. Certainly in this criticism we have "psychologizing," and there is not much of it that we need quarrel with. When, however, we turn to Coleridge on the same subject, we see how much fur-ther and deeper the criticism of both hero and play can go.

Coleridge's Shakespeare criticism consists mainly of margi-nalia that he wrote in copies of the plays, of brief notes for lec-tures he was to deliver, and of reports of those lectures made by other hands. The selection included in this volume gives nearly all of his marginalia on *Hamlet* together with some notes for a lecture on the play.[20] Although some prominence is given to Coleridge's share in character-criticism, the marginalia suffi-ciently indicate that his approach to the play was wide-ranging. He has a good deal to say on the language of *Hamlet*—noting how Shakespeare, in the cock passage in Act I, scene i, teaches young poets "*how* to elevate a thing almost mean by its famil-iarity";[21] observing with rare acuteness the variety of impulses and occasions that may lead to punning;[22] insisting that often a passage in Shakespeare cannot be properly interpreted with-out reference to the character and to the character's mood and situation;[23] and seeing Shakespeare's need to use a different kind of language in *The Murder of Gonzago* from that used in the play proper,[24] and his occasional securing of a special effect through the adumbration, rather than full expression, of meaning.[25] Coleridge can praise the passage where Horatio

[20] A newspaper report of this lecture is printed by Raysor, II, 272–75.

[21] See p. 28.   [22] See pp. 28–29.   [23] See pp. 31–32.

[24] See p. 42. De Quincey similarly drew attention to this distinction in "Theory of Greek Tragedy" (1840) (*Works*, ed. David Masson [1896–97], X, 344–45).

[25] See p. 32.

tells Hamlet of the ghost as being "the purest poetry and yet the most natural language, equally distant from the inkhorn and the provincial plough,"[26] here reminding us of Dryden's praise of the speech he quoted from *Richard II;* and at the same time he can see the Pyrrhus speech as a "superb" example of the epic style used appropriately in drama.[27]

Indeed, Coleridge recognizes the mingled character of Shakespeare's dramatic writing, some parts of the play being fully dramatic in the sense of directly concerned with the presentation of character in action, and others being predominantly in the epic or lyric mode.[28] Noting Hamlet's dialogue with the players, he admires "Shakespeare's power of diversifying the scene while he is carrying on the plot,"[29] and he speaks with eloquence of the mingling of the everyday with the strange in the play's opening scene.[30] He insists that we are not meant to see Claudius through Hamlet's eyes, and he shows both a respect for the usurper as a man and a sense of his importance in the play as Hamlet's adversary.[31] He can contrast Hamlet's spontaneous mental activity with the gravediggers' jesting, which shows "the traditional wit valued like truth for its antiquity, and treasured up, like a tune, for use."[32] He notices the ghost's gradual "accrescence of objectivity" through repeated appearance,[33] and the careful balancing of effect in the handling of Laertes, so that his imperfections are made clear while we are allowed to accept as just the praise which Hamlet gives him.[34] Less happy are his two attempts to make an irregular line come closer to the metrical norm, where he seems for a moment to follow Pope's practices with the text.[35]

But Coleridge's account of *Hamlet* is best remembered, of course, for what he has to say about the hero's character. He admitted in his *Table Talk* that he found in himself "a smack of Hamlet,"[36] and certainly the portrait is of a kind that Coleridge should recognize. It is not merely that he sees a man given to "brooding over the world within him" and with an

[26] See p. 41.

[27] See p. 32.

[28] See p. 29, and also p. 34.

[29] See p. 34.

[30] See pp. 26–27.

[31] See pp. 28, 38.

[32] See p. 39.

[33] See p. 30.

[34] See pp. 38, 39.

[35] See pp. 29, 33.

[36] Raysor, II, 352.

"aversion to externals": he sees him, too, as a poet whose "prodigality of beautiful words" represents "the half embodyings of thoughts," whose utterances combine a degree of expression ("an outness") with a "correspondence and shadowy approach to the images and movements within":[37] the embodyings are only "half" such, the approach to what is within is "shadowy." It is the poet of *Kubla Khan* who thus finds himself in Elsinore; and when in the nunnery scene Coleridge discerns "a wild upworking of love, sporting with opposites with a wilful self-tormenting irony,"[38] we may be reminded of the speculation, in the "conclusion" to Part II of *Christabel*, on the "words of unmeant bitterness" that a father may speak to a loved child: one of the causes suggested for the phenomenon is the pleasure we may experience from the "sweet recoil of love and pity" that comes with the utterance of "each wild word." Yet, if we cannot agree that Hamlet is to be explained as an inhibited intellectual, he is certainly the most thoughtful of Shakespeare's heroes; if he is not a poet tormented by the impossibility of fully achieving either expression or truth to an inner vision, he is a man both voluble and often unable to achieve communion. Coleridge makes him out to be more unsociable than he is, and says little of his violence of word and deed. The portrait is none the less illuminating, and it goes much deeper than any previous comment.

In particular, Coleridge's awareness of different levels of consciousness in the character is finely used—not only in the nunnery scene already referred to, but in the scene in which Hamlet meets the ghost, where the talk arising from the wassail music allows him to gather his strength for the encounter and where the continuing dependence on a marginal consciousness of his friends' presence and companionship can help to explain his courage and his ready eloquence.[39] Coleridge follows Richardson in his account of the prayer scene,[40] and some more recent comments on this (illustrated in Raysor's footnote) disregard the fact that to equate Hamlet with Greene's Cutwolf is surely to brutalize him beyond easy reconcilement with his general presentation in the play: that he could dally with the thought of securing Claudius's damnation, and thus

[37] See p. 41.
[38] See p. 34.
[39] See p. 30.
[40] See p. 36.

have "reason" for turning away, is similar to the common exercise of the fancy in which we may imagine the deaths of those who have affronted us.[41] Hamlet's jesting and wildness Coleridge sees as partly a reaction after a period of high tension, the ludicrous being complementarily associated with the terrible, but partly too he sees the wildness as only "half-false" and exclaims that a manifest assumption of a certain kind of behavior can be caused by our being almost compelled to that behavior:[42] here Coleridge is close to Richardson again, but with a surer understanding. Moreover, he preserves the distinction in Hamlet's conduct between the voluntary and the compelled, a distinction always fine in tragedy but particularly relevant to our experience of this play.

The patriotic winding-up for the *Hamlet* lecture[43] may startle us (as may Coleridge's laborious finding of a moral in the play[44]), but what he has written here exhibits a finely sensitive response to the tragedy as a whole. What is totally missing is any proper recognition of performance: the "pit and gallery would be malcontent" if an "actor were capable of catching" the shades of characterization in Polonius,[45] and "the managers" appear to see Claudius in the simple terms of Hamlet's view of him.[46] It was to be a long time before Shakespeare criticism was to become again what it was with Dryden, a compound of the fruits of reading and seeing the plays.

The wealth of writing on the tragedies in the later nineteenth century, both in England and in Germany, cannot be represented here, but—apart from Hazlitt's book already mentioned —there must be reference to Dowden's *Shakspere: A Critical Study of His Mind and Art* (1875) and to R. G. Moulton's *Shakespeare as a Dramatic Artist* (1885). Dowden is today most remembered for his use of the plays to construct a spiritual biography of the playwright, yet his book is without much doubt the most considerable attempt in English (and before Bradley) to interpret and assess Shakespeare's achievement. To him we owe the long-surviving division of the plays into four

---

[41] Cf. a detailed example in Malcolm Lowry's *Ultramarine* (1963), pp. 145–50.

[42] See p. 42.

[43] See p. 42.

[44] See p. 40.

[45] See p. 30.

[46] See p. 38.

"periods," and his sentimentality in this and other matters does not blind him to Shakespeare's craftsmanship in the tragedies and elsewhere. Moulton aimed at establishing criticism as an "inductive" science, whose operative laws are to be traced in the objects under consideration—i.e., the plays. Though he lacked sharpness and economy of expression, Moulton often showed a subtler sense of dramatic pattern than can be found among his contemporary critics, and his analysis of *Lear* is in this respect among the best things in his book. But of course Dowden and Moulton could have written as they did without ever seeing a play or imagining a performance.

So, for that matter, could Bradley. In the comparatively short extract here printed he refers twice to reading Shakespeare, as if there were no other way of encountering him.[47] *Shakespearean Tragedy* is rightly seen as the summation of nineteenth-century Shakespeare criticism: it is a book on the grand scale, not only for the sharpness of its insight into character and motive, but for the sense of the plays' magnitude that continuously yet unobtrusively informs it. Meres and Jonson and Dryden, we have seen, compared Shakespeare with major dramatists of antiquity: Bradley's assumption is that we have here a body of work comparable in quality with Greek tragedy and not totally dissimilar in implication. Among the many quarrels with Bradley that later critics have enjoyed is a disputing of the terms of this relationship. It has seemed useful, therefore, to represent Bradley in this volume by the passage at the end of Lecture I where he discusses the universe which he believes the tragedies imply. He recognizes how difficult it is for us to see this without some tainting from convention or from personal predilection:[48] we want Shakespeare's world to be the world as we have ourselves come to see it. Moreover, he points out that the world of tragedy is restricted to the compass of non-theological observation, and that a tragic writer may, outside the composition of his tragedies, supplement with "additional ideas" the experience there embodied.[49]

With those caveats put before us, he argues against both the notion that Shakespeare's tragic world is controlled by a moral order and the notion that it is controlled by a cruel or blind

---

[47] See pp. 44, 48.   [48] See pp. 43–44.   [49] See p. 44.

fate.[50] Rather, it is a world where we find a justice which is harsh and by no means "poetic,"[51] where the action is partly of human contriving,[52] where there is no sense of a doom-on-the-house.[53] Yet the evil in man that precipitates disaster is itself part of the cosmic order: in destroying evil, that order is destroying part of itself and is thus, in advance, responsible for the evil. Bradley arrives at the idea that this mysterious order (and tragedy, he says, is the celebration of "a painful mystery"[54]) exhibits a passion for perfection in itself which leads to a destruction in no way corresponding to human desert.[55] In the presentation of such a universe the judging of particular men becomes irrelevant: when Macbeth or Richard III commits his crimes, we are moved and horrified, but we are in no way impelled to pass sentence or to deduce a lesson.[56]

It is a picture of things we might derive from Hardy's *The Dynasts:* perhaps it is too systematized, too elaborately conscious for the ten plays (or so) that we know as Shakespeare's tragedies. It does not sufficiently allow for the complications induced by Christian feelings and Stoic philosophy. It disregards what appears indubitable, that tragic figures live more fully through being tragic—a consideration that does not, however, permit us to condone the way things are, or to find that after all Dr. Pangloss was right. A world that denied man the tragic status would be a smaller world—a consideration that makes heaven shrink. In any event, Bradley's account of this matter shows clearly enough that *Shakespearean Tragedy* is not concerned merely with characterization or—as it sometimes is in the notes—with speculation about what the characters may be doing when they are not before our eyes.

Nevertheless, the book is severely limited, neglecting not only the theater but the poetry of the plays, and it has largely been the function of later twentieth-century critics to make good these defects. Running counter to a book to which such powerful prestige was attached, they have frequently exaggerated Bradley's failings and carried defiance as a banner. Thus L. C. Knights's *How Many Children Had Lady Macbeth?* (1933)

[50] See pp. 44–45.

[51] See p. 49.

[52] See p. 48.

[53] See p. 47.

[54] See p. 54.

[55] See pp. 53–54.

[56] See pp. 49–50.

not only burlesqued a Bradley-note in its title but insisted that a Shakespearian tragedy, in this particular instance *Macbeth*, should be read as a poem about light and darkness, good and evil, and not at all as a record of conflict and interaction between "characters." But the shift of emphasis had been seen earlier, in G. Wilson Knight's *The Wheel of Fire* (1930) and in the preliminary studies of Caroline Spurgeon that led to her formidable book *Shakespeare's Imagery and What It Tells Us* (1935). Miss Spurgeon was primarily concerned to achieve some insight into Shakespeare's mind from the clues unconsciously given by his frequent use of particular images. Her work was quickly followed by Wolfgang Clemen's *Shakespeares Bilder* (1936), where attention is directed to the part played by imagery in the economy of an individual play: this book appeared in English in a considerably revised and expanded form, as *The Development of Shakespeare's Imagery* (1951), from which one section is here reprinted. Edward A. Armstrong's *Shakespeare's Imagination* (1946), taking a hint from Caroline Spurgeon, concerned itself with the tracing of "image-clusters"—i.e., the recurrence in the plays as a whole of certain groups of images, at first sight without apparent relation to one another but resultant from the regular setting off of particular trains of association in Shakespeare's mind. These writers together—some of them important as critics, others concerned rather with an attempt to reach Shakespeare through his moments of self-betrayal—have exercised a dominant influence on current discussion of the tragedies, and it is now rare to find an extended study of a Shakespeare play which does not give substantial room to a consideration of its imagery. R. B. Heilman's books on *Lear* and *Othello—This Great Stage* (1948) and *Magic in the Web* (1956)—have exemplified the trend and enriched it.

Of all these critics Wilson Knight has been the most influential and the most prolific. As is apparent in the chapter from *The Imperial Theme* (1931) that is here reprinted, he makes use of what he calls the "spatial" method of interpretation, associating words and images that may be widely apart in a play without immediate or necessary reference to their different places in the temporal pattern. He has a sharp sense of a play's individuality and, for example, more than any other critic he has made modern readers aware of the special character of *Pericles* through his chapter on that play in *The Crown of Life* (1947). Yet for him the works of Shakespeare exist as a single *œuvre*, so that he has been able to speak of Shakespeare giving us his *Inferno* and *Purgatorio* in the tragedies and dark comedies and his *Paradiso* in the romances. In the essay here reprinted he presents *Macbeth* and *Antony and Cleopatra* as opposed and complementary plays, and finally brings them into a tripartite pattern with *Lear*.

Knight's views are never overcautious or compromising, so he can speak of "the optimism of all high tragedy,"[57] can declare the story of Antony's and Cleopatra's love to be one "which receives universal sanction,"[58] and can see Cleopatra's death simply and splendidly as "an added glory to life."[59] Certainly his view of tragedy is very different from Bradley's, though in the enlarged edition (1949) of *The Wheel of Fire* he declared that he first saw his aims as "the application to Shakespeare's work in general of the methods applied by Bradley to certain outstanding plays." For him, all tragedy implies, however discreetly, a happy ending: in *Macbeth* "the child of peace and life" is "struggling to be born"; in *Lear* there is "at long last, victory"; in *Antony and Cleopatra* "life conquers death." Nevertheless, Knight's view of the plays does not disregard difficulty. He sees that there is evil in Cleopatra,[60] and that in *Lear* "our vision is constricted to the earth."[61] The plays for him are about human life, but they scarcely employ human beings. Of *Antony and Cleopatra* he says: "We must, of course, never forget that the persons, ultimately, are not human at all, but purely symbols of a poetic vision."[62] Despite the "purely," there is much virtue in the "ultimately." Wilson Knight is a man with wide experience of acting and directing, and he knows that immediately, though not "ultimately," we see the action as involving particular people who engage our attention. So, though we may not always be convinced by his interpretations of specific plays, and may find his total presentation of Shakespeare too close to the Dowdenesque (as we may find Harold S. Wilson's shrewd and sensitive book, *On the Design of Shakespearian Tragedy* (1957), with its ingenious presentation of the tragedies under "The Order of Faith"

[57] See p. 70.   [59] See p. 79.   [61] See p. 81.

[58] See p. 79.   [60] See pp. 70, 78.   [62] See p. 78.

and "The Order of Nature" and "Synthesis"), we can understand that Knight's criticism should have exercised a generally wholesome influence in the contemporary theater. He can give to a director a sense of the special character of a particular play and of its relations with other parts of the canon.

But of course there were other critics who thought more immediately in terms of the theater. Most notably, Harley Granville-Barker—actor, director, dramatist, as well as critic—gave in his *Prefaces to Shakespeare* (1927–54) the theater-worker's view of a play's essence and the way it might be conveyed in action. His Prefaces to *Hamlet, Othello, Lear, Coriolanus,* and *Antony and Cleopatra* made his readers see them in terms of the contemporary stage and have become required reading for any director. The plays are presented in human rather than in cosmic terms, though Granville-Barker was familiar enough with the more purely professional kind of Shakespeare scholarship. Rarely has a man of the theater contributed so powerfully to the criticism of a major author. His theater, however, was the theater of the twentieth century. There were other writers at work who were anxious to remind us of the peculiarities of Shakespeare's own theater and to insist that our interpretations were likely to go astray if we did not keep always in view the special conventions that operated there.

Earliest among these was Levin L. Schücking, whose *Character Problems in Shakespeare's Plays* (1919, translated 1922) urged that we should recognize various principles or conventions as governing dramatic presentation in Shakespeare's time —among them "direct self-explanation" in soliloquies (which should prevent us from attributing cynicism to Iago or Richard III) and "episodic intensification" (as explanatory of Shakespeare's factual contradictions from scene to scene). In the section on *Lear* here reprinted, his case is that we are presented with a picture of mental disintegration and that we should not assume anything approaching the choric in Lear's new concern with the suffering of the poor and with the handy-dandy relation between judge and criminal. We may object that such sentiments of Lear do not stand alone in the play, that by providing a parallel in Gloucester's new vision Shakespeare has forced us to consider them *in vacuo.* And we may add that there comes a point where a sentiment rings too true for it to be explained away as a customary utterance of the Melancholy Man, which for Schücking has become Lear's status in this part of the play.[63] Nevertheless, Schücking's insistence that we must see Lear against the background provided by Hieronimo and Titus Andronicus and D'Amville is valid and important: we may still question whether in any of these instances we should rightly see the dramatist as the fully detached presenter. The insistence on the degree of grossness and violence to be found in Lear's conduct is, moreover, a healthy reminder of a sometimes willingly forgotten aspect of the play.

E. E. Stoll, too, thought in terms of the Elizabethan theater and its conventions, but he was preoccupied by drama of other periods as well as Shakespeare's, and his doctrines are those of a man fascinated by—and in many respects deeply aware of —theater-effects of all kinds. For him, every theater has its unexpressed conventions: for the Elizabethans the calumniator was always credited; the soliloquizing character (as in Schücking) described himself for the audience's benefit and without regard for the implications of such self-portrayal if it took place in real life; and for the sake of making the action plain there would be moments of clairvoyance which did not imply supernatural aid or peculiar gift.[64] Though Ibsen's plays may possess "depth and volume," Shakespeare's have rather "extension and expanse."[65] His tragedies do not develop out of character or from the working of fate: rather, they are dependent on a contrived intrigue.[66] The audience is to sympathize or to condemn, but not to analyze.[67]

In the extract printed here from J. I. M. Stewart's book, *Character and Motive in Shakespeare* (1949), Stoll's views are sharply dealt with: they would, suggests Stewart, reduce Shakespearian tragedy to a purely "sensational" form of theater, in which all that we are offered is a skilfully exciting show.[68] And it must be confessed that when Stoll declares Shakespeare's genius to be "tragic rather than comic"[69] we are bound to wonder what sense he attaches to "tragic." The

[63] See p. 64.
[64] See pp. 85–86.
[65] See p. 84.
[66] See p. 87.

[67] See p. 91.
[68] See p. 106.
[69] See p. 96.

term is rarely used in criticism without some reference to a view of the cosmic order, and yet Stoll's idea of the tragedies is merely that they expertly give us a wide-ranging display of possible human actions and emotions, fitted into a framework of playhouse conventions. For him it would be nonsense to describe *Othello* as "in some ways" Shakespeare's "most disquieting tragedy," is D. A. Traversi does,[70] or to take *Coriolanus* as a serious comment on the world of politics, as A. P. Rossiter does.[71] It would be equally wrong to take the tragedies, or any of them, as implying a notion of the cosmos, as Bradley and Wilson Knight and most writers from Dowden onward (and earlier in Germany) have done. In A. P. Rossiter's essay on *Coriolanus* here reprinted, we are reminded of Caroline Helstone's comment, in Charlotte Brontë's *Shirley*, to the effect that the function of Shakespearian tragedy is to stir us, to give us new sensations, to make us feel strongly.[72] Rossiter rejects it as not even conceivably appropriate for *Coriolanus*, but to Stoll it should have seemed the right response to all the tragedies. Nevertheless, he is not consistent: when discussing the crediting of a calumniator in the essay here reprinted, he draws attention to the plausibility with which Shakespeare has presented the crediting of Iago,[73] and in a passage quoted by J. I. M. Stewart he obscurely implies that, somehow, a vision of the world is communicated through the display of unlikely behavior.[74]

With all this, Stoll displays a remarkable sense of theater effect. His notion of tragedy seems to have been nearer to the grandly exciting strains of opera than to that darker and endless, that still and yet destructive conflict that most of us recognize. But his most coherent and successful book, *Art and Artifice in Shakespeare* (1933), has more to teach us concerning the range of possibilities in the theater than most other critical writings of our time.

In yet a third way critics of this century have moved in a different direction from Bradley. This is by seeking illumination on Shakespeare's plays through the extensive study of the writings of his predecessors and contemporaries. Sometimes it

[70] See p. 175.

[71] See pp. 226–42.

[72] See p. 229.

[73] See p. 94.

[74] See p. 107.

is the dramatists and poets who are related to him, as in M. C. Bradbrook's *Shakespeare and Elizabethan Poetry* (1951) and Robert Ornstein's *The Moral Vision of Jacobean Tragedy* (1960); more often it is the Homilies, the *Mirror for Magistrates*, *The French Academie*, *The Gouernour*, that are put under contribution. The danger is that Shakespeare will be seen as necessarily echoing the common notions of his age, and that his plays will shrink to faithful demonstrations of a party line: D. G. James does well to protest that "the creativeness of the rare and great mind" is "a major brute fact."[75] To see Shakespeare and his tragedies against the background of his age should, nevertheless, be a necessary step in the scholar's task, and interpretation should suffer no harm if the "brute fact" is kept steadily before us. In the essay on *Timon* here in part reprinted from *Shakespeare's Tragic Frontier* (1950), Willard Farnham draws on a deep knowledge of Shakespeare's cultural inheritance without losing sight of the nature of the tragic or of the individual effect produced by the play under consideration.

And there are neo-Bradleyans of recent years who have been concerned with character or with structure or with a meaning permanently available, paying little attention to imagery, or theatrical effects and conditions, or the background of thought and writing in Shakespeare's day. These writers do not often claim to express a total view of the tragedies, but they are ready to challenge criticism that neglects what they see as a timeless fidelity to general nature. Thus Stewart in *Character and Motive in Shakespeare* draws on the findings of modern psychology to demonstrate the accuracy of Shakespeare's presentation of human beings: we are, he suggests, in a position to recognize the apparently unlikely as well within the scope of our behavior. Thus we can accept the reality of Macbeth's murder of Duncan because we know, or should know, that the skin of civilized life is always thin; and his crimes can be recognized as the product, not of a hardening of the heart, but of the compelling as well as terrifying fascination of a criminality not as yet achieved.[76] In his concern with motives below the level of consciousness Stewart has

[75] See p. 155.

[76] See p. 116. See also the similar view of Robert Ornstein, p. 224.

obvious relations with the Freudian interpreters of Shakespeare, and Ernest Jones's definitive contribution on this subject, *Hamlet and Oedipus,* appeared in the same year. Stewart, however, is not concerned with the application of a formula: his insistence on the range of human possibility is accompanied by a sense of "an actual mystery in things,"[77] and this linking of psychological probing with metaphysical wonder is, of course, something that Bradley would approve.

William Rosen, in *Shakespeare and the Craft of Tragedy* (1960), recognizes the effect of the poetry in our response to *Antony and Cleopatra* but argues that this goes against the implications of the play's structure and that we must therefore not be led astray by it.[78] He is with Bradley in urging that Shakespeare is not concerned with separating out the strands of experience to provide a moral lesson, "a practical guide for living,"[79] and at the same time his insistence on our detachment from the characters in this play[80] puts him at the furthest extreme from Wilson Knight, for whom the "characters" become symbols of a triumph that, afar off, we can share.

For D. G. James, in *The Dream of Learning* (1951), the prime importance of Shakespearian tragedy is the meaning available to, and relevant to, us in our twentieth-century predicament. *Hamlet* expresses a doubt concerning the basic metaphysical question (the nature of the cosmos) and concerning the conflicting claims of passion and judgment. The hero admires Horatio but cannot emulate his friend's willing sufferance; he envies Fortinbras, but cannot put aside the reason that tells him Fortinbras's prize is an eggshell. For James, the play is independent of its age and yet makes a special appeal to us; at the same time it is for him the supreme expression of Renaissance doubt, transcending in kind—because supremely in degree—related utterances of its age.

No attempt can be made here to provide a comprehensive survey of twentieth-century opinion on this subject: many important critics have not been mentioned. Nevertheless, the variety illustrated in this volume is indeed remarkable. Wilson

---

[77] See p. 114.

[78] See p. 201.

[79] See p. 203.

[80] See p. 206.

Introduction

Knight and William Rosen present views of *Antony and Cleopatra* that no ingenuity could reconcile, and the total concepts of Shakespearian tragedy that underlie the writings of E. E. Stoll and D. G. James have almost no point of contact. The writers differ, too, in manner as well as in approach and in final interpretation: we have prose ranging from the scholarly and weighted to the easy and graceful, and thence to the familiar and nervously muscular. It is interesting to recall that every one of the post-Bradleyan writers represented in this book holds or has held a teaching post in the English department of a university. In many ways, indeed, the variations are healthy, and the disagreements provide a challenge to all scholars, all readers and spectators of Shakespeare, to examine the grounds for their own case. Yet it is difficult to end even so sketch-like an account as this without considering a few of the directions in which the study of Shakespearian tragedy needs to be strengthened, so that our own confusions may be put at least into a clearer light.

First, recognizing the value of the impetus given in their different ways by Granville-Barker and Schücking and Stoll, we need to have the relation of the plays to the theater constantly in mind. This means not only the Elizabethan and Jacobean theater, though indeed we need to learn as much as possible about that, but the theater in general as a mode of creation. If we consider some recent experiments in the use of the stage—incorporating many varieties of speech (from the frankly rhetorical to the naturalistic), veering between illusionist action and inclosed dialogue on the one hand and detached commentary and symbolic movement on the other, telescoping time and juxtaposing inherently remote localities— it is remarkable that many Shakespeare critics should retain a narrow conception of the "dramatic." Clemen, for example, sees Shakespeare's earlier use of imagery as "undramatic," compared with its use in the mature tragedies:[81] drama for him is fully achieved when fusion of all elements has taken place and when it is only as a result of energetic analysis that those elements can, for convenience, be discussed in isolation. D. A. Traversi in *An Approach to Shakespeare* (rev. ed., 1956) finds *Othello* "more truly dramatic" than *Hamlet* because it is more "objective," the conflict being externalized in the two figures

[81] See pp. 149–150.

Othello and Iago.[82] And he argues that in the presentation of Othello's fall, the dramatist, in order to make the process "strictly dramatic," had to insure that the hero's vulnerability was congruent with his utterances in the earlier part of the play.[83] A similar view of the dramatic essence underlies most of the essays in Una Ellis-Fermor's posthumous volume, *Shakespeare the Dramatist* (1961), where we are almost led to the assumption that Shakespeare did not achieve mastery of his medium until he had come to write in the fashion of Ibsen.

Now these are distinguished scholars and critics, and we have to recognize that the kind of drama characterized by causal connection and the fully-woven thread is, in general terms, the mode of *Othello*. But we may doubt whether it is certainly the mode of *Hamlet* and *Lear* and *Macbeth* and *Timon*, and we may fail to see an inherent inferiority in the drama less manifestly "fused." Coleridge, we have seen, pointed out the use of the epic and the lyric strains in *Hamlet*, and in a recent article here reprinted, William Frost has drawn attention to the variation in *Lear* between ritual, interrupted ritual, seemingly casual talk, action suggestive of disorder, and anti-ritual. Frost does not defend the mixed kind of dramatic writing for its own sake, seeing ritual as often an easy device for exciting interest and a way of blurring a play's essential line of thought. But he briefly brings out something of the technical range of *Lear*, not forgetting the part that characterization has in the total impact.[84] For many critics, despite their professional concern with imagery, the dramatic norm is still the naturalistic play: we are likely to understand *Lear* and *Timon* better, however, if performances of the plays of Brecht and Dürrenmatt are part of our remembered experience.

And we can be helped in this if we extend our knowledge of the tragedies of Shakespeare's contemporaries—not for the sake of finding in one of the minor playwrights a direct exposition of an idea which we can then import into our interpretation of a Shakespeare play, but for the sake of comparing major dramatists working at the same time in similar conditions. Of course, Shakespeare is supreme among them, but Marlowe and Jonson and Chapman and Webster (and at least one or two others) are dramatists of high stature indeed. A

[82] See p. 171. [83] See p. 175. [84] See p. 193.

consideration of what they did in tragedy, and in some forms of comedy, will make us more sensitive to the different but related things that Shakespeare did. We have had notable help in this direction from Ornstein's *The Moral Vision of Jacobean Tragedy*, but it is still not uncommon for a Shakespeare critic either to disregard other playwrights altogether or to make a casual and contemptuous reference to one of them by way of offering a tribute which Shakespeare might not have welcomed. Nor can the non-dramatic poets be safely left out of account. M. C. Bradbrook's *Shakespeare and Elizabethan Poetry* and W. B. C. Watkins's *Shakespeare and Spenser* (1950) are rare instances of a wish to see Shakespeare in relation to some of the major things available for his reading. Nicholas Brooke's essay on *Titus* and *Romeo*, included in this volume, draws on the non-dramatic poetic tradition in its examination of the early tragedies.

Finally, the critic of Shakespearian tragedy must face the challenge of the term "tragedy" itself. We have seen how the notion of a "moral" was present for critics from Dryden to Coleridge, and in some of the later writings in this volume it is still referred to. Traversi thinks that *Othello* may be "lacking in a proper moral balance" and therefore may not "give complete satisfaction as a work of art": its "prevailing tenor is still destructive," he finds, and he looks to *Macbeth* and the romances for a "decisive orientation," a "full, balanced ordering of experience."[85] On the other hand, we see Rosen denying a "moral lesson" to *Antony and Cleopatra*, Ornstein asserting bluntly that Shakespeare "did not preach,"[86] and Rossiter expressing confidence that "moral answers . . . cannot be the tragic heart of a tragedy."[87] For Wilson Knight, as we have noted, the supreme tragedy is ultimately a story of triumph, or at least it belongs within an *œuvre* where that triumph is finally asserted. In contrast, Rossiter sees an ending for *Coriolanus* in "utter darkness," and Ornstein sees *Macbeth* as offering only fragile affirmations in a similarly grim universe. It would be sanguine indeed to suggest that Shakespeare critics will come to agree on the meaning of "tragedy," or rather (for the question is more complex) on the range of meanings that the word can continue to bear without losing all practical value.

[85] See p. 189.   [86] See p. 215.   [87] See p. 229.

At least the uncommitted reader, however, may ask what significance it had for those responsible for putting it on the title page of the First Folio, along with "comedy" and "history," what relation exists between these tragedies and certain other plays of other times that regularly carry the description, what it may have meant to Shakespeare when he started the composition of a play with the description in mind. And these questions, of course, are related to the basic question: Does the word imply merely a particular kind of story or does it have reference to a particular view of the world? Some recent books can substantially help us at least to know where we stand on some of these issues: among them are H. D. F. Kitto's *Form and Meaning in Drama* (1956), Richard B. Sewall's *The Vision of Tragedy* (1959), and the collection of essays edited by Sewall and Lawrence Michel, *Tragedy: Modern Essays in Criticism* (1963).

JOHN DRYDEN

Preface Containing the Grounds of Criticism in Tragedy

The poet Æschylus was held in the same veneration by the Athenians of after ages as Shakespeare is by us; and Longinus has judged, in favour of him, that he had a noble boldness of expression, and that his imaginations were lofty and heroic; but, on the other side, Quintilian affirms that he was daring to extravagance. 'Tis certain that he affected pompous words, and that his sense too often was obscured by figures; notwithstanding these imperfections, the value of his writings after his decease was such, that his countrymen ordained an equal reward to those poets who could alter his plays to be acted on the theatre, with those whose productions were wholly new, and of their own. The case is not the same in England; though the difficulties of altering are greater, and our reverence for Shakespeare much more just, than that of the Grecians for Æschylus. In the age of that poet, the Greek tongue was arrived to its full perfection; they had then amongst them an exact standard of writing and of speaking: the English language is not capable of such a certainty; and we are at present so far from it, that we are wanting in the very foundation of it, a perfect grammar. Yet it must be allowed to the present age, that the tongue in general is so much refined since Shakespeare's time, that many of his words, and more of his phrases, are scarce intelligible. And of those which we understand, some are ungrammatical, others coarse; and his whole style is so pestered with figurative expressions, that it is as affected as it

From the Preface to Dryden's version of *Troilus and Cressida* [1679], *Essays of John Dryden*, ed. W. P. Ker (Oxford: Clarendon Press, 1900), I, 202–29. The first extract is the opening paragraph of the Preface, the remainder comes from the long concluding section headed "The Grounds of Criticism in Tragedy."

is obscure. 'Tis true, that in his latter plays he had worn off somewhat of the rust; but the tragedy which I have undertaken to correct was in all probability one of his first endeavours on the stage.

After all, if any one will ask me, whether a tragedy cannot be made upon any other grounds than those of exciting pity and terror in us;—Bossu, the best of modern critics, answers thus in general: That all excellent arts, and particularly that of poetry, have been invented and brought to perfection by men of transcendent genius; and that, therefore, they, who practise afterwards the same arts, are obliged to tread in their footsteps, and to search in their writings the foundation of them; for it is not just that new rules should destroy the authority of the old. But Rapin writes more particularly thus, that no passions in a story are so proper to move our concernment as fear and pity; and that it is from our concernment we receive our pleasure, is undoubted; when the soul becomes agitated with fear for one character, or hope for another, then it is that we are pleased in Tragedy, by the interest which we take in their adventures.

Here, therefore, the general answer may be given to the first question, how far we ought to imitate Shakespeare and Fletcher in their plots; namely, that we ought to follow them so far only as they have copied the excellencies of those who invented and brought to perfection Dramatic Poetry; those things only excepted, which religion, custom of countries, idioms of languages, etc., have altered in the superstructures, but not in the foundation of the design.

How defective Shakespeare and Fletcher have been in all their plots, Mr. Rymer has discovered in his criticisms: neither can we, who follow them, be excused from the same, or greater errors; which are the more unpardonable in us, because we want their beauties to countervail our faults. The best of their designs, the most approaching to antiquity, and the most conducing to move pity, is the *King and No King;* which, if the farce of Bessus were thrown away, is of that inferior sort of tragedies, which end with a prosperous event. It is probably derived from the story of Œdipus, with the character of Alexander the Great, in his extravagances, given to Arbaces. The taking of this play, amongst many others, I cannot wholly ascribe to the excellency of the action; for I find it moving when it is read: 'tis true, the faults of the plot are so evidently proved, that they can no longer be denied. The beauties of it must therefore lie either in the lively touches of the passion; or we must conclude, as I think we may, that even in imperfect plots there are less degrees of Nature, by which some faint emotions of pity and terror are raised in us: as a less engine will raise a less proportion of weight, though not so much as one of Archimedes's making; for nothing can move our nature, but by some natural reason, which works upon passions. And, since we acknowledge the effect, there must be something in the cause.

The difference between Shakespeare and Fletcher in their plotting seems to be this; that Shakespeare generally moves more terror, and Fletcher more compassion: for the first had a more masculine, a bolder and more fiery genius; the second, a more soft and womanish. In the mechanic beauties of the plot, which are the observation of the three Unities, Time, Place, and Action, they are both deficient; but Shakespeare most. Ben Johnson reformed those errors in his comedies, yet one of Shakespeare's was regular before him; which is, *The Merry Wives of Windsor*. For what remains concerning the design, you are to be referred to our English critic. That method which he has prescribed to raise it, from mistake, or ignorance of the crime, is certainly the best, though it is not the only; for amongst all the tragedies of Sophocles, there is but one, *Œdipus*, which is wholly built after that model.

After the plot, which is the foundation of the play, the next thing to which we ought to apply our judgment, is the manners; for now the poet comes to work above ground. The groundwork, indeed, is that which is most necessary, as that upon which depends the firmness of the whole fabric; yet it strikes not the eye so much, as the beauties or imperfections of the manners, the thoughts, and the expressions.

The first rule which Bossu prescribes to the writer of an Heroic Poem, and which holds too by the same reason in all Dramatic Poetry, is to make the moral of the work; that is, to lay down to yourself what that precept of morality shall be, which you would insinuate into the people; as, namely, Homer's (which I have copied in my *Conquest of Granada*), was, that union preserves a commonwealth, and discord destroys it; Sophocles, in his *Œdipus*, that no man is to be accounted happy before his death. 'Tis the moral that directs the whole action of the play to one centre; and that action or fable is the example built upon the moral, which confirms the truth of it to our experience: when the fable is designed, then, and not before, the persons are to be introduced, with their manners, characters, and passions.

The manners, in a poem, are understood to be those inclinations, whether natural or acquired, which move and carry us to actions, good, bad, or indifferent, in a play; or which incline the persons to such or such actions. I have anticipated part of this discourse already, in declaring that a poet ought not to make the manners perfectly good in his best persons; but neither are they to be more wicked in any of his characters than necessity requires. To produce a villain, without other reason than a natural inclination to villainy, is, in Poetry, to produce an effect without a cause; and to make him more a villain than he has just reason to be, is to make an effect which is stronger than the cause.

The chief character or hero in a tragedy, as I have already shown, ought in prudence to be such a man who has so much more of virtue in him than of vice, that he may be left amiable to the audience, which otherwise cannot have any concernment for his sufferings; and it is on this one character, that the pity and terror must be principally, if not wholly, founded: a rule which is extremely necessary, and which none of the critics, that I know, have fully enough discovered to us. For terror and compassion work but weakly when they are divided into many persons. If Creon had been the chief character in *Œdipus*, there had neither been terror nor compassion moved; but only detestation of the man, and joy for his punishment; if Adrastus and Eurydice had been made more appealing characters, then the pity had been divided, and lessened on the part of Œdipus: but making Œdipus the best and bravest person, and even Jocasta but an underpart to him, his virtues, and the punishment of his fatal crime, drew both the pity and the terror to himself.

By what has been said of the manners, it will be easy for a reasonable man to judge whether the characters be truly or falsely drawn in a tragedy; for if there be no manners appearing in the characters, no concernment for the persons can be raised; no pity or horror can be moved, but by vice or virtue; therefore, without them, no person can have any business in the play. If the inclinations be obscure, it is a sign the poet is in the dark, and knows not what manner of man he presents to you; and consequently you can have no idea, or very imperfect, of that man; nor can judge what resolutions he ought to take; or what words or actions are proper for him. Most comedies made up of accidents or adventures are liable to fall into this error; and tragedies with many turns are subject to it; for the manners can never be evident, where the surprises of fortune take up all the business of the stage; and where the poet is more in pain to tell you what happened to such a man, than what he was. 'Tis one of the excellencies of Shakespeare, that the manners of his persons are generally apparent, and you see their bent and inclinations. Fletcher comes far short of him in this, as indeed he does almost in everything: there are but glimmerings of manners in most of his comedies, which run upon adventures; and in his tragedies, Rollo, Otto, the King and No King, Melantius, and many others of his best, are but pictures shown you in the twilight; you know not whether they resemble vice or virtue, and they are either good, bad, or indifferent, as the present scene requires it. But of all poets, this commendation is to be given to Ben Johnson, that the manners, even of the most inconsiderable persons in his plays, are everywhere apparent.

If Shakespeare be allowed, as I think he must, to have made his characters distinct, it will easily be inferred that he understood the nature of the passions: because it has been proved already that confused passions make undistinguishable characters: yet I cannot deny that he has his failings; but they are not so much in the passions themselves, as in his manner of expression: he often obscures his meaning by his words, and sometimes makes it unintelligible. I will not say of so great a poet, that he distinguished not the blown puffy style from true sublimity; but I may venture to maintain, that the fury of his fancy often transported him beyond the bounds of judgment, either in coining of new words and phrases, or racking words which were in use, into the violence of a catachresis. It is not that I would explode the use of metaphors from passion, for

Longinus thinks 'em necessary to raise it: but to use 'em at
every word, to say nothing without a metaphor, a simile, an
image, or description, is, I doubt, to smell a little too strongly
of the buskin. I must be forced to give an example of expressing passion figuratively; but that I may do it with respect to
Shakespeare, it shall not be taken from anything of his: 'tis an
exclamation against Fortune, quoted in his *Hamlet* but written
by some other poet—

> Out, out, thou strumpet, Fortune! all you gods,
> In general synod, take away her power;
> Break all the spokes and felleys from her wheel,
> And bowl the round nave down the hill of Heav'n,
> As low as to the fiends.

And immediately after, speaking of Hecuba, when Priam was
killed before her eyes—

> The mobbled queen
> Threatning the flame, ran up and down
> With bisson rheum; a clout about that head
> Where late the diadem stood; and for a robe,
> About her lank and all o'er-teemed loins,
> A blanket in th' alarm of fear caught up.
> Who this had seen, with tongue in venom steep'd
> 'Gainst Fortune's state would treason have pronounced;
> But if the gods themselves did see her then,
> When she saw Pyrrhus make malicious sport
> In mincing with his sword her husband's limbs,
> The instant burst of clamour that she made
> (Unless things mortal move them not at all)
> Would have made milch the burning eyes of heaven,
> And passion in the gods.

What a pudder is here kept in raising the expression of
trifling thoughts! Would not a man have thought that the poet
had been bound prentice to a wheelwright, for his first rant?
and had followed a ragman, for the clout and blanket in the
second? Fortune is painted on a wheel, and therefore the
writer, in a rage, will have poetical justice done upon every
member of that engine: after this execution, he bowls the nave
down-hill, from Heaven, to the fiends (an unreasonable long
mark, a man would think); 'tis well there are no solid orbs
to stop it in the way, or no element of fire to consume it: but
when it came to the earth, it must be monstrous heavy, to

break ground as low as the centre. His making milch the burning eyes of heaven was a pretty tolerable flight too: and I think no man ever drew milk out of eyes before him: yet, to make the wonder greater, these eyes were burning. Such a sight indeed were enough to have raised passion in the gods; but to excuse the effects of it, he tells you, perhaps they did not see it. Wise men would be glad to find a little sense couched under all these pompous words; for bombast is commonly the delight of that audience which loves Poetry, but understands it not: and as commonly has been the practice of those writers, who, not being able to infuse a natural passion into the mind, have made it their business to ply the ears, and to stun their judges by the noise. But Shakespeare does not often thus; for the passions in his scene between Brutus and Cassius are extremely natural, the thoughts are such as arise from the matter, the expression of 'em not viciously figurative. I cannot leave this subject, before I do justice to that divine poet, by giving you one of his passionate descriptions: 'tis of Richard the Second when he was deposed, and led in triumph through the streets of London by Henry of Bullingbrook: the painting of it is so lively, and the words so moving, that I have scarce read anything comparable to it in any other language. Suppose you have seen already the fortunate usurper passing through the crowd, and followed by the shouts and acclamations of the people; and now behold King Richard entering upon the scene: consider the wretchedness of his condition, and his carriage in it; and refrain from pity, if you can—

> As in a theatre, the eyes of men,
> After a well-graced actor leaves the stage,
> Are idly bent on him that enters next,
> Thinking his prattle to be tedious:
> Even so, or with much more contempt, men's eyes
> Did scowl on Richard: no man cried, God save him:
> No joyful tongue gave him his welcome home,
> But dust was thrown upon his sacred head,
> Which with such gentle sorrow he shook off,
> His face still combating with tears and smiles
> (The badges of his grief and patience),
> That had not God (for some strong purpose) steel'd
> The hearts of men, they must perforce have melted,
> And barbarism itself have pitied him.

To speak justly of this whole matter: 'tis neither height of thought that is discommended, nor pathetic vehemence, nor any nobleness of expression in its proper place; but 'tis a false measure of all these, something which is like them, and is not them; 'tis the Bristol-stone, which appears like a diamond; 'tis an extravagant thought, instead of a sublime one; 'tis roaring madness, instead of vehemence; and a sound of words, instead of sense. If Shakespeare were stripped of all the bombasts in his passions, and dressed in the most vulgar words, we should find the beauties of his thoughts remaining; if his embroideries were burnt down, there would still be silver at the bottom of the melting-pot: but I fear (at least let me fear it for myself) that we, who ape his sounding words, have nothing of his thought, but are all outside; there is not so much as a dwarf within our giant's clothes. Therefore, let not Shakespeare suffer for our sakes; 'tis our fault, who succeed him in an age which is more refined, if we imitate him so ill, that we copy his failings only, and make a virtue of that in our writings which in his was an imperfection.

For what remains, the excellency of that poet was, as I have said, in the more manly passions; Fletcher's in the softer: Shakespeare writ better betwixt man and man; Fletcher, betwixt man and woman: consequently, the one described friendship better; the other love: yet Shakespeare taught Fletcher to write love: and Juliet and Desdemona are originals. 'Tis true, the scholar had the softer soul; but the master had the kinder. Friendship is both a virtue and a passion essentially; love is a passion only in its nature, and is not a virtue but by accident: good nature makes friendship; but effeminacy love. Shakespeare had an universal mind, which comprehended all characters and passions; Fletcher a more confined and limited: for though he treated love in perfection, yet honour, ambition, revenge, and generally all the stronger passions, he either touched not, or not masterly. To conclude all, he was a limb of Shakespeare.

I had intended to have proceeded to the last property of manners, which is, that they must be constant, and the characters maintained the same from the beginning to the end; and from thence to have proceeded to the thoughts and expressions suitable to a tragedy: but I will first see how this will relish with the age. It is, I confess, but cursorily written; yet the judgment, which is given here, is generally founded upon experience: but because many men are shocked at the name of rules, as if they were a kind of magisterial prescription upon poets, I will conclude with the words of Rapin, in his *Reflections* on Aristotle's work *of Poetry:* "If the rules be well considered, we shall find them to be only to reduce Nature into method, to trace her step by step, and not to suffer the least mark of her to escape us: 'tis only by these, that probability in fiction is maintained, which is the soul of poetry. They are founded upon good sense, and sound reason, rather than on authority; for though Aristotle and Horace are produced, yet no man must argue, that what they write is true, because they writ it; but 'tis evident, by the ridiculous mistakes and gross absurdities which have been made by those poets who have taken their fancy only for their guide, that if this fancy be not regulated, it is a mere caprice, and utterly incapable to produce a reasonable and judicious poem."

II

THOMAS RYMER

Reflections on the *Julius Caesar*

In the former Play, our Poet might be the bolder, the persons being all his own Creatures, and meer fiction. But here he sins not against Nature and Philosophy only, but against the most known History, and the memory of the Noblest Romans, that ought to be sacred to all Posterity. He might be familiar with *Othello* and *Iago*, as his own natural acquaintance: but *Cæsar* and *Brutus* were above his conversation. To put them in Fools Coats, and make them Jack-puddens in the *Shakespear* dress, is a *Sacriledge*, beyond any thing in *Spelman*. The Truth is, this authors head was full of villainous, unnatural images, and history has only furnish'd him with great names, thereby to recommend them to the World; by writing over them, *This is* Brutus; *this is* Cicero; *this is* Cæsar. But generally his History flies in his Face; And comes in flat contradiction to the Poets imagination. As for example: of *Brutus* says *Antony*, his Enemy,

> Ant.—*His life was gentle, and the Elements*
> *So mixt in him, that Nature might stand up,*
> *And say to all the World, this was a Man.*

And when every body judg'd it necessary to kill *Antony*, our Author in his *Laconical* way, makes *Brutus* speak thus:

> Bru. *Our Course will seem too bloody*, Caius Cassius,
> *To cut the Head off, and then hack the Limbs,*
> *Like wrath in death, and envy afterwards;*
> *For* Antony *is but a Limb of* Cæsar:
> *Let's be Sacrificers, but not Butchers,* Caius,
> *We all stand up against the Spirit of* Cæsar,

From *A Short View of Tragedy; It's Original, Excellency, and Corruption. With some Reflections on Shakespear, and other Practitioners for the Stage,* by Thomas Rymer (London, 1693), pp. 148–59. A few changes in punctuation have been made where the original printing obscures the sense.

10

> *And in the Spirit of man there is no blood;*
> *O that we then cou'd come by* Cæsars *Spirit,*
> *And not dismember* Cæsar; *but, alas!*
> Cæsar *must bleed for it. And gentle friends,*
> *Let's kill him boldly but not wrathfully;*
> *Let's carve him, as a dish fit for the Gods,*
> *Not hew him, as a Carkass fit for Hounds.*
> *And let our Hearts, as subtle Masters do,*
> *Stir up their Servants to an act of rage,*
> *And after seem to chide 'em. This shall make*
> *Our purpose necessary, and not envious:*
> *Which so appearing to the common eyes,*
> *We shall be call'd Purgers, not murderers.*
> *And for* Mark Antony *think not of him:*
> *For he can do no more than* Cæsars *arm,*
> *When* Cæsars *head is off.*

In these two speeches we have the true character of *Brutus*, according to History. But when *Shakespear*'s own blundering Maggot of self contradiction works, then must *Brutus* cry out,

> Bru.—*Stoop*, Romans, *stoop*,
> *And let us bath our hands in* Cæsars *blood*
> *Up to the Elbows—*

Had this been spoken by some King of *France*, we might remember *Villon:*

> *Se fusse des hoirs Hue Capel,*
> *Qui fut extrait de boucherie,*
> *On m' eut parmy ce drapel,*
> *Fait boire de l' escorcherie.*

And what *Dante* has recorded:

> *Chiamato fui di là Ugo ciapetta,*
> *Di me son Nati i Philippi, e' Loigi,*
> *Per cui novellamente e' Francia retta,*
> *Figlivol fui d' un Beccaio di Parigi—*

For, indeed, that Language which *Shakespear* puts in the Mouth of *Brutus* wou'd not suit, or be convenient, unless from some son of the Shambles, or some natural offspring of the Butchery. But never any Poet so boldly and so barefac'd, flounced along from contradiction to contradiction. A little preparation and forecast might do well now and then. For his *Desdemona*'s Marriage, He might have helped out the proba-

bility by feigning how that some way, or other, a Black-amoor
Woman had been her Nurse, and suckl'd her: Or that once,
upon a time, some *Virtuoso* had transfus'd into her Veins the
Blood of a black Sheep: after which she might never be at
quiet till she is, as the Poet will have it, *Tupt with an old black
ram.*

But to match this pithy discourse of *Brutus;* see the weighty
argumentative oration, whereby *Cassius* draws him into the
Conspiracy:

> Cas.—Brutus, *and* Cæsar: *what shou'd be in that* Cæsar?
> *Why shou'd that name be sounded more than yours?*
> *Write them together: yours is as fair a name:*
> *Sound them, it doth become the mouth as well.*
> *Weigh them, it is as heavy: conjure with them,*
> Brutus *will start a Spirit as soon as* Cæsar.
> *Now, in the names of all the Gods at once,*
> *Upon what meat doth this our* Cæsar *feed,*
> *That he is grown so great? Age, thou art sham'd;*
> Rome *thou hast lost the breed of noble bloods.*
> *When went there by an Age since the great flood,*
> *But it was fam'd with more, than with one man?*
> *When could they say (till now) that talk'd of* Rome,
> *That her wide Walls encompass'd but one man?*
> *Now it is* Rome *indeed, and room enough*
> *When there is in it but one only Man—*

One may Note that all our Authors Senators, and his Orators
had their learning and education at the same school, be they
Venetians, Black-amoors, Ottamites, or noble Romans. *Brutus*
and *Cassius* here, may *cap sentences*, with *Brabantio,* and the
Doge of *Venice,* or any *Magnifico* of them all. We saw how the
Venetian Senate spent their time, when, amidst their alarms,
call'd to Counsel at midnight. Here the Roman Senators, the
midnight before *Cæsar*'s death (met in the Garden of *Brutus,* to
settle the matter of their Conspiracy) are gazing up to the Stars,
and have no more in their heads than to wrangle about which is
the East and West:

> Decius. *Here lies the East, doth not the day break here?*
> Caska. *No.*
> Cinna. *O, pardon, Sir, it doth, and yon grey lines,*
> *That fret the Clouds, are Messengers of Day.*
> Caska. *You shall confess, that you are both deceiv'd:*
> *Here as I point my Sword, the Sun arises,*

Which is a great way growing on the South,
Weighing the youthful season of the year,
Some two months hence, up higher toward the North,
He first presents his fire, and the high East
Stands as the Capitol directly here.

This is directly, as *Bays* tells us, to *shew the World a Pattern here, how men shou'd talk of Business.* But it wou'd be a wrong to the Poet, not to inform the reader, that on the Stage, the Spectators see *Brutus* and *Cassius* all this while at *Whisper* together. That is the importance, that deserves all the attention. But the *grand question* wou'd be: does the *Audience hear 'em Whisper?*

     Ush. *Why, truly I can't tell: there's much to be said upon the word Whisper—*

Another Poet wou'd have allow'd the noble *Brutus* a Watch-Candle in his Chamber this important night, rather than have puzzel'd his Man *Lucius* to grope in the dark for a Flint and Tinder-box, to get the Taper lighted. It wou'd have been no great charge to the Poet, however. Afterwards, another night, the Fiddle is in danger to be broken by this sleepy Boy:

     Bru. *If thou dost nod thou break'st thy Instrument.*

But pass we to the famous Scene, where *Brutus* and *Cassius* are by the Poet represented acting the parts of *Mimicks:* from the Nobility and Buskins, they are made the *Planipedes;* are brought to daunce *bare-foot,* for a Spectacle to the people. Two Philosophers, two generals, (*imperatores* was their title) the *ultimi Romanorum,* are to play the Bullies and Buffoon, to shew their Legerdemain, their *activity* of face, and divarication of Muscles. They are to play a prize, a tryal of skill in huffing and swaggering, like two drunken Hectors, for a two-penny reckoning.

When the Roman Mettle was somewhat more allaid, and their Stomach not so very fierce, in *Augustus*'s time; *Laberius,* who was excellent at that sport, was forced once by the Emperor to shew his Talent upon the Stage: in his Prologue, he complains that

     Necessity has no law.
     It was the will of Cæsar *brought me hither,*
     What was imagin'd for me to deny
     This Cæsar; *when the Gods deny him nothing?*

But says he,

—Ego bis tricenis annis actis sine nota,
Eques Romanus lare egressus meo,
Domum revertor Mimus. *Nimirum hac die*
Una plus vixi mihi quam vivendum fuit—

Twice thirty years have I liv'd without blemish;
From home I came a Roman Gentleman,
But back shall go a Mimick. *This one day*
Is one day longer than I shou'd have liv'd.

This may shew with what indignity our Poet treats the noblest *Romans*. But there is no other cloth in his Wardrobe. Every one must be content to wear a Fools Coat, who comes to be dressed by him. Nor is he more civil to the Ladies. *Portia*, in good manners, might have challeng'd more respect: she that shines, a glory of the first magnitude in the Gallery of Heroick Dames, is with our Poet, scarce one remove from a Natural: She is the own Cousin German, of one piece, the very same impertinent silly flesh and blood with *Desdemona*. *Shakespears* genius lay for Comedy and Humour. In Tragedy he appears quite out of his Element; his Brains are turn'd, he raves and rambles, without any coherence, any spark of reason, or any rule to controul him, or set bounds to his phrenzy. His imagination was still running after his Masters, the Coblers, and Parish Clerks, and *Old Testament Stroulers*. So he might make bold with *Portia*, as they had done with the Virgin Mary. Who, in a Church Acting their Play call'd *The Incarnation*, had usually the *Ave Mary* mumbl'd over to a stradling wench (for the blessed Virgin) straw-hatted, blew-apron'd, big-bellied, with her Immaculate Conception up to her chin.

The Italian Painters are noted for drawing the *Madonna*'s by their own Wives or Mistresses; one might wonder what sort of *Betty Mackerel, Shakespear* found in his days, to sit for his *Portia*, and *Desdemona;* and Ladies of a rank, and dignity, for their place in Tragedy. But to him a Tragedy in *Burlesk*, a merry Tragedy, was no Monster, no absurdity, nor at all preposterous: all colours are the same to a Blind man. The Thunder and Lightning, the Shouting and Battel, and alarms every where in this play, may well keep the Audience awake; otherwise no Sermon wou'd be so strong an Opiate. But since the memorable action by the *Putney Pikes*, the *Hammersmith Bri-*

gade, and the *Chelsey Cuirassiers:* one might think, in a modest Nation, no Battel wou'd ever presume to shew upon the Stage agen, unless it were at *Perin* in *Cornwal,* where the story goes that, some time before the year 88. the *Spaniards* once were landing to burn the Town, just at the nick when a Company of *Stroulers* with their Drums and their shouting were setting *Sampson* upon the *Philistines,* which so scar'd Mr. Spaniard, that they Scampered back to their Galions, as apprehending our whole *Tilbury* Camp had lain in Ambush, and were coming souse upon them.

At *Athens* (they tell us) the Tragedies of *Æsculus, Sophocles,* and *Euripides* were enroll'd with their Laws, and made part of their Statute-Book.

We want a law for Acting the *Rehearsal* once a week, to keep us in our senses, and secure us against the Noise and Nonsense, the Farce and Fustian which, in the name of Tragedy, have so long invaded, and usurp our Theater.

Tully defines an Orator to be, *Vir bonus dicendique peritus.* Why must he be a *good Man,* as if a bad Man might not be a good Speaker? But what avails it to Speak well, unless a man is well heard? To gain attention *Aristotle* told us, it was necessary that an Orator be a *good Man;* therefore he that writes Tragedy should be careful that the persons of his *Drama,* be of consideration and importance, that the Audience may readily lend an Ear, and give attention to what they say, and act. Who would thrust into a crowd to hear what Mr. *Iago, Roderigo,* or *Cassio,* is like to say? From a Venetian Senate, or a Roman Senate one might expect great matters: But their Poet was out of sorts; he had it not for them; the Senators must be no wiser than other folk.

Ben. Johnson, knew to distinguish men and manners, at an other rate. In *Catiline* we find our selves in *Europe,* we are no longer in the *Land of Savages,* amongst Blackamoors, Barbarians, and Monsters.

III

WILLIAM RICHARDSON

Additional Observations
on
Shakespeare's
Dramatic Character of Hamlet
in a Letter to a Friend

DEAR SIR,

I thank you for your remarks on my account of Hamlet. Yet I frankly confess that, notwithstanding their ingenuity, I still adhere to my opinion; and, as I am solicitous that you should agree with me, I shall, as briefly as possible, lay my reasons before you. Nor have I any doubt, but that the same candour which dictated the objections, will procure attention to the reply. Allow me, then, to plead in behalf of Hamlet; and of Shakespeare*, if he need such aid; and of the Public, who, by always interesting themselves in the fate of Hamlet, have, in this most unequivocal manner, as on many other occasions, expressed their approbation of Shakespeare.

The strongest feature in the mind of Hamlet, as exhibited in the tragedy, is an exquisite sense of moral conduct. He displays, at the same time, great sensibility of temper; and, is therefore, most "tremblingly alive" to every incident or event that befalls him. His affections are ardent, and his attachments lasting. He also displays a strong sense of character; and therefore, a high

From *Essays on Some of Shakespeare's Dramatic Characters, to Which Is Added an Essay on the Faults of Shakespeare*, by William Richardson (5th ed.; London, 1797), pp. 121–41. The essay here reprinted was first published in 1784.

* Si tali auxilio.

regard for the opinions of others. His good sense, and excellent dispositions, in the early part of his life, and in the prosperous state of his fortune, rendered him amiable and beloved. No misfortune had hitherto befallen him; and, though he is represented as susceptible of lively feelings, we have no evidence of his having ever shewn any symptoms of a morose or melancholy disposition. On the contrary, the melancholy which throws so much gloom upon him in the course of the play, appears to his former friends and acquaintance altogether unusual and unaccountable.

> —— Something have you heard
> Of Hamlet's transformation: so I call it;
> Since nor th' exterior, nor the inward man,
> Resembles that it was.

In the conduct, however, which he displays, in the progress of the tragedy, he appears irresolute and indecisive; he accordingly engages in enterprizes in which he fails; he discovers reluctance to perform actions, which, we think, needed no hesitation; he proceeds to violent outrage, where the occasion does not seem to justify violence; he appears jocular where his situation is most serious and alarming; he uses subterfuges not consistent with an ingenuous mind; and expresses sentiments not only immoral, but inhuman.

This charge is heavy: yet every reader, and every audience, have hitherto taken part with Hamlet. They have not only pitied, but esteemed him; and the voice of the people, in poetry as well as politics, deserves some attention. Let us enquire, therefore, whether those particulars which have given such offence, may not be considered as the infirmities of a mind constituted like that of Hamlet, and placed in such trying circumstances, rather than indications of folly, or proofs of inherent guilt. If so, he will still continue the proper object of our compassion, of our regret, and esteem. The award of the public will receive confirmation.

Consider, then, how a young person of good sense, of strong moral feelings, possessing an exquisite sense of character, great sensibility, together with much ardour and constancy of affection, would be apt to conduct himself, in a situation so peculiar as that of Hamlet. He loses a respectable father; nay, he has some reason to suspect, that his father had been treacherously murdered; that his uncle was the perpetrator of the cruel deed;

and that his mother, whom he tenderly loved, was an accomplice in the guilt: he sees her suddenly married to the suspected murderer; he is himself excluded from his birth-right; he is placed in a conspicuous station; the world expects of him that he will resent or avenge his wrongs: while in the mean time he is justly apprehensive of his being surrounded with spies and informers. In these circumstances, and of such a character, if the poet had represented him as acting with steady vigour and unexceptionable propriety, he would have represented not Hamlet, but a creature so fanciful, as to have no prototype in human nature. We are not therefore to expect that his conduct is to proceed according to the most infallible rules of discretion or of propriety. We must look for frailties and imperfections; but for the frailties and imperfections of Hamlet.

The injuries he has sustained, the guilt of Claudius, and the perversion of Gertrude, excite his resentment, and indignation. Regard for the opinions of others, who expect such resentment in the Prince of Denmark, promotes the passion. He therefore meditates, and resolves on vengeance. But the moment he forms his resolution, the same virtuous sensibility, and the same regard to character, that roused his indignation, suggest objections. He entertains a doubt concerning the ground of his suspicions, and the evidence upon which he proceeds.

> ——— The spirit that I've seen
> May be a devil; and the devil hath power
> T' assume a pleasing shape; yea, and, perhaps,
> Out of my weakness and my melancholy,
> (As he is very potent with such spirits),
> Abuses me to damn me. I'll have grounds
> More relative than this.

In this manner he becomes irresolute and indecisive. Additionally, therefore, to the sorrow and melancholy which he necessarily feels for the situation of his family, and which his peculiar frame of mind renders unusually poignant, the harassment of such an inward struggle aggravates his affliction. His sense of duty, a regard to character, and feelings of just resentment, prompt him to revenge: the uncertainty of his suspicions, the fallacious nature of the evidence on which he proceeds, and the dread of perpetrating injustice, embarrass and arrest his purpose.

> The time is out of joint—O cursed spight,
> That ever I was born to set it right.

This irresolution, which indeed blasts his designs, but does not lessen our regard for his character, nor our compassion for his misfortunes, and the misery with which it afflicts him, are pathetically described and expressed, in the famous soliloquy consequent to the representation of the Players.

> What's Hecuba to him, or he to Hecuba,
> That he should weep for her? What would he do,
> Had he the motive and the cue for passion
> That I have? &c.—Yet I, &c.

In that particular mood, when he sees his own wrongs and the guilt of Claudius in a striking light, his resentment is inflamed, the evidence seems convincing, and he acts with a violence and precipitation very dissimilar to, though not inconsistent with, his native temper. In these circumstances, or at a time when he tells us he

> ——— Could drink hot blood!
> And do such bitter business, as the day
> Would quake to look on!

in such a situation and state of mind he slew Polonius: he mistook him for the king: and so acted with a violence and precipitation of which he afterwards expresses his repentance. In a similar situation, when he had no leisure nor inclination to weigh and examine appearances, he wrote the death-warrant of Rosencrantz and Guildenstern.

> Being thus benetted round with villanies,
> Or I could make a prologue to my brains,
> They had begun the play: I sat me down,
> Devis'd a new commission, &c.
> An earnest conjuration from the king,
> As England was his faithful tributary,—
> That on the view and knowing of these contents,
> He should the bearers put to sudden death.

Rosencrantz and Guildenstern had been employed as spies upon Hamlet: under the disguise of friendship for him, they had accepted of this infamous office; they were in some measure accessary to his intended assassination: "they made love to this employment;" and therefore, as "the defeat grew from their own insinuation," there was no occasion why it "should sit near to Hamlet's conscience." If leisure had been given him to reflect, perhaps he would not have sacrificed them; but having done the deed, he does not charge himself with deliberate guilt. He does not contend that his conduct was entirely blameless; he only tells us,

> They are not *near* my conscience.

Thus agitated by external circumstances, torn by contending emotions, liable to the weaknesses nearly allied to extreme sensibility, and exhausted by the contests of violent passions, is it wonderful that he should exhibit dejection of mind, and express disrelish for every human enjoyment? This extreme is no less consistent with his character than his temporary violence. "I have of late," he tells Rosencrantz and Guildenstern, "lost all my mirth; forgone all custom of exercises; and, indeed, it goes so heavily with my disposition, that this goodly frame, the earth, seems to me a sterile promontory; this most excellent canopy, the air, look you, this brave o'erhanging firmament; this majestical roof fretted with golden fire; why, it appears no other thing to me than a foul and pestilent congregation of vapours." &c. In like manner, the same state of internal contest leads him to a conduct directly opposite to that of violence or precipitancy; and when we expect that he will give full vent to his resentment, he hesitates and recedes. This is particularly illustrated in the very difficult scene where Hamlet, seeing Claudius kneeling and employed in devotion, utters the following soliloquy:

> Now might I do it pat, now he is praying;
> And now I'll do it;—and so he goes to heaven;
> And so am I reveng'd? That would be scann'd;
> A villain kills my father, and for that,
> I, his sole son, do this same villain send
> To heaven.
> Why, this is hire and salary, not revenge.
> He took my father grossly, full of bread,
> With all his crimes broad blown, as flush as May;
> And, how his audit stands, who knows, save heaven?
> But, in our circumstance and course of thought,
> 'Tis heavy with him: and am I then reveng'd,
> To take him in the purging of his soul,
> When he is fit and season'd for his passage?

You ask me, why he did not kill the Usurper? And I answer, because he was at that instant irresolute. This irresolution arose from the inherent principles of his constitution, and is to be accounted natural: it arose from virtuous, or at least from amiable sensibility, and therefore cannot be blamed. His sense of justice, or his feelings of tenderness, in a moment when his violent emotions were not excited, overcame his resentment. But you will urge the inconsistency of this account, with the inhuman sentiments he expresses:

> Up, sword, and know thou a more horrid hent:
> When he is drunk, asleep, or in his rage, &c.
> Then trip him, &c.

In reply to this difficulty, and it is not inconsiderable, I will venture to affirm, that these are not his real sentiments. There is nothing in the whole character of Hamlet that justifies such savage enormity. We are therefore bound, in justice and candour, to look for some hypothesis that shall reconcile what he now delivers, with his usual maxims and general deportment. I would ask, then, whether, on many occasions, we do not alledge those considerations as the motives of our conduct, which really are not motives? Nay, is not this sometimes done almost without our knowledge? Is it not done when we have no intention to deceive others; but when, by the influences of some present passion, we deceive ourselves? The fact is confirmed by experience, if we commune with our own hearts; and by observation, if we look around. When the profligate is accused of enormities, he will have them pass for manly spirit, or love of society; and imposes this opinion not upon others, but on himself. When the miser indulges his love of wealth, he says, and believes, that he follows the maxims of a laudable œconomy. So also, while the censorious and invidious slanderer gratifies his malignity, he boasts, and believes, that he obeys the dictates of justice. Consult Bishop Butler, your favourite, and the favourite of every real enquirer into the principles of human conduct, and you will be satisfied concerning the truth of the doctrine.—Apply it, then, to the case of Hamlet: sense of supposed duty, and a regard to character, prompt him to slay his uncle; and he is withheld at that particular moment, by the ascendant of a gentle disposition; by the scruples, and perhaps weakness, of extreme sensibility. But how can he answer to the world, and to his sense of duty, for missing this opportunity? The real motive cannot be urged. Instead of excusing, it would expose him, he thinks, to censure; perhaps to contempt. He looks about for a motive; and one better suited to the opinions of the multitude, and better calculated to lull resentment, is immediately suggested. He indulges, and shelters himself under the subterfuge. He alledges, as direct causes of his delay, motives that could never influence his conduct; and thus exhibits a most exquisite picture of amiable self-deceit. The lines and colours are, indeed, very fine; and not very obvious to cursory observation. The beauties of Shakespeare, like genuine beauty of every kind, are often veiled; they are not forward nor obtrusive. They do not demand, though they claim attention.

I would now offer some observations concerning Hamlet's counterfeited or real madness: and as they are also intended to justify his moral conduct, let me beg of you to keep still in view, the particular circumstances of his situation, and the peculiar frame of his mind.

Harassed from without, and distracted from within, is it wonderful, if, during his endeavour to conceal his thoughts, he should betray inattention to those around him; incoherence of speech and manner; or break out inadvertently, into expressions of displeasure? Is it wonderful that he should "forego all mirth," become pensive, melancholy, or even morose? Surely, such disorder of mind, in characters like that of Hamlet, though not amounting to actual madness, yet exhibiting reason in extreme perplexity, and even trembling on the brink of madness, is not unusual. Meantime, Hamlet was fully sensible how strange those involuntary improprieties must appear to others: he was conscious he could not suppress them; he knew he was surrounded with spies; and was justly apprehensive, lest his suspicions or purposes should be discovered. But how are these consequences to be prevented? By counterfeiting an insanity which in part exists. Accordingly, to Ophelia, to Polonius, and others, he displays more extravagance than his real disorder would have occasioned. This particular aspect of the human mind is not unnatural; but is so peculiar and so exquisitely marked, that he alone who delineated the commencing madness, the blended reason and distraction of Lear, has ventured to pourtray its lineaments. That Hamlet really felt some disorder, that he studied concealment, and strove to hide his distraction under appearances of madness, is manifest in the following passage, among others of the same kind, where he discovers much earnestness and emotion, and at the same time, an affectation of sprightliness and unconcern:

> Swear by my sword
> Never to speak of this that you have heard.
> *Ghost.* Swear by his sword.
> *Ham.* Well said, old mole! can'st work i' the earth so fast?
> A worthy pioneer! Once more remove, good friends.
> *Hor.* O day and night, but this is wond'rous strange!
> *Ham.* And therefore, as a stranger, give it welcome.
> There are more things in heaven and earth, Horatio,
> Than are dreamt of in your philosophy.—
> But come;—
> Here, as before, never, so help you mercy!
> *Ghost.* Swear, &c.
> *Ham.* Rest, rest, perturbed spirit!

If we allow that the poet actually intended to represent Hamlet as feeling some distraction of mind; and was thus led to extravagancies which he affected to render still more extravagant, why, in his apology to Laertes, need we charge him with deviation from truth?

> This presence knows, and you must needs have heard,
> How I am punish'd with a sore distraction.
> What I have done,
> That might your nature, honour, and exception,
> Roughly awake, I here proclaim was madness.
> Was't Hamlet wrong'd Laertes? Never, Hamlet.
> If Hamlet from himself be ta'en away,
> And, when he's not himself, does wrong Laertes,
> Then Hamlet does it not; Hamlet denies it.

Hamlet, no doubt, put to death Polonius; but without intention, and in the frenzy of tumultuous emotion. He might therefore say, both of that action and of the consequent madness of Ophelia,

> Let my disclaiming from a purpos'd evil,
> Free me so far in your most generous thoughts,
> That I have shot my arrow o'er the house,
> And hurt my brother.

Neither is his conduct at the funeral of Ophelia to be construed into any design of insulting Laertes. His behaviour was the effect of violent perturbation; and he says so afterwards, not only to Laertes, but to Horatio:

> —— I am very sorry, good Horatio,
> That to Laertes I forgot myself, &c.
> But sure, the bravery of his grief did put me
> Into a tow'ring passion.

To this he alludes in his apology:

> If Hamlet from himself be ta'en away,
> And, when he's not himself, does wrong Laertes,
> Then Hamlet does it not; Hamlet denies it.

The whole of his behaviour at the funeral, shews a mind exceedingly disordered, and thrown into very violent agitation. But his affection for Ophelia appears sincere; and his regard for Laertes genuine. On recovery from his transport, to which, however, Laertes provoked him, how pathetic is the following expostulation:

> —— Hear you, Sir,
> What is the reason that you us'd me thus?
> I lov'd you ever.

I have been the more minute in considering those particulars, that not only you, but Commentators of great reputation, have charged Hamlet, in this part of his conduct, with falsehood and inhumanity.*

It remains that I should offer a few observations concerning Hamlet's jocularity. You seem to think it strange, that he should affect merriment when his situation is miserable, and when he feels his misery. Alas! it is a symptom, too unambiguous, of his affliction. He is so miserable, that he has no relish for any enjoyment; and is even weary of his existence.

> O that this too, too solid flesh would melt,
> Thaw, and resolve itself into a dew! &c.

Thinking himself incapable of happiness, he thinks he should be quite unconcerned in any human event. This is another aspect of self-deceit: for in truth he is not unconcerned. Yet acting as if it were so, he affects to regard serious, and even important matters, with a careless indifference. He would laugh:

---

* With high respect and sincere esteem for one of the most enlightened critics, and most useful moral philosophers that ever appeared in England, this and some other remarks in the Essay on the character of Hamlet, are intended, as the attentive reader will perceive, to remove some strong objections urged by Dr. Johnson against both the play, and the character.

but his laughter is not that of mirth. Add to this, that in those moments when he fancies himself indifferent or unconcerned, he endeavours to treat those actions which would naturally excite indignation, with scorn or contempt. This, on several occasions, leads him to assume the appearance of an ironical, but melancholy gaiety. This state of mind is exquisitely delineated in the following passage, where his affected melancholy betrays itself: and his gaiety and indifference, notwithstanding his endeavours to preserve them, relapse into his usual mood.

> *Hor.* My Lord, I came to see your father's funeral.
> *Ham.* I pray thee do not mock me, fellow student:
> I think it was to see my mother's wedding.
> *Hor.* Indeed, my lord, it follow'd hard upon.
> *Ham.* Thrift, thrift, Horatio! the funeral bak'd meats
> Did coldly furnish forth the marriage tables.
> Would I had met my dearest foe in heaven,
> Or ever I had seen that day, Horatio.

If, however, this account of the matter should not seem to you satisfactory, I must refer you to the preceding essay on the character of Hamlet: for I confess that I think the explanation given in that place is altogether sufficient. Hamlet assumes an air of ease, familiarity, and cheerful unconcern; and therefore jests with his friends, not only to conceal his designs, but that he may suit the complexion of his own mind to that of the unconcerned spectator; nor exhibit in his behaviour, any thing strange, improper, or unbecoming.

From these remarks, I hope you will now agree with me, that Hamlet deserves compassion; and that Horatio may say of him, with propriety,

> ——— Good night, sweet Prince;
> And flights of angels sing thee to thy rest.

The character is consistent. Hamlet is exhibited with good dispositions, and struggling with untoward circumstances. The contest is interesting. As he endeavours to act right, we approve and esteem him. But his original constitution renders him unequal to the contest: he displays the weaknesses and imperfections to which his peculiar character is liable; he is unfortunate; his misfortunes are in some measure occasioned by his weakness: he thus becomes an object not of blame, but of genuine and tender regret.

IV

S. T. COLERIDGE

Hamlet

Compare the easy language of common life in which this drama opens, with the wild wayward lyric of the opening of *Macbeth*. The language is familiar: no poetic descriptions of night, no elaborate information conveyed by one speaker to another of what both had before their immediate perceptions (such as the first distich in Addison's *Cato*,[1] which is a translation into poetry of "Past four o'clock, and a damp morning")—yet nothing bordering on the comic on the one hand, and no striving of the intellect on the other. It is the language of *sensation* among men who feared no charge of effeminacy for feeling what they felt no want of resolution to bear. Yet the armour, the dead silence, the watchfulness that first interrupts it, the welcome relief of guard, the cold, the broken expressions as of a man's compelled attention to bodily feelings allowed no man,—all excellently accord with and prepare for the after gradual rise into tragedy—but above all into a tragedy the interest of which is eminently *ad et apud intra*, as *Macbeth* . . .[?] is *ad extra*.

The preparation *informative* of the audience [is] just as much as was precisely necessary: how gradual first, and with the uncertainty appertaining to a question—

What, has *this thing* appeared *again* to-night.

From *Coleridge's Shakespearean Criticism*, ed. Thomas Middleton Raysor (London: Constable, 1930), I, 20–40. Apart from its concluding section, the passage consists of notes marginally inserted by Coleridge either in the copy of Theobald's edition which belonged to Morgan or in the Stockdale Shakespeare that was Coleridge's own property. The insertions in square brackets are by Professor Raysor, as are the footnotes. In the present reprint a few of the less interesting observations are omitted, and some of the footnotes are abbreviated.

[1] "*Port*. The dawn is over-cast, the morning lours,/And heavily in clouds brings on the day."

Even the word "again" has its *credibilizing* effect. Then the representative of the ignorance of the audience, Horatio (not himself but [quoted by] Marcellus to Bernardo) anticipates the common solution, " 'tis but our phantasy." But Marcellus rises secondly into "[this] dreaded sight." Then this "thing" becomes at once an "apparition," and that too an intelligent spirit that is to be *spoken* to.

> Tush, tush! 'twill not appear.

Then the shivery feeling, at such a time, with two eye-witnesses, of sitting down to hear a story of a ghost, and this, too, a ghost that had appeared two nights before [at] about this very time. The effort of the narrator to master his own imaginative terrors; the consequent elevation of the style, itself a continuation of this effort; the turning off to an *outward* object, "yon same star." O heaven! words are wasted to those that feel and to those who do not feel the exquisite judgement of Shakespeare.

Hume himself could not but have faith in *this* Ghost dramatically, let his anti-ghostism be as strong as Samson against ghosts less powerfully raised.

> [I. i. 70–72.
> *Mar.* Good now, sit down, and tell me, he that knows,
> Why this same strict and most observant watch
> So nightly toils the subject of the land.]

The exquisitely natural transit into the narration retrospective. [When the Ghost re-appears, note] Horatio's increased courage from having translated the late individual spectre into thought and past experience, and Marcellus' and Bernardo's sympathy with it [Horatio's courage] in daring to strike, while yet the former feeling returns in

> We do it wrong [being so majestical,
> To offer it the show of violence.]

> [I. i. 149–52.
>   I have heard,
> The cock, that is the trumpet to the morn,
> Doth with his lofty and shrill-sounding throat
> Awake the god of day.]

No Addison more careful to be poetical in diction than Shakespeare in providing the grounds and sources of its propriety. But *how* to elevate a thing almost mean by its familiarity, young poets may learn in the cock-crow.

> [I. i. 169–71.
> Let us impart what we have seen to-night
> Unto young Hamlet; for, upon my life,
> This spirit, dumb to us, will speak to him.]

The unobtrusive and yet fully adequate mode of introducing the main character, *young* Hamlet, upon whom transfers itself all the interest excited for the acts and concerns of the king, his father.

[I. ii] Relief by change of scene to the royal court. This [relief is desirable] on any occasion; but how judicious that Hamlet should not have to take up the leavings of exhaustion. The set, pedantically antithetic form of the king's speech—tho' in the concerns that galled the heels of conscience, rhetorical below a king, yet in what follows, not without majesty. Was he not a royal brother?

> [I. ii. 42. The King's speech.
> And now, Laertes, what's the news with you?]

Shakespeare's art in introducing a most important but still subordinate character first. Milton's Beelzebub.[2] So Laertes, who is yet thus graciously treated from the assistance given to the election of the king's brother instead of son by Polonius.

> [I. ii. 65–67.
> *Ham.* [*Aside.*] A little more than kin, and less than kind.
> *King.* How is it that the clouds still hang on you?
> *Ham.* Not so, my lord; I am too much i' the sun.]

Play on words either [due] to 1. exuberant activity of mind, as in Shakespeare's higher comedy; [or] 2. imitation of it as a fashion, which has this to say for it—"Why is not this now better than groaning?"[3]—or 3. contemptuous exultation in minds vul-

---

[2] Coleridge's memory seems to have played him false on this point.

[3] "Why is not this better now than groaning for love" (*Romeo and Juliet* II. iv. 85–86).

garized and overset by their success, [like] Milton's Devils;[4] or
4. as the language of resentment, in order to express contempt
—most common among the lower orders, and [the] origin of
nicknames; or lastly, as the language of suppressed passion, especially of hardly smothered dislike. Three of these combine in
the present instance; and doubtless Farmer is right in supposing
the equivocation carried on into "too much in the *sun*."

> [I. ii. 74.
> *Ham.* Ay, madam, it is common.]

Suppression prepares for overflow.

> [I. ii. 120.
> *Ham.* I shall in all my best obey you, madam.]

Hamlet's silence to the long speech of the king, and general answer to his mother.

[I. iii] This scene must be regarded as one of Shakespeare's
lyric movements in the play, and the skill with which it is in-
terwoven with the dramatic parts is peculiarly an excellence of
our poet. You experience the sensation of a pause without the
sense of a stop. You will observe in Ophelia's short and general
answer to the long speech of Laertes the natural carelessness of
innocence, which cannot think such a code of cautions and pru-
dences necessary to its own preservation.

> [I. iii. 115–17.
> *Pol.*   . . . I do know,
> When the blood burns, how prodigal the soul
> Lends the tongue vows: these blazes, daughter, etc.]

A spondee has, I doubt not, dropt out of the text. After "vows"
insert either "Go to" or "mark you!" If the latter be preferred, it might end the line.

> "Lends the tongue vows. Go to! these blazes, daughter,"

or

> "Lends the tongue vows. These blazes, daughter, mark you."

N.B. Shakespeare never introduces a catalectic line without in-
tending an equivalent to the foot omitted, in the pauses, or the

---

[4] *Paradise Lost* vi. 609–27.

dwelling emphasis, or the diffused retardation. I do not, however, deny that a good actor might by employing the last mentioned, viz., the retardation or solemn knowing drawl, supply the missing spondee with good effect. But I do not believe that in this or the foregoing speeches Shakespeare meant to bring out the senility or weakness of Polonius's mind. In the great ever-recurring dangers and duties of life, where to distinguish the fit objects for the application of the maxims collected by the experience of a long life requires no fineness of tact, as in the admonitions to his son and daughter, Polonius is always made respectable. But if the actor were capable of catching these shades in the character, the pit and gallery would be malcontent.

[I. iv] In addition to the other excellencies of Hamlet's speech concerning the wassail music, so finely revealing the predominant idealism, the ratiocinative meditativeness of his character, it has the advantage of giving nature and probability to the impassioned continuity of the speech instantly directed to the Ghost. The momentum had been given to his mental activity, the full current of the thoughts and words had set in, and the very forgetfulness, in the fervor of his argumentation, of the purpose for which he was there, aided in preventing the appearance from benumbing the mind. Consequently, it acted as a new impulse, a sudden stroke which increased the velocity of the body already in motion, while it altered the direction. The co-presence of Horatio, Marcellus, and Bernardo is most judiciously contrived, for it renders the courage of Hamlet and his impetuous eloquence perfectly intelligible. The knowledge, the *unthought* of consciousness, the *sensation*, of human auditors, of flesh and blood sympathists, acts as a support, a stimulation *a tergo*, while the *front* of the mind, the whole consciousness of the speaker, is filled by the solemn apparition. Add, too, that the apparition itself has by its frequent previous appearances been brought nearer to a thing of this world. This accrescence of objectivity in a ghost that yet retains all its ghostly attributes and fearful subjectivity, is truly wonderful.

[I. v. 92–112. The speech of Hamlet as the Ghost vanishes.
Ham. O all you host of heaven! O earth! what else?
And shall I couple hell? O, fie! Hold, hold, my heart; etc.]

I remember nothing equal to this burst unless it be the first speech of Prometheus,[5] after the exit of Vulcan and the two Afrites, in Aeschylus. But Shakespeare alone could have produced the vow of Hamlet to make his memory a blank of all maxims and generalized truths that "observation had copied there," followed by the immediate noting down of the generalized fact,

> That one may smile, and smile, and be a villain.

[II. i. Polonius and Reynaldo. Polonius and Ophelia.] In all things dependent on, or rather made up of, fine address, the *manner* is no more or otherwise rememberable than the light motions, steps, and gestures of youth and health. But this is almost everything; no wonder, therefore, if that which can be *put down by rule* in the memory should appear mere poring, maudlin-eyed cunning, slyness blinking thro' the watery eye of superannuation. So in this admirable scene, Polonius, who is throughout the skeleton of his own former skill and statecraft, hunts the trail of policy at a dead scent, supplied by the weak fever-smell in his own nostrils.

[II. ii. 172–73.
Pol. Do you know me, my lord?
Ham. Excellent well; you are a fishmonger.]

"Fishmonger"; *i.e.* you are sent to *fish* out the secret. This is Hamlet's meaning. The purposely obscure lines—

For if the sun [breed maggots in a dead dog, being a god kissing carrion—Have you a daughter?]

I rather think refer to some thought in Hamlet's mind contrasting the lovely daughter with such a tedious old fool, her father, as *he* represents Polonius to himself. "Why, fool as he is, he is some degrees in rank above a dead dog's carcase; and if the sun, being a god that kisses carrion, can raise life out of a dead dog, why may [not] good fortune, that favors fools, have raised a lovely girl out of this dead-alive old fool."

Warburton is often led astray in his interpretations by his attention to general positions without the due Shakespearian reference to what is probably passing in the mind of his speaker,

[5] *Prometheus Bound* 88–127.

characteristic and expository of his particular character and present mood. In confirmation of my preceding note, see

O Jephthah, judge of Israel! what a treasure hadst thou, etc.

[II. ii. 398–403]

[II. ii. 212–16.
Pol. . . . I will most humbly take my leave of you.
Ham. You cannot, sir, take from me any thing that I will more willingly part withal: except my life, except my life, except my life.]

The repetition of "except my life" is most admirable.

[II. ii. 262–64.
Ham. Then are our beggars bodies, and our monarchs and outstretched heroes the beggars' shadows. Shall we to the court? for, by my fay, I cannot reason.]

I do not understand this; and Shakespeare seems to have intended the meaning not to be more than snatched at: "By my fay! I cannot reason."

[II. ii. 446–512.
"The rugged Pyrrhus, he whose sable arms," etc.]

This admirable substitution of the epic for the dramatic, giving such a *reality* to the impassioned dramatic diction of Shakespeare's own dialogue,[6] and authorized too by the actual style of the tragedies before Shakespeare (*Porrex and Ferrex, Titus Andronicus*, etc.) is worthy of notice. The fancy that a burlesque was intended, sinks below criticism. The lines, as *epic* narrative, are superb.

[II. ii. 543–601. Hamlet's soliloquy:
O, what a rogue and peasant slave am I!]

---

[6] For this fine observation Coleridge is indebted to Schlegel, though with alterations. Schlegel's excellent treatment of this problem is worth reading in its entirety, but space forbids quotation of more than two sentences which Coleridge used. "They [Shakespeare's commentators] have not considered that this speech must not be judged by itself but in the place where it stands. That which is meant to appear as dramatic invention in the play itself, must contrast with the play's dignified poetry in the same degree as theatrical elevation with simple nature." *Werke*, VI, 251.

Here, after the recapitulation and character of Hamlet, recommence the particular criticism, as these lines contain Shakespeare's own attestation of the truth of the idea I have started.
Turn likewise to [Act IV, Scene iv, Hamlet's soliloquy,

How all occasions do inform against me,]

as [evidence of] Hamlet's character self-attested.

> [II. ii. 594–99.
> *Ham.*   . . . The spirit that I have seen
> May be the devil; and the devil hath power
> To assume a pleasing shape; yea, and perhaps
> Out of my weakness and my melancholy,
> As he is very potent with such spirits,
> Abuses me to damn me.]

[See] Sir Thomas Browne: "Those apparitions and ghosts of departed persons are not the wandering souls of men, but the unquiet walks of devils, prompting and suggesting us unto mischief, blood, and villainy," etc., *Religio Medici* [Part I], sect. 37, *ad finem*.

> [III. i. 48–49.
> *Pol.*   . . . we do sugar o'er
> The devil himself.
> *King.* [*Aside.*] O, 'tis too true!]

The "O" here is to be so pronounced as to be equal in effect of sound to a spondee or at least a trochaic dissyllable; and the metre to be thus restored—

> The devil himself. Ŏh! it is too true
> How smart a lash that speech doth give my conscience.

> [III. i. 56–88. Hamlet's soliloquy.
> To be, or not to be: that is the question.]

Of such universal interest, and yet to which of all Shakespeare's characters could it have [been] *appropriately* given but to Hamlet? For Jaques it would have been too deep; for Iago, too habitual a communion with the *heart*, that belongs or ought to belong, to all mankind.

> [III. i. 103.
> *Ham.* Ha, ha! are you honest?]

Here it is evident that the penetrating Hamlet perceived, from the strange and forced manner of Ophelia, that the sweet girl was not acting a part of her own—in short, saw into the stratagem—and his after speeches are not directed to Ophelia, but to the listeners and spies.

Hamlet here discovers that he is watched, and Ophelia a decoy. Even this in a mood so anxious and irritable accounts for a certain harshness in him; and yet a wild upworking of love, sporting with opposites with a wilful self-tormenting irony, is perceptible throughout: *ex. gr.* "I did love you" and [his reference to] the faults of the sex from which Ophelia is so characteristically free that the freedom therefrom constitutes her character. Here again Shakespeare's charm of constituting female character by absence of characters, [of] outjuttings.

[III. i. 146–49. Hamlet to Ophelia.
. . . I say, we will have no more marriages: those that are married already, all but one, shall live; the rest shall keep as they are.]

The dallying with the inward purpose that of one who had not brought his mind to the steady acting point, would fain *sting* the uncle's mind,—but to stab the body!

The soliloquy of Ophelia is the perfection of love—so exquisitely unselfish!

[III. ii. The dialogue of Hamlet with the players.] One and among the happiest [instances] of Shakespeare's power of diversifying the scene while he is carrying on the plot.

[III. ii. 100–103.
Pol. I did enact Julius Caesar: I was killed i' the Capitol;
Brutus killed me.
Ham. It was a brute part of him to kill so capital a calf there.]

In any direct form to have kept Hamlet's love for Ophelia before the audience, would have made a breach in the unity of the interest; but yet to the thoughtful reader it is suggested by his spite to poor Polonius, whom he cannot let rest.

[III. ii. The play.] As in the first interview with the players by *epic* verse, so here [the style of the play performed before the court is distinguished] by rhyme.

[III. ii. 326–27.
Ros. My lord, you once did love me.
Ham. So I do still, by these pickers and stealers.]

I never heard an actor give this word its proper emphasis—
Shakespeare's meaning is—"Lov'd *you? * Hum? *So* I do still," etc.
There has been no *change* in my opinion. Else Hamlet tells an
ignoble falsehood, and a useless one, as the last speech to
Guildenstern, "Why, look you now," proves.

[III. ii. 380–82. Hamlet's soliloquy.
. . . now could I drink hot blood,
And do such bitter business as the day
Would quake to look on.]

The utmost Hamlet arrives to is a disposition, a mood, to do
something. What is still left undecided, while every word he
utters tends to betray his disguise.

The perfect equal to any call of the moment is Hamlet, let it
only not be for a future.

[III. iii. 11–15.
Ros. The single and peculiar life is bound
With all the strength and armour of the mind
To keep itself from noyance; but much more
That spirit upon whose weal depends and rests
The lives of many.]

To bring all possible good out of evil, yet [also] how characteristically is this just sentiment placed in the mouth of Rosencrantz.

[III. iii. 27–29.
Pol. My lord, he's going to his mother's closet:
Behind the arras I'll convey myself,
To hear the process.]

Polonius's volunteer obtrusion of himself into this business,
while it is appropriate to his character, still letching after former importance, removes all likelihood that Hamlet should suspect his presence, and prevents us from making his death injure
Hamlet in our opinion.

[III. iii. 36–72. The king's remorse.
O, my offence is rank, it smells to heaven.]

The king's speech well marks the difference between crime and guilt of habit. The conscience is still admitted to audience. Nay, even as an audible soliloquy, it is far less improbable than is supposed by such as have watched men only in the beaten road of their feelings. But it deserves to be dwelt on, that final "All may be well"; a degree of merit [is] attributed by the self-flattering soul to its own struggle, tho' baffled, and to the indefinite half-promise, half-command, to persevere in religious duties. The divine medium of the Christian doctrine of expiation [is] in this: not what you have done, but what you *are*, must determine. Metanoia.[7]

[III. iii. 73–96. Hamlet spares the king because he finds him at prayer, and, therefore, safe from damnation.

> *Ham.* Now might I do it pat, now he is praying;
> . . . and am I then revenged,
> To take him in the purging of his soul,
> When he is fit and season'd for his passage?
> No.]

Dr. Johnson's mistaking of the marks of reluctance and procrastination for impetuous, horror-striking fiendishness![8] Of such importance is it to understand the *germ* of a character. But the interval taken up by Hamlet's speech is truly awful! and then—

> My words fly up, [my thoughts remain below.]

O what a lesson concerning the essential difference between wishing and willing, and the folly of all motive-mongering, while the individual self remains.

---

[7] Μετάνοια, repentance.

[8] Not merely in Dr. Johnson did eighteenth-century humanitarianism so express itself. Cf. [Hanmer?], *Some Remarks on the Tragedy of Hamlet* (1736), p. 41; a "Well-wisher and Admirer" of Garrick's in 1742, *Private Correspondence of David Garrick* (1831), i. 14; Francis Gentleman, *The Dramatic Censor* (1770), i. 46; Tom Davies, *Dramatic Miscellanies* (1785), iii. 104. Dr. Johnson is nearer to the Elizabethans on this point than Coleridge, who did not have the general knowledge of Elizabethan literature which was necessary to support historical criticism, though he preached the historical point of view. Analogies in Elizabethan literature show that contemporaries of Shakespeare would not be horrified at such a motive in a revenge play, but also that they would take it seriously, as Johnson did. See chap. iv, *Hamlet: An Historical and Comparative Study*, by E. E. Stoll.

[III. iv. 28–30.
Ham. A bloody deed! almost as bad, good mother,
As kill a king, and marry with his brother.
Queen. As kill a king!]

I confess that Shakespeare has left the character of the queen in an unpleasant perplexity. Was she or was she not conscious of the fratricide?

[IV. ii. 14–16.
Ros. Take you me for a sponge, my lord?
Ham. Ay, sir; that soaks up the king's countenance, his rewards, his authorities.]

Hamlet's madness is made to consist in the full utterance of all the thoughts that had past thro' his mind before—in telling home truths.

[IV. v. Ophelia's singing.] The conjunction here of these two thoughts that had never subsisted in disjunction, the love for Hamlet and her filial love, and the guileless floating on the surface of her pure imagination of the cautions so lately expressed and the fears not too delicately avowed by her father and brother concerning the danger to which her honor lay exposed.

Thought and affliction, passion, murder[9] itself,
She turns to favor and to prettiness.
[IV. v. 184–85]

This play of association is sweetly instanced in the close—

. . . My brother shall know of it: and [so] I thank you for your good *counsel.*
[IV. v. 68–69]

[IV. v. 100–103. The revolt of Laertes is announced to the king:
And, as the world were now but to begin,
Antiquity forgot, custom not known,
The ratifiers and props of every word,
They cry 'Choose we; Laertes shall be king!']

Fearful and self-suspicious as I always feel when I seem to see an error of judgement in Shakespeare, yet I cannot reconcile the cool, [and, as Warburton calls it,] "rational and consequential" reflection in these three lines with the anonymousness or the alarm of the messenger.

[9] *Read* "*hell.*"

[IV. v. 120–21. The king faces Laertes:
There's such divinity doth hedge a king,
That treason can but peep to what it would.]

Proof, as indeed all else is, that Shakespeare never intended us to see the king with Hamlet's eyes, tho', I suspect, the managers have long done so.

[IV. v. 128. Laertes to the king:
To hell, allegiance! vows, to the blackest devil!

Warburton's note: "*Laertes* is a good character; but he is here in actual rebellion," etc.]

Mercy on Warburton's notions of goodness! See [the seventh scene

Laer. . . . I will do 't
And for that purpose I'll anoint my sword.]

especially [treacherous?] after the king's description of Hamlet—

. . . he, being remiss,
Most generous and free from all contriving,
[Will not peruse the foils.]

Shakespeare evidently wishes as much as possible to spare the character of Laertes, to break the extreme turpitude of his consent to become an agent and accomplice of the king's treacheries—and to this end works the re-introduction of Ophelia [at the end of this scene].

[IV. vi. Hamlet's capture by the pirates, as explained in his letter.] Almost the only play of Shakespeare, in which mere accidents, independent of all will, form an essential part of the plot; but here how judiciously in keeping with the character of the over-meditative Hamlet, ever at last determined by accident or by a fit of passion.

[IV. vii. 81–106. The king] first awakens Laertes' vanity by the praises of the report[er], then gratifies it by the report itself, and then [comes to the point—

. . . Sir, this report of his]
Did Hamlet so envenom with his envy
[That he could nothing do but wish and beg
Your sudden coming o'er, to play with him.]

And that Laertes might be excused in some degree for not cooling, the act concludes with the affecting death of Ophelia. Who does not see [her], like a little projection of land into a lake or stream, covered with spring-flowers, lying quietly reflected in the great waters, but at length [being] undermined and loosened, becomes a floating faery isle, and after a brief vagrancy sinks almost without an eddy!

[V. i] The contrast between the clowns and Hamlet as two extremes—the [clowns'] mockery of logic, the traditional wit valued like truth for its antiquity, and treasured up, like a tune, for use.

> [V. i. 270. Hamlet to Laertes.
> Woo't drink up eisel?

"Eisel" is Theobald's emendation for "Esill" or "Esile."]

"Eisil," I suppose, is the word; but I suspect that Hamlet alluded to the cup of anguish at the Cross, and that it should be "the Eisel"; *i.e.* would'st drink it *up?* Christ simply tasted it. Theobald does not explain the "drink *up!*" We do not say drink up vinegar, but drink vinegar.

[V. i–ii] Shakespeare seems to mean *all* Hamlet's character, to be brought together before his final disappearance from the scene—his meditative excess in the grave-digging [scene], his yielding to passion, his love for Ophelia blazing out, his tendency to generalize on all occasions in the dialogue with Horatio, his fine gentlemanly manners with Osrick, and his and Shakespeare's fondness for presentiment[10]—"O my prophetic soul" [I. v. 40], and his "Most generous and free from all contriving" in his fencing-duel—and all at last done by . . . [?] and accident at the conclusion.

THE CHARACTER OF HAMLET[11]

Shakespeare's mode of conceiving characters out of his own intellectual and moral faculties, by conceiving any one intel-

[10] V. ii. 204–16.

[11] This manuscript is from a transcript by E. H. Coleridge of one of Coleridge's notebooks. The original notebook has escaped the editor's search for it. The transcript indicates that this is a lecture prepared for the Bristol series of 1813.

lectual or moral faculty in morbid excess and then placing himself, thus mutilated and diseased, under given circumstances. This we shall have repeated occasion to re-state and enforce. In Hamlet I conceive him to have wished to exemplify the moral necessity of a due balance between our attention to outward objects and our meditation on inward thoughts—a due balance between the real and the imaginary world. In Hamlet this balance does not exist—his thoughts, images, and fancy [being] far more vivid than his perceptions, and his very perceptions instantly passing thro' the medium of his contemplations, and acquiring as they pass a form and color not naturally their own. Hence great, enormous, intellectual activity, and a consequent proportionate aversion to real action, with all its symptoms and accompanying qualities.

> Action is transitory, a step, a blow,[12] etc.

Then as in the first instance proceed with a cursory survey thro' the play, with comments, etc.

(1) The easy language of ordinary life, contrasted with the direful music and wild rhythm of the opening of *Macbeth.* Yet the armour, the cold, the dead silence, all placing the mind in the state congruous with tragedy.

(2) The admirable judgement and yet confidence in his own marvellous powers in introducing the ghost twice, each rising in solemnity and awfulness before its third appearance to Hamlet himself.

(3) Shakespeare's tenderness with regard to all innocent superstition: no Tom Paine declarations and pompous philosophy.

(4) The first words that Hamlet speaks—

> A little more than kin, and less than kind.

He begins with that play of words, the complete absence of which characterizes *Macbeth* . . . [?]. No one can have heard quarrels among the vulgar but must have noticed the close connection of punning with angry contempt. Add too what is highly characteristic of superfluous activity of mind, a sort of playing with a thread or watch chain or snuff box.

---

[12] "Action is transitory—a step, a blow, . . .
Suffering is permanent, obscure and dark,
And shares the nature of infinity."
Wordsworth *The Borderers* III. v.

(5) And [note] how the character develops itself in the next speech—the aversion to externals, the betrayed habit of brooding over the world within him, and the prodigality of beautiful words, which are, as it were, the half embodyings of thoughts, that make them more than thoughts, give them an outness, a reality *sui generis*, and yet retain their correspondence and shadowy approach to the images and movements within.

(6) The first soliloquy [I. ii

O, that this too too solid flesh would melt.]

[The] reasons why *taedium vitae* oppresses minds like Hamlet's: the exhaustion of bodily feeling from perpetual exertion of mind; that all mental form being indefinite and ideal, realities must needs become cold, and hence it is the indefinite that combines with passion.

(7) And in this mood the relation is made [by Horatio, who tells Hamlet of his father's ghost], of which no more than [that] it is a perfect model of dramatic narration and dramatic style, the purest poetry and yet the most natural language, equally distant from the inkhorn and the provincial plough.

(8) Hamlet's running into long reasonings [while waiting for the ghost], carrying off the impatience and uneasy feelings of expectation by running away from the *particular* in[to] the *general*. This aversion to personal, individual concerns, and escape to generalizations and general reasonings a most important characteristic.

Besides that, it does away with surprizing[13] all the ill effects that the two former appearances of the ghost would have produced by rendering the ghost an expected phenomenon, and restores to it all the suddenness essential to the effect.

(9) The ghost [is] a superstition connected with the most [sacred?] truths of revealed religion and, therefore, O how contrasted from the withering and wild language of the [witches in] *Macbeth*.

(10) The instant and over violent resolve of Hamlet—how he wastes in the efforts of resolving the energies of action. Compare this with the . . . [?] of Medea; and [note] his quick relapse into the satirical and ironical vein [after the ghost disappears].

[13] That is, by means of the consequent surprise when the ghost appears.

(11) Now comes the difficult task, [interpreting the jests of Hamlet when his companions overtake him].

The familiarity, comparative at least, of a brooding mind with shadows is something. Still more the necessary alternation when one muscle long strained is relaxed; the antagonist comes into action of itself. Terror [is] closely connected with the ludicrous; the latter [is] the common mode by which the mind tries to emancipate itself from terror. The laugh is rendered by nature itself the language of extremes, even as tears are. Add too, Hamlet's wildness is but *half-false*. O that subtle trick to pretend the *acting* only when we are very near *being* what we act. And this explanation of the same with Ophelia's vivid images [describing Hamlet's desperation when he visits her]; nigh akin to, and productive of, temporary mania. [See II. i. 75–100, the speeches of] Ophelia [which were just mentioned] proved by [Hamlet's wildness at Ophelia's grave, V. i. 248–78].

(12) Hamlet's character, as I have conceived [it, is] described by himself [in the soliloquy after the players leave him—

O, what a rogue and peasant slave am I, etc.]

But previous to this, speak of the exquisite judgement in the diction of the introduced play. Absurd to suppose it extracted in order to be ridiculed from [an] old play. It is in thought and even in the separate parts of the diction highly poetical, so that this is its fault, that it is too poetical, the language of lyric vehemence and epic pomp, not of the drama. But that if Shakespeare had made the language truly dramatic? Where would have been the contrast between *Hamlet* and the play of *Hamlet?*

(13) And then conclude with the objections; see the cover and first page of this book.[14] Schlegel, III, 67, 69.

(14) After this whether it will not do to speak of the honest pride of our Englishmen—Milton, Shakespeare, Bacon, Newton, and now Wellington—and how the glorious events of the day[15] all are [?] deducible from the attack on England.

[14] A reference to the fragment on *Macbeth* in the same notebook.

[15] Wellington was just beginning his invasion of southern France, after driving Soult out of Spain.

V

A. C. BRADLEY

The Substance of Shakespearean Tragedy

In this tragic world, where individuals, however great they may
be and however decisive their actions may appear, are so evidently not the ultimate power, what is this power? What account can we give of it which will correspond with the imaginative impressions we receive? This will be our final question.

The variety of the answers given to this question shows how
difficult it is. And the difficulty has many sources. Most people,
even among those who know Shakespeare well and come
into real contact with his mind, are inclined to isolate and exaggerate some one aspect of the tragic fact. Some are so much
influenced by their own habitual beliefs that they import them
more or less into their interpretation of every author who is
"sympathetic" to them. And even where neither of these causes
of error appears to operate, another is present from which it is
probably impossible wholly to escape. What I mean is this. Any
answer we give to the question proposed ought to correspond
with, or to represent in terms of the understanding, our imaginative and emotional experience in reading the tragedies. We
have, of course, to do our best by study and effort to make this
experience true to Shakespeare; but, that done to the best of
our ability, the experience is the matter to be interpreted, and
the test by which the interpretation must be tried. But it is extremely hard to make out exactly what this experience is, because in the very effort to make it out, our reflecting mind, full
of everyday ideas, is always tending to transform it by the
application of these ideas, and so to elicit a result which, instead of representing the fact, conventionalises it. And the

From Lecture I in *Shakespearean Tragedy* by A. C. Bradley (London,
1904), pp. 24–39. Reprinted by permission of Macmillan and Co., Ltd.,
St. Martin's Press, Inc., New York, and the Macmillan Company of Canada,
Ltd.

consequence is not only mistaken theories; it is that many a man will declare that he feels in reading a tragedy what he never really felt, while he fails to recognise what he actually did feel. It is not likely that we shall escape all these dangers in our effort to find an answer to the question regarding the tragic world and the ultimate power in it.

It will be agreed, however, first, that this question must not be answered in "religious" language. For although this or that dramatis persona may speak of gods or of God, of evil spirits or of Satan, of heaven and of hell, and although the poet may show us ghosts from another world, these ideas do not materially influence his representation of life, nor are they used to throw light on the mystery of its tragedy. The Elizabethan drama was almost wholly secular; and while Shakespeare was writing he practically confined his view to the world of non-theological observation and thought, so he represents it substantially in one and the same way whether the period of the story is pre-Christian or Christian.[1] He looked at this "secular" world most intently and seriously; and he painted it, we cannot but conclude, with entire fidelity, without the wish to enforce an opinion of his own, and, in essentials, without regard to anyone's hopes, fears, or beliefs. His greatness is largely due to this fidelity in a mind of extraordinary power; and if, as a private person, he had a religious faith, his tragic view can hardly have been in contradiction with this faith, but must have been included in it, and supplemented, not abolished, by additional ideas.

Two statements, next, may at once be made regarding the tragic fact as he represents it: one, that it is and remains to us something piteous, fearful, and mysterious; the other, that the representation of it does not leave us crushed, rebellious or desperate. These statements will be accepted, I believe, by any reader who is in touch with Shakespeare's mind and can observe his own. Indeed such a reader is rather likely to complain that they are painfully obvious. But if they are true as well as obvious, something follows from them in regard to our present question.

From the first it follows that the ultimate power in the tragic world is not adequately described as a law or order which we can see to be just and benevolent—as, in that sense, a "moral

[1] I say substantially, but the concluding remarks on *Hamlet* [later in *Shakespearean Tragedy*] will modify a little the statements above.

order"—for in that case the spectacle of suffering and waste could not seem to us so fearful and mysterious as it does. And from the second it follows that this ultimate power is not adequately described as a fate, whether malicious and cruel or blind and indifferent to human happiness and goodness, for in that case the spectacle would leave us desperate or rebellious. Yet one or other of these two ideas will be found to govern most accounts of Shakespeare's tragic view or world. These accounts isolate and exaggerate single aspects, either the aspect of action or that of suffering; either the close and unbroken connection of character, will, deed and catastrophe, which, taken alone, shows the individual simply as sinning against, or failing to conform to, the moral order and drawing his just doom on his own head; or else that pressure of outward forces, that sway of accident, and those blind and agonised struggles, which, taken alone, show him as the mere victim of some power which cares neither for his sins nor for his pain. Such views contradict one another, and no third view can unite them; but the several aspects from whose isolation and exaggeration they spring are both present in the fact, and a view which would be true to the fact and to the whole of our imaginative experience must in some way combine these aspects.

Let us begin, then, with the idea of fatality and glance at some of the impressions which give rise to it, without asking at present whether this idea is their natural or fitting expression. There can be no doubt that they do arise and that they ought to arise. If we do not feel at times that the hero is, in some sense, a doomed man; that he and others drift struggling to destruction like helpless creatures borne on an irresistible flood towards a cataract; that, faulty as they may be, their fault is far from being the sole or sufficient cause of all they suffer; and that the power from which they cannot escape is relentless and immovable; we have failed to receive an essential part of the full tragic effect.

The sources of these impressions are various, and I will refer only to a few. One of them is put into words by Shakespeare himself when he makes the player-king in *Hamlet* say:

> Our thoughts are ours, their ends none of our own;

"their ends" are the issues or outcomes of our thoughts, and these, says the speaker, are not our own. The tragic world is a world of action, and action is the translation of thought into reality. We see men and women confidently attempting it. They strike into the existing order of things in pursuance of their ideas. But what they achieve is not what they intended; it is terribly unlike it. They understand nothing, we say to ourselves, of the world on which they operate. They fight blindly in the dark, and the power that works through them makes them the instrument of a design which is not theirs. They act freely, and yet their action binds them hand and foot. And it makes no difference whether they meant well or ill. No one could mean better than Brutus, but he contrives misery for his country and death for himself. No one could mean worse than Iago, and he too is caught in the web he spins for others. Hamlet, recoiling from the rough duty of revenge, is pushed into blood-guiltiness he never dreamed of, and forced at last on the revenge he could not will. His adversary's murders, and no less his adversary's remorse, bring about the opposite of what they sought. Lear follows an old man's whim, half-generous, half-selfish; and in a moment it looses all the powers of darkness upon him. Othello agonises over an empty fiction, and, meaning to execute solemn justice, butchers innocence and strangles love. They understand themselves no better than the world about them. Coriolanus thinks that his heart is iron, and it melts like snow before a fire. Lady Macbeth, who thought she could dash out her own child's brains, finds herself hounded to death by the smell of a stranger's blood. Her husband thinks that to gain a crown he would jump the life to come, and finds that the crown has brought him all the horrors of that life. Everywhere in this tragic world, man's thought, translated into act, is transformed into the opposite of itself. His act, the movement of a few ounces of matter in a moment of time, becomes a monstrous flood which spreads over a kingdom. And whatsoever he dreams of doing, he achieves that which he least dreamed of, his own destruction.

All this makes us feel the blindness and helplessness of man. Yet by itself it would hardly suggest the idea of fate, because it shows man as in some degree, however slight, the cause of his own undoing. But other impressions come to aid it. It is aided by everything which makes us feel that a man is, as we say, terribly unlucky; and of this there is, even in Shakespeare, not a little. Here come in some of the accidents already considered: Juliet's waking from her trance a minute too late, Desdemona's loss of her handkerchief at the only moment when the loss would have mattered, that insignificant delay which cost Cordelia's life. Again, men act, no doubt, in accordance with their characters; but what is it that brings them just the one problem which is fatal to them and would be easy to another, and sometimes brings it to them just when they are least fitted to face it? How is it that Othello comes to be the companion of the one man in the world who is at once able enough, brave enough, and vile enough to ensnare him? By what strange fatality does it happen that Lear has such daughters and Cordelia such sisters? Even character itself contributes to these feelings of fatality. How could men escape, we cry, such vehement propensities as drive Romeo, Antony, Coriolanus, to their doom? And why is it that a man's virtues help to destroy him, and that his weakness or defect is so intertwined with everything that is admirable in him that we can hardly separate them even in imagination?

If we find in Shakespeare's tragedies the source of impressions like these, it is important, on the other hand, to notice what we do *not* find there. We find practically no trace of fatalism in its more primitive, crude, and obvious forms. Nothing, again, makes us think of the actions and sufferings of the persons as somehow arbitrarily fixed beforehand without regard to their feelings, thoughts, and resolutions. Nor, I believe, are the facts ever so presented that it seems to us as if the supreme power, whatever it may be, had a special spite against a family or an individual. Neither, lastly, do we receive the impression (which, it must be observed, is not purely fatalistic) that a family, owing to some hideous crime or impiety in early days, is doomed in later days to continue a career of portentous calamities and sins. Shakespeare, indeed, does not appear to have taken much interest in heredity, or to have attached much importance to it.

What, then, is this "fate" which the impressions already considered lead us to describe as the ultimate power in the tragic world? It appears to be a mythological expression for the whole system or order, of which the individual characters form an inconsiderable and feeble part; which seems to determine, far more than they, their native dispositions and their circumstances, and through these, their action; which is so vast and complex that they can scarcely at all understand it or control its workings; and which has a nature so definite and fixed that whatever changes take place in it produce other changes inevitably and without regard to men's desires and regrets. And whether this system or order is best called by the name of fate or no,[2] it can hardly be denied that it does appear as the ultimate power in the tragic world, and that it has such characteristics as these. But the name "fate" may be intended to imply something more—to imply that this order is a blank necessity, totally regardless alike of human weal and of the difference between good and evil or right and wrong. And such an implication many readers would at once reject. They would maintain, on the contrary, that this order shows characteristics of quite another kind from those which made us give it the name of fate, characteristics which certainly should not induce us to forget those others, but which would lead us to describe it as a moral order and its necessity as a moral necessity.

Let us turn, then, to this idea. It brings into the light those aspects of the tragic fact which the idea of fate throws into the shade. And the argument which leads to it in its simplest form may be stated briefly thus: "Whatever may be said of accidents, circumstances and the like, human action is, after all, presented to us as the central fact in tragedy, and also as the main cause of the catastrophe. That necessity which so much impresses us is, after all, chiefly the necessary connection of actions and consequences. For these actions we, without even raising a question on the subject, hold the agents responsible; and the tragedy would disappear for us if we did not. The critical action is, in greater or less degree, wrong or bad. The catastrophe is, in the main, the return of this action on the head of the agent. It is an example of justice; and that order which, present alike within the agents and outside them, infallibly brings it

---

[2] I have raised no objection to the use of the idea of fate, because it occurs so often both in conversation and in books about Shakespeare's tragedies that I must suppose it to be natural to many readers. Yet I doubt whether it would be so if Greek tragedy had never been written; and I must in candour confess that to me it does not often occur while I am reading, or when I have just read, a tragedy of Shakespeare. Wordsworth's lines, for example, about

> poor humanity's afflicted will
> Struggling in vain with ruthless destiny . . .

do not represent the impression I receive, much less do images which compare man to a puny creature helpless in the claws of a bird of prey. The reader should examine himself closely on this matter.

about, is therefore just. The rigour of its justice is terrible, no doubt, for a tragedy is a terrible story; but, in spite of fear and pity, we acquiesce, because our sense of justice is satisfied."

Now, if this view is to hold good, the "justice" of which it speaks must be at once distinguished from what is called "poetic justice." "Poetic justice" means that prosperity and adversity are distributed in proportion to the merits of the agents. Such "poetic justice" is in flagrant contradiction with the facts of life, and it is absent from Shakespeare's tragic picture of life; indeed, this very absence is a ground of constant complaint on the part of Dr. Johnson. Δράσαντι παθεῖν, "the doer must suffer"—this we find in Shakespeare. We also find that villainy never remains victorious and prosperous at the last. But an assignment of amounts of happiness and misery, an assignment even of life and death, in proportion to merit, we do not find. No one who thinks of Desdemona and Cordelia, or who remembers that one end awaits Richard III and Brutus, Macbeth and Hamlet, or who asks himself which suffered most, Othello or Iago, will ever accuse Shakespeare of representing the ultimate power as "poetically" just.

And we must go further. I venture to say that it is a mistake to use at all these terms of "justice" and "merit" or "desert." And this for two reasons. In the first place, essential as it is to recognise the connection between act and consequence, and natural as it may seem in some cases (e.g., Macbeth's) to say that the doer only gets what he deserves, yet in very many cases to say this would be quite unnatural. We might not object to the statement that Lear deserved to suffer for his folly, selfishness and tyranny; but to assert that he deserved to suffer what he did suffer is to do violence not merely to language but to any healthy moral sense. It is, moreover, to obscure the tragic fact that the consequences of action cannot be limited to that which would appear to us to follow "justly" from them. And, this being so, when we call the order of the tragic world just, we are either using the word in some vague and unexplained sense, or we are going beyond what is shown us of this order and are appealing to faith.

But, in the second place, the ideas of justice and desert are, it seems to me, in *all* cases—even those of Richard III and of Macbeth and Lady Macbeth—untrue to our imaginative experience. When we are immersed in a tragedy, we feel towards dispositions, actions, and persons such emotions as attraction and repulsion, pity, wonder, fear, horror, perhaps hatred; but we do not *judge*. This is a point of view which emerges only when, in reading a play, we slip, by our own fault or the dramatist's, from the tragic position, or when, in thinking about the play afterwards, we fall back on our everyday legal and moral notions. But tragedy does not belong, any more than religion belongs, to the sphere of these notions; neither does the imaginative attitude in presence of it. While we are in its world we watch what is, seeing that so it happened and must have happened, feeling that it is piteous, dreadful, awful, mysterious, but neither passing sentence on the agents nor asking whether the behaviour of the ultimate power towards them is just. And, therefore, the use of such language in attempts to render our imaginative experience in terms of the understanding is, to say the least, full of danger.[3]

Let us attempt then to restate the idea that the ultimate power in the tragic world is a moral order. Let us put aside the ideas of justice and merit, and speak simply of good and evil. Let us understand by these words, primarily, moral good and evil, but also everything else in human beings which we take to be excellent or the reverse. Let us understand the statement that the ultimate power or order is "moral" to mean that it does not show itself indifferent to good and evil, or equally favourable or unfavourable to both, but shows itself akin to good and alien from evil. And, understanding the statement thus, let us ask what grounds it has in the tragic fact as presented by Shakespeare.

Here, as in dealing with the grounds on which the idea of fate rests, I choose only two or three out of many. And the most important is this: In Shakespearean tragedy the main source of the convulsion which produces suffering and death is

[3] It is dangerous, I think, in reference to all really good tragedies, but I am dealing here only with Shakespeare's. In not a few Greek tragedies it is almost inevitable that we should think of justice and retribution not only because the dramatis personae often speak of them but also because there is something casuistical about the tragic problem itself. The poet treats the story in such a way that the question, Is the hero doing right or wrong? is almost forced upon us. But this is not so with Shakespeare. *Julius Caesar* is probably the only one of his tragedies in which the question suggests itself to us, and this is one of the reasons why that play has something of a classic air. Even here, if we ask the question, we have no doubt at all about the answer.

never good: good contributes to this convulsion only from its tragic implication with its opposite in one and the same character. The main source, on the contrary, is in every case evil; and, what is more (though this seems to have been little noticed), it is in almost every case evil in the fullest sense, not mere imperfection but plain moral evil. The love of Romeo and Juliet conducts them to death only because of the senseless hatred of their houses. Guilty ambition, seconded by diabolic malice and issuing in murder, opens the action in *Macbeth*. Iago is the main source of the convulsion in *Othello;* Goneril, Regan, and Edmund in *King Lear*. Even when this plain moral evil is not the obviously prime source within the play, it lies behind it: the situation with which Hamlet has to deal has been formed by adultery and murder. *Julius Caesar* is the only tragedy in which one is even tempted to find an exception to this rule. And the inference is obvious. If it is chiefly evil that violently disturbs the order of the world, this order cannot be friendly to evil or indifferent between evil and good, any more than a body which is convulsed by poison is friendly to it or indifferent to the distinction between poison and food.

Again, if we confine our attention to the hero and to those cases where the gross and palpable evil is not in him but elsewhere, we find that the comparatively innocent hero still shows some marked imperfection or defect—irresolution, precipitancy, pride, credulousness, excessive simplicity, excessive susceptibility to sexual emotions, and the like. These defects or imperfections are certainly, in the wide sense of the word, evil, and they contribute decisively to the conflict and catastrophe. And the inference is again obvious. The ultimate power which shows itself disturbed by this evil and reacts against it, must have a nature alien to it. Indeed its reaction is so vehement and "relentless" that it would seem to be bent on nothing short of good in perfection, and to be ruthless in its demand for it.

To this must be added another fact, or another aspect of the same fact. Evil exhibits itself everywhere as something negative, barren, weakening, destructive, a principle of death. It isolates, disunites, and tends to annihilate not only its opposite but itself. That which keeps the evil man[4] prosperous, makes him

---

[4] It is most essential to remember that an evil man is much more than the evil in him. I may add that in this paragraph I have, for the sake of clearness, considered evil in its most pronounced form; but what is said would apply, *mutatis mutandis,* to evil as imperfection, etc.

succeed, even permits him to exist, is the good in him (I do not mean only the obviously "moral" good). When the evil in him masters the good and has its way, it destroys other people through him, but it also destroys *him*. At the close of the struggle he has vanished and has left behind him nothing that can stand. What remains is a family, a city, a country—exhausted, pale and feeble, but alive through the principle of good which animates it—and within it, individuals who, if they have not the brilliance or greatness of the tragic character, still have won our respect and confidence. And the inference would seem clear. If existence in an order depends on good, and if the presence of evil is hostile to such existence, the inner being or soul of this order must be akin to good.

These are aspects of the tragic world at least as clearly marked as those which, taken alone, suggest the idea of fate. And the idea which they in their turn, when taken alone, may suggest, is that of an order which does not indeed award "poetic justice," but which reacts through the necessity of its own "moral" nature both against attacks made upon it and against failure to conform to it. Tragedy, on this view, is the exhibition of that convulsive reaction; and the fact that the spectacle does not leave us rebellious or desperate is due to a more or less distinct perception that the tragic suffering and death arise from collision, not with a fate or blank power, but with a moral power, a power akin to all that we admire and revere in the characters themselves. This perception produces something like a feeling of acquiescence in the catastrophe, though it neither leads us to pass judgment on the characters nor diminishes the pity, the fear, and the sense of waste, which their struggle, suffering, and fall evoke. And, finally, this view seems quite able to do justice to those aspects of the tragic fact which give rise to the idea of fate. They would appear as various expressions of the fact that the moral order acts not capriciously or like a human being, but from the necessity of its nature, or, if we prefer the phrase, by general laws—a necessity or law which of course knows no exception and is as "ruthless" as fate.

It is impossible to deny to this view a large measure of truth. And yet without some amendment it can hardly satisfy. For it does not include the whole of the facts, and therefore does not wholly correspond with the impressions they produce. Let it be granted that the system or order which shows itself omnipotent against individuals is, in the sense explained, moral. Still—at any rate for the eye of sight—the evil against which it asserts itself, and the persons whom this evil inhabits, are not really something outside the order, so that they can attack it or fail to conform to it; they are within it and a part of it. It itself produces them—produces Iago as well as Desdemona, Iago's cruelty as well as Iago's courage. It is not poisoned, it poisons itself. Doubtless it shows by its violent reaction that the poison *is* poison, and that its health lies in good. But one significant fact cannot remove another, and the spectacle we witness scarcely warrants the assertion that the order is responsible for the good in Desdemona, but Iago for the evil in Iago. If we make this assertion we make it on grounds other than the facts as presented in Shakespeare's tragedies.

Nor does the idea of a moral order asserting itself against attack or want of conformity answer in full to our feelings regarding the tragic character. We do not think of Hamlet merely as failing to meet its demand, of Antony as merely sinning against it, or even of Macbeth as simply attacking it. What we feel corresponds quite as much to the idea that they are *its* parts, expressions, products; that in their defect or evil *it* is untrue to its soul of goodness, and falls into conflict and collision with itself; that, in making them suffer and waste themselves, *it* suffers and wastes itself; and that when, to save its life and regain peace from this intestinal struggle, it casts them out, it has lost a part of its own substance—a part more dangerous and unquiet, but far more valuable and nearer to its heart, than that which remains—a Fortinbras, a Malcolm, an Octavius. There is no tragedy in its expulsion of evil: the tragedy is that this involves the waste of good.

Thus we are left at last with an idea showing two sides or aspects which we can neither separate nor reconcile. The whole or order against which the individual part shows itself powerless seems to be animated by a passion for perfection: we cannot otherwise explain its behaviour towards evil. Yet it appears to engender this evil within itself; and in its effort to overcome and expel it, it is agonised with pain, and driven to mutilate its own substance and to lose not only evil but priceless good. That this idea, though very different from the idea of a blank fate, is no solution of the riddle of life is obvious; but why should we expect it to be such a solution? Shakespeare was not attempting to justify the ways of God to men, or to show the universe as a Divine Comedy. He was writing tragedy, and tragedy would not be tragedy if it were not a painful mystery. Nor can he be said even to point distinctly, like some writers of tragedy, in any direction where a solution might lie. We find a few references to gods or God, to the influence of the stars, to another life: some of them certainly, all of them perhaps, merely dramatic—appropriate to the person from whose lips they fall. A ghost comes from purgatory to impart a secret out of the reach of its hearer—who presently meditates on the question whether the sleep of death is dreamless. Accidents once or twice remind us strangely of the words, "There's a divinity that shapes our ends." More important are other impressions. Sometimes from the very furnace of affliction a conviction seems borne to us that somehow, if we could see it, this agony counts as nothing against the heroism and love which appear in it and thrill our hearts. Sometimes we are driven to cry out that these mighty or heavenly spirits who perish are too great for the little space in which they move and that they vanish not into nothingness but into freedom. Sometimes from these sources and from others comes a presentiment, formless but haunting and even profound, that all the fury of conflict, with its waste and woe, is less than half the truth, even an illusion, "such stuff as dreams are made on." But these faint and scattered intimations that the tragic world, being but a fragment of a whole beyond our vision, must needs be a contradiction and no ultimate truth, avail nothing to interpret the mystery. We remain confronted with the inexplicable fact, or the no less inexplicable appearance, of a world travailing for perfection, but bringing to birth, together with glorious good, an evil which it is able to overcome only by self-torture and self-waste. And this fact or appearance is tragedy.[5]

[5] Partly in order not to anticipate later passages, I abstained from treating fully here the question why we feel, at the death of the tragic hero, not only pain but also reconciliation and sometimes even exultation. As I cannot at present make good this defect, I would ask the reader to see "Hegel's Theory of Tragedy," in *Oxford Lectures on Poetry*, especially pp. 90, 91.

VI

LEVIN L. SCHÜCKING

Character and Action: *King Lear*

Though Shakespeare usually to a surprising degree adapts himself to the given action, we yet see in a few instances that he departs from the course prescribed by it. The most remarkable case of this kind is *King Lear*. It is true that here the playwright found a story which was of very doubtful value as a dramatic plot—a king who makes the division of his realm among his children depend on the magniloquence of their protestations of love—the idea strikes one as though it had been invented by the author of *The Playboy of the Western World*, and can, indeed, have arisen only in a nation which is inclined to be intoxicated by fine and well-set phrases.[1] The various versions and arrangements of this theme in existence before Shakespeare's time had not attempted to render the subsequent course of the action psychologically consistent with the initial situation. Everywhere the King is treated cruelly by the daughters he has preferred, until he flees, degraded to the condition of a beggar, to the daughter who had been disowned by him, but who wins back his kingdom for him and puts him on the throne again. The strangeness of the introductory action compelled the dramatist either to provide different motives for the issue of the conflict, or to adjust the subsequent course of the action to the first part of it. The author of the older play of *King Leir*, which was hardly used by Shakespeare, adopted the former alternative, Shakespeare the latter. Many details of this perplexing tangle of vicissitudes may have suited his mood at

From *Character Problems in Shakespeare's Plays: A Guide to the Better Understanding of the Dramatist*, by Levin L. Schücking (London, 1922), pp. 176–90. Reprinted by permission of the author and George G. Harrap & Co., Ltd.

[1] The story is first related by the Welshman, Geoffrey of Monmouth, in the *Historia regum Britanniae, ca.* 1136. The name of Lear is Celtic. the subject possibly Irish. *Cf.* Rhys in Craig's edition, pp. xxxv f.

the time. It was that period of his creative activity when his aim was to represent the overthrow of a great nature brought about by a certain blindness to things which to the common sense of the average mind cannot appear for a moment otherwise than in their true aspect. In this way, for example, his Othello works his own ruin and his infatuated Antony runs his head against the wall.

Not only in the world of the poet's own thoughts do we find figures closely related to King Lear. The suggestions to which this character is due, at least in its most comprehensive outlines, came to him from the works of other poets, a very common occurrence with him, as we know. The old man who goes mad with continual fretting had already fascinated the public in the guise of Kyd's old marshal Hieronimo, and to a lesser degree in that of Titus Andronicus. Furthermore, it is evident that immediately before the creation of Lear the author's mind had had stamped upon it the image of another strong-willed old man who believes himself superior to his whole environment, and then, struck by fate just where he is most vulnerable, knows no limit to his rage, kicks against the pricks, and is driven into madness by his futile resistance to his destiny. This is the Atheist in Tourneur's drama.[2]

The decisive impression, however, of his figure of Lear Shakespeare had received from the story itself. There the behaviour of the King, especially in the initial action, shows an extraordinary irascibility. On this fundamental trait Shakespeare based the whole character. Only a short, though important, passage is devoted to giving reasons for Lear's behaviour, the device employed being the reflection of his character in the minds of Goneril and Regan. We learn that he was hot-headed, "the best and soundest of his time hath been but rash," that "he hath ever but slenderly known himself," but that now age has weakened still further his "poor judgment" and makes his choleric disposition break out in "inconstant starts." Though this review of the situation is given by the two wicked sisters, yet the poet's technique leaves no doubt that it is to be taken as substantially correct. Still, this is not much; we are not given more than a hint, which is not sufficient to explain the much

[2] Cf. the author's essay "Eine Anleihe Shakespeares bei Tourneur," *Englische Studien*, I, 80 f.

disputed introductory action. Here the question as to the relation of character and action once more becomes very acute. The critics, indeed, hold divergent views. Rümelin[3] designates the whole scene as absurd, saying that the introduction is good enough for a fairy tale but not for a soul-stirring tragedy. A renowned old king, he thinks, ought long to have known the disposition of his children, and could not deprive a beloved daughter of her inheritance merely because her simple words did not come up to the exaggerations of her sisters. Who acts thus, in Rümelin's opinion, has not much reason to lose and is probably not quite responsible from the very beginning. Kreyssig[4] also thinks little of the scene. According to him the first words of the King are those of a man who has "a screw loose." Brandes,[5] who in important questions mostly follows Kreyssig, also considers the action as absolutely contrary to reason, and possible only in the world of fairy tales. Others, however, have thought it necessary to defend Shakespeare. Thus, for instance, Vischer[6] thinks he can invalidate Rümelin's objections by saying that this critic cannot get away from a purely realistic conception of the events of the play. His own view is that the introductory action should be taken more symbolically, and that it only condenses into a short space of time what in reality was spread over many years. The King's yearning for tenderness, Cordelia's shy reluctance to show her love, the adroit utilization of the father's weakness by the other daughters, according to this critic presuppose a fairly long time without which they could not bring about the King's final resolve to disinherit Cordelia. Vischer concludes, therefore, that the poet wished to create a symbolical scene by concentrating all these actions into one dramatic moment.

This explanation, however, is untenable because it distorts the facts—a practice which makes so much symbolical interpretation of an art which is essentially realistic appear extremely doubtful. It would be scarcely possible, for instance, to explain the famous scene between Richard III and Anne in which he woos the widow of his victim at the very bier of her husband

3 *Shakespeare-Studien eines Realisten* (1874), p. 60.

4 *Vorlesungen über Shakespeare* (1877), II, 113.

5 *William Shakespeare* (1895–96), p. 642.

6 *Shakespeare Vorträge* (1899), III, 286 f.

by the theory that it is not so much to be taken in a literal sense as to be considered the first beginning of a new love affair that springs up beside the corpse of the victim. This would be taking away the whole point of the scene. It is much the same in the case of Lear. The very suddenness of the resolution is the decisive point. Vischer's idea is a psychological process of an altogether different kind. Shakespeare did not dream of making Cordelia's reserve and coyness the cause of a slow estrangement between herself and her father. Had he wished to express this he could have made Lear designate his action as a kind of final test to which he intended to put her. We know, however, that on the contrary Lear is so full of tender love for Cordelia until the moment when she opens her mouth to utter the fatal words that he markedly prefers her to the other sisters.

In this manner, therefore, it is impossible to solve the difficulties described above, and Vischer's confident assertion that Schiller and Goethe would certainly have pronounced the piece to have a wonderful exposition could not count on finding much credence, even if there did not exist a statement made by Goethe, as unfortunately there does, to the effect that the exposition is simply absurd. The question must also be raised whether Bradley[7] has really mastered these difficulties, which he probably underestimates,[8] in considering the opening scene as *not at all incredible* and describing the marriage of Othello, the Moor, and Desdemona, the daughter of the Venetian senator, as not less strange. He finds a good reason for Lear's behaviour in the "unfortunate speech" of Cordelia, who, he thinks, is not quite aware that saying less than the truth may also be equivalent to *not* telling it, and who is also partly to blame for the consequences on account of the disappointment and disgrace she has caused her father at the great moment he had so carefully planned. To this view we must object that it misjudges the problem. Nobody will dispute that the thwarting of his most eccentric plan by Cordelia was apt to put her father out of humour, even to anger him, but that it should change his love for his daughter to savage hate would be inconceivable, even if his love for Cordelia had been on a par with that which he felt for his other daughters. The fact that she is his darling, how-

---

[7] *Shakespearean Tragedy* (1904), p. 249.
[8] *Ibid.*, p. 71.

ever, shows that he is well aware of her superior worth. How is it possible, then, that this knowledge could be extinguished by a single outburst of ill-humour and be replaced by the most sense-less misconception of her character? Bradley replies: The King has a long life of absolute power behind him, in which he has been flattered to an almost incredible extent; as a consequence, an arrogant self-will has been bred in him, the slightest opposition to which makes him fly into a passion. But a domineering spirit and an excessive vanity need not necessarily destroy all power of judgment. For the rest, the dragging in of previous events not mentioned by the poet is always a most questionable undertaking. Besides, all those critics who are so fond of depicting a reign of the King which was filled with flattery seem entirely to forget the Fool and the good Kent, no less than the honest Gloster.

The problem cannot be solved in this way. What we have to decide is rather *whether the behaviour of the King towards his daughter can be brought into agreement, not with the laws of reason, but with the rest of his conduct.* The question whether this behaviour itself is reasonable or lunatic, whether the assumption of madness might eventually be detrimental to the tragic effect, etc., may in the meantime be left out of consideration altogether.

Now it is impossible to overlook the fact that Shakespeare has certainly tried very carefully to bring about an agreement between the behaviour of Lear in the introductory scene and the subsequent part of the action. The first indication of this endeavour is found in the conversation of the sisters, who report what we are told again later on,[9] that the abnormal excitement and exaltation is now beginning to be much more noticeable in his behaviour than before. Then in the banishment of the faithful Kent we witness a further instance of this change, which is hardly less remarkable than the preceding incident had been. In both he is equally immoderate. He is not satisfied with banishing Kent, but must, in addition, threaten him with capital punishment. He does not merely withdraw his favour from Cordelia, but immediately goes so far as to treat her like the scum of the earth; the "barbarous Scythian" is as dear to him as she,

---

[9] "These dispositions, which *of late* transport you/From what you rightly are" (I. iv. 242).

and he spitefully designates her as "new adopted to our hate." This attack is not followed by any return to a saner attitude.

The same traits are manifested by Lear when, after his abdication, he is living on the charity of others. His impatience, lack of self-control, capriciousness, and arrogance remain unchanged. When the Fool fails to respond to a sign given by him he reviles the whole world for being asleep. To the remarks made by the faithful Fool he repeatedly replies by threatening him with a whip. When Kent, in disguise, applies to him in order to rejoin his service, unknown to him, he uses such language as a policeman might use to a burglar, and then promises magnanimously to take him into his service if, after he has dined, he finds that he still likes him. Such being his treatment of his faithful followers, he naturally behaves with still greater rudeness toward those who provoke him. He strikes Goneril's gentleman-in-waiting, he insults the negligent steward with the words, "You whoreson dog! you slave! you cur!" and is delighted when Kent trips the fellow up and throws him to the ground. Thereupon, when Goneril dares to remonstrate with him, certainly not out of any feeling of kindness, but at least provisionally observing the forms of outward politeness, he considers himself highly offended in his dignity even by this slight rebuke, and breaks out in a paroxysm of fury that makes him weep with rage and hurl a veritable flood of execrations at his daughter, cursing not only her as a degenerate bastard, but the very child in her womb (I. iv. 295). Not satisfied with having given the most unsparing expression to his indignation, he adds scorn to insult by asking the woman who has offended him: "Your name, fair gentlewoman?" The same love of theatrical ostentation is shown later in the scene with Regan (II. iii), when in order to heighten the effect of his bitter words he kneels down, by way of trial, as he says. (This is a most ingenious and successful way of following up the theatrical idea which had induced Lear to arrange the opening scene.) Then, after Regan has finally disillusioned him, he is seized and shaken in every limb by such a fit of frenzy that even he perceives himself to be struggling with a malady, and makes violent efforts to free himself from the *hysterica passio* (a term frequently used in that time to designate cramp in the stomach). The enormous excitement of the ensuing scenes, in which he is degraded to the condition of a beggar, throws his reason completely out of gear.

Every one of these actions shows a remarkable lack of moderation, just as his behaviour to Kent and his undiminished confidence in Regan—despite his experiences with Goneril—betray, to put it mildly, a total lack of judgment, and both of these qualities are in perfect harmony with his conduct in the opening scene. Nevertheless, the poet evidently does not wish him to forfeit thereby the sympathy of the spectator, though it is put to a very severe test. There are several things not only in the mental condition but also in the character of Lear which at first sight repel our modern feeling and which are not quite compatible with the ideal picture, gradually evolved by a long tradition, of the poor, noble, dignified King who is so cruelly treated by his children. We have already drawn attention to the traits which are indicative of a certain brutality, fierceness, arrogance, and capriciousness; to them we must add also a distinctly vindictive spirit which makes him find consolation in the hope that he will one day be able to pay back his daughters in their own coin. Further, it has been suggested by Kreyssig[10] that to be unspeakably offended by ingratitude is not a sign of a very noble character. Though ingratitude hurts, yet one who does good merely from inward compulsion, to whom the generous deed is an end in itself—and only such a character can we call truly unselfish—will find no venom in his disappointment. None will become incensed and embittered by ingratitude but he who has acted from calculation and has seen his calculation fail. There can be no doubt that Lear is embittered to a high degree. Lastly, we may see an unpleasant trait in the habit which the old King has of pitying himself. No one speaks so much of his venerable white hairs as he.

All these things might induce us to regard Lear from a point of view different from what the poet intended. For this reason it is important to bear in mind that in the play itself no sympathetic figure reproaches Lear for any of the traits mentioned; they all look at the situation entirely from his standpoint, and this is also what Shakespeare wishes the spectator to do. The predominant impression is to be that of the monstrous irreverence shown to three of the most venerable human qualities here united in one person: fatherhood, old age, and kingship. Stress is laid, above all, on the unspeakable insult offered to the pride of a king who yet retains his dignity in his association with

[10] Kreyssig, II, 115.

beggars as well as in his madness. This trait has been given an especial prominence. It agrees with the thought we constantly find in Shakespeare, that the true king is best shown by the way in which he preserves his dignity. (Katharine, the wife of Henry VIII, is a model of humility and Christian charity; yet even she, though on the point of death, dismisses from her service a messenger [IV. ii] merely because in his hurry he had entered without kneeling, and with the address "Your Grace" instead of "Your Highness.")

Lear thus appears like an old, gnarled, stubborn oak tree, vigorously resisting the tempest, unyielding, majestic, deep-rooted, upheld only by its own strength, and towering above all its fellows. His weaknesses may almost be said to be the necessary concomitants of his strong qualities. His vindictiveness appears to be a result of his strength; his savage maledictions seem due to his fiery temperament; his behaviour to people of lower rank would not have dishonoured him in that period, when, as is well known, Queen Elizabeth herself boxed her servants' ears with her own hands, and the Merchant of Venice, that model of "ancient Roman honour," publicly spat on the Jew. King Lear, therefore, is meant to be a sublime and truly noble figure, and the Earl of Gloster has good reasons for designating him in his madness as a "ruin'd piece of nature."

This view does not exclude what Kreyssig says of him: "He can conceive of no other relation between himself and society than that on his side there should be the right to claim obedience and service and the power of dispensing mercy, and on the other the duties of supplication, gratitude, and devotion." A convinced royalist like Shakespeare would see no disparagement in this criticism, for this is practically his own conception of the proper relation between king and subject.[11] The attitude of the spectator, however, to the facts described above is sure to be influenced by this consideration, and the degree of his sympathy will largely depend on whether he looks for the humanly valuable part of a tragic character in some feeling which he considers as worthy from a social point of view or whether he

---

[11] Cf. the passage, which is perhaps the most significant one in this respect, in *Henry V*, Act IV, scene i, where it is even denied that the king is responsible to God for those about to be killed in the war he has set on foot, the fallacious reason being given that heaven may let the victims perish on this occasion because of their sins.

would be prepared to regard such a character in actual life with nothing more than an aesthetic interest.

It is true that a number of expositors (Dowden, Bradley, etc.) see in Lear's tragedy a great process of purification, by means of which he is freed from the dross of vanity and selfishness and is led out of his blindness to a proper recognition of the true values of life. It is just his sufferings, they think, which draw him closer to us by bringing out his true human nature. By way of proof they adduce the words in which he shows for the Fool a sympathy formerly unknown to him, and further the passage in which, being himself exposed to the inclemency of the weather, he for the first time remembers the houseless wretches who have to roam about with no protection:

> Poor naked wretches wheresoe'er you are,
> That bide the pelting of this pitiless storm,
> How shall your houseless heads and unfed sides,
> Your loop'd and window'd raggedness, defend you
> From seasons such as these? O! I have ta'en
> Too little care of this. Take physic, pomp;
> Expose thyself to feel what wretches feel,
> That thou mayst shake the superflux to them
> And show the heavens more just.
>
> (III. iv)

They also point to the recognition and contempt of empty appearance which are the products of his madness, his magnificent trenchant criticism of authority that lacks true moral sanction: "Thou hast seen a farmer's dog bark at a beggar? And the creature run from the cur? There thou might'st behold the great image of authority: a dog's obeyed in office." Lastly, his deepened sensibility is mentioned, as revealed by his preferring the company of Cordelia in his prison to all other joys in the world.

But the question is whether it is really consistent with Shakespeare's philosophy to see in this sequence of events an ascent of the character to a higher plane, a process of purification and perfection.

If we take up and examine singly the supposed stages of this upward evolution we cannot unreservedly agree with this conception. Does Shakespeare, for instance, associate compassion for the poor and wretched with a higher moral standpoint? We know that the social sense was very little developed in him. If in this manifestation of pity for the poor naked wretches the emergence of a higher morality was to be shown, we ought really to wonder why it stands quite alone in his works. This fact, indeed, tends to justify Crosby when he accuses Shakespeare of a total lack of social sense, because we seek in vain throughout his works for a single admission that poor people are sometimes unjustly left to starve and suffer want, that they occasionally raise just complaints, and that their endeavours to make these heard, so far from being ridiculous, are indeed the most serious facts of history. There is no passage where Shakespeare formulates a demand corresponding to the spirit of Lear's reflection in describing an ideal figure or laying down rules of life (like those given to Laertes by his father). It is quite probable that Lear's words are intended to furnish him with a sympathetic trait—that, as Edgar in the same drama once says of himself (IV. vi), he is "by the art of known and feeling sorrows" "pregnant to good pity." But we may be quite sure that Shakespeare, for the reasons adduced, would never have taken this matter so seriously as to see in it a purification from adherent dross, whatever his interpreters may do!

That Lear in the further course of his madness comes to reject all that is unnatural and all claims that are morally unjustified, though sanctioned by tradition and authority, cannot be disputed. But it must be noticed that in this he does little more than follow the beaten track of the melancholy type, whose "humour" especially delights in unmasking all kinds of shams; and the fact of his being greatly attracted by the naked Edgar, the "thing in itself," is a further manifestation of the Melancholy Man's predilection for the Diogenes attitude. Lear shows himself a truer representative of the melancholy type in yet another respect, viz., in his arguing and railing against women. His furious tirade against the unchastity of women—

> Down from the waist they are Centaurs
> Though women all above . . .
>
> (IV. vi)

—has really nothing to do with his own affairs.

Undoubtedly Lear's criticism shows profound insight; but this recognition, as it stands here, is but an aspect of a mood and dependent on a state of mental derangement which may under certain circumstances disappear again, as is shown by the example of other melancholy characters. It would have to be confirmed by him in some form or other after his reason had been restored to sanity in order to make us see in it a real revolution of his philosophic outlook and a stage of his development.

This condition seems perhaps to be fulfilled indirectly by his behaviour to Cordelia, whose love he accepts with the unrestrained happiness of one who has got to know the world too well to expect from it anything further. But even his relation to Cordelia, when regarded from this point of view, would appear in a false light. What attracts Lear to Cordelia and makes him regard a life with her in the quiet dungeon as supremely desirable is doubtless the recognition of the true worth of her love, and his deeply pathetic cry when she is dead, "Howl, howl, howl, howl! O! you are men of stones!" shows that by her death the innermost core of his existence has been destroyed. But this change is not to be regarded as a development of his character. That he has completely given up every idea of his kingdom, that he shows no further outburst of vindictiveness or indignation at the insults he has received, is really contrary to his nature and is due to the state of physical decrepitude into which he has fallen after his madness has left him. The thunderstorm has felled the oak. *His predominant feeling is one of weariness.* He is no longer able completely to grasp what is happening. He must make an effort to render the course of events clear to himself. When he recognizes Cordelia, who tenderly and with hot tears in her eyes bends over him, he so misunderstands the situation that he says: "If you have poison for me I will drink it." Gradually his mind becomes more lucid again. But when he says of himself, "Pray you now, forget and forgive: I am old and foolish," this recognition contains a sad truth, especially in view of his former high opinion of himself. Nothing is more touching than the fact that he is no longer the old Lear.

Edmund, too, now calls him the "old and miserable king" (V. iii. 47). Extreme weakness and helplessness, an infinitely pathetic relapse into childish ways of thinking and feeling, make him find supreme felicity in Cordelia's tenderness:

No, no, no, no! Come, let's away to prison;
We two alone will sing like birds i' the cage:
When thou dost ask me blessing, I'll kneel down,
And ask of thee forgiveness: so we'll live,
And pray, and sing, and tell old tales, and laugh
At gilded butterflies, and hear poor rogues
Talk of court news; and we'll talk with them too,
Who loses and who wins; who's in, who's out . . .
                              and we'll wear out,
In a wall'd prison, packs and sects of great ones
That ebb and flow by the moon.

This is not a purified Lear from whose character the flame of unhappiness has burnt away the ignoble dross, but a nature completely transformed, whose extraordinary vital forces are extinguished, or about to be extinguished.

This is the whole course of the drama: the story of a breakdown, of a decay accompanied by the most wonderful and fascinating phenomena, comparable to the autumn decline of the year when the dying leaves appear in their most beautiful colours. It is not a development, but a decadence manifesting itself in a variety of forms, among others in that feeling of weakness which creates in the masterful old man, who so far has been centred entirely in himself, a sympathetic interest in the distress of others which he has never known before. Shakespeare's astonishing wisdom and experience of life are shown by the fact that he does not describe the great mental revolutions without reference to the corresponding physical alterations.

It is therefore a complete misunderstanding of the true state of affairs to regard Lear as greater at the close than at the beginning. He has become a different person; he is nearing his end. This is why Shakespeare had no use for the conclusion of the story of Lear as it had been handed down by tradition. According to the legend the old King, after the victory of Cordelia's troops, ascended his throne again as "a sadder and a wiser man," so to speak, and occupied it for some years more. For Shakespeare's broken old man this was unthinkable. The conflict between the action and the character would have been too patent, even grotesque. He had therefore to bring Lear's life to an end. This he did, anticipating at the same time the end of Cordelia, but still maintaining a certain connexion with the original source, because from Spenser's *Faerie Queene* we learn that after a long and happy reign, when smitten at last by misfortune, she had hanged herself in prison. By converting her voluntary death into a murder which cost Lear his life he did indeed heap a load of tragedy on the spectator's mind, a thing against which the latter had been rebelling for centuries as against an intolerable excess of horror.[12] On the other hand, however, he secured by this issue, better than by any other, the possibility of working out the process of dissolution in Lear to its last stage. His master-hand even succeeded in building up on this foundation the most tragic effects of the whole play. A soul-stirring anticlimax is produced as his mental fire, which is slowly flickering out and again and again being obscured by the clouds of insanity, is once more fanned into a short, violent flame by the cruelty of the injuries he receives, a flame in which the last sparks of the powerful self-consuming passions flash forth, followed by eternal night. Here the action and the character-drawing are harmoniously blended in one perfect close.

[12] Tate's version, made in 1681, which makes the conflict end in a conciliatory manner, held undisputed sway until 1768, and later on still appeared occasionally on the English stage.

VII

G. WILSON KNIGHT

Macbeth and *Antony and Cleopatra*

I have remarked elsewhere that "in point of imaginative pro-
fundity *Macbeth* is comparable alone to *Antony and Cleopatra*" and that "*Macbeth* forces us to a consciousness more
exquisitely unified and sensitive than any of the great tragedies
but its polar opposite, *Antony and Cleopatra.*" Here I shall expand and justify the implicit assertion that these two plays have
a certain powerful similarity of exact opposition.

Both plays are clearly dominated by a woman. In no other
play do we find just this relation existent between hero and
heroine. Lady Macbeth and Cleopatra each possess a unique
power and vitality which is irresistible and expressly feminine:
their mastery is twined with their femininity. Each is very
feminine: we might note that both faint at crucial moments.
Each rules her man in somewhat similar fashion and with somewhat similar results. In Macbeth and Antony we find, too, a
very definite masculine weakness and strength alternate. Both
are fine warriors; both are plastic to their women. They fail in
warriorship and practical affairs in proportion as they absorb
and are absorbed by the more spiritual forces embodied in their
women. Antony grows strong in love, Macbeth in evil. Macbeth is aware of the similarity. Banquo—we might aptly substitute Macduff or Malcolm—is his Octavius:

> . . . under him,
> My Genius is rebuked; as, it is said,
> Mark Antony's was by Caesar.

> (III. i. 55)

From *The Imperial Theme: Further Interpretations of Shakespeare's
Tragedies including the Roman Plays* by G. Wilson Knight (London,
1931), pp. 327–42. Reprinted by permission of the author and Methuen
and Co. A few changes in wording have been made at the kind suggestion
of Professor Wilson Knight.

In point of world affairs both become weak, though they endure spirit-adventures which quite dwarf the superficial successes of Octavius and Malcolm. Those two are similar in youth and inexperience. Compare

> I will not yield,
> To kiss the ground beneath young Malcolm's feet. . . .
>
> (*Macbeth* V. viii. 27)

with

> To the boy Caesar send this grizzled head,
> And he will fill thy wishes to the brim
> With principalities.
>
> (*Antony and Cleopatra* III. xiii. 16)

There is reference in both plays to the disgrace of being captured alive, relating often to Cleopatra in the one play, and Macbeth, exhibited as "rarer monsters are" (V. viii. 25) "to be baited with the rabble's curse" (V. viii. 29), in the other. Macbeth again explicitly stimulates our sense of similarity by his words on suicide, his determination not to "play the Roman fool" (V. viii. 1). We find a somewhat similar conquest of hardened but weakening prowess by youthful integrity in each. Yet, in spiritual adventure, both Macbeth and Antony are indeed rich, and ripened for death. Macbeth is "ripe for shaking" (IV. iii. 237); he is fallen "into the sear, the yellow leaf" (V. iii. 23). So, too, Antony cries that his followers

> . . . melt their sweets
> On blossoming Caesar, and this pine is bark'd,
> That over-topp'd them all.
>
> (IV. xii. 22)

Which again insistently recalls Lennox's words on Malcolm. Caithness speaks:

> Meet we the medicine of the sickly weal,
> And with him pour we in our country's purge
> Each drop of us.

To which Lennox replies:

> Or so much as it needs,
> To dew the sovereign flower and drown the weeds.
>
> (V. ii. 27)

Caesar and Malcolm are both "flowers" to be watered by their followers' support. Caesar wears "the rose of youth upon him" (III. xiii. 20). Antony is like an old lion dying (III. xiii. 95), Macbeth like a bear at the stake (V. vii. 1). Antony is seen to sacrifice all reason to love just as Macbeth sacrifices all reason to evil. And these tremendous spiritual principles are embodied exactly in their women. The one pair of protagonists are "in love with" each other, both together blended in a reality transcending persons; the other pair are similarly "in evil with" each other. We should observe that Macbeth and Lady Macbeth are joint partners in evil: it is twined with their love, itself a kind of unholy love. Macbeth commits his crime partly through his wife's influence over him, his love for her: and it has been often remarked that she desires it primarily for her lord's, not for her own, sake. After the crime the evil bond is yet for a while strong between them. It is impossible clearly to dissociate their evil from their love. Their love gives place to evil, which is itself powerfully binding as love, and yet eventually drives them, it seems, apart. Thus a mighty spiritual force broods over each pair. They are lost in it, through and in each other and themselves: yet it is greater, more universal, than they. This force is radiant and life-giving in the one play, black and death-dealing in the other. In *Macbeth* the intellect is baffled and the emotions at every turn troubled. In *Antony and Cleopatra* the intellectual and emotional elements are closely harmonized, and both contribute to a single positive directness that makes the optimism of all high tragedy here explicit. The intellect is satisfied, the emotions pleased. Moreover, the one vision fills, the other empties, its own universe. The two visions may thus be ranged as opposites.

There are further imaginative correspondences, not very easy to characterize. Cleopatra has something of the paralysing, serpentine grace and attraction of the *Macbeth*-evil, which further relates her to Lady Macbeth and the Weird Sisters. Lady Macbeth prays to "spirits" in her invocation to evil; and those spirits, as they appear to Macbeth, are feminine. The *Macbeth*-evil clearly has its roots in femininity. Now Cleopatra is called a "witch" (IV. xii. 47), a "great fairy" (IV. viii. 12). And there is a recurrent "serpent" suggestion in both plays. Lady Macbeth urges her lord to be "the serpent" under "the innocent flower" (I. v. 66). She is herself serpentine, a temptress, like Eve, serpent-beguiled, serpent-propelled. Serpents and similar reptilian or poisonous creatures are often suggested in *Macbeth* (III. ii. 13, 36; III. iv. 29; IV. i. 6, 12, 14, 16, 17). So, too, Cleopatra is the "serpent of old Nile"; and crocodiles, serpents, and "the worm of Nilus" are frequently mentioned in *Antony and Cleopatra*. Here they are not nearly so powerfully impregnated with evil as in *Macbeth*, and are often purely picturesque. In exactly this sense, evil in *Antony and Cleopatra* is subdued to a strange beauty.

Moreover, both plays stress "air" and air-life. Such references I have already observed in *Antony and Cleopatra*. In *Macbeth* we have a large proportion of air-life in our animal-suggestion: sparrows, eagles, the raven, owl, falcon, hawk, the "crow" and its "rooky wood," "night's black agents" preying, "maws of kites," maggot-pies, choughs, rooks, "howlet," the wren fighting the owl, the hell-kite swooping on chickens, the "temple-haunting martlet," the bat and his "cloister'd flight," the "shard-borne beetle." These are either evil, or sweet in contrast. We also have violent and ominous, or sweet, air imagery. We have Macbeth's vision of innocence desecrated:

> And pity, like a naked new-born babe,
> Striding the blast, or heaven's cherubim, horsed
> Upon the sightless couriers of the air,
> Shall blow the horrid deed in every eye,
> That tears shall drown the wind.
>
> (I. vii. 21)

Both good and evil spirits ride on the wind, and disorder in the elements is violent. The Weird Sisters "hover through the fog and filthy air" (I. i. 12). Again Macbeth cries:

> Infected be the air whereon they ride. . . .
>
> (IV. i. 138)

The winds of chaos are loosed:

> This night has been unruly; where we lay,
> Our chimneys were blown down; and, as they say,
> Lamentings heard i' the air; strange screams of death. . . .
>
> (II. iii. 59)

Macbeth draws a picture of wholesale destruction in terms of wind:

> Though you untie the winds and let them fight
> Against the churches. . . .
>
> (IV. i. 52)

And later:

> Though bladed corn can be lodged and trees blown down. . . .
>
> (IV. i. 55)

All this is an aspect of the usual Shakespearian "tempest." Here "air" and "wind" are stressed. And this leads on to the thought of "vast regions" observed by Caroline Spurgeon, who notes as a typical *Macbeth*-idea "the reverberation of sound echoing over vast regions, even into the limitless spaces beyond the confines of the universe," and quotes a passage where heaven itself rings with the horror of Scotland's suffering, and another where words of Macbeth's crime should

> . . . be howl'd out in the desert air,
> Where hearing should not latch them.
>
> (IV. iii. 194)

Air, wind and vast spaces—all are then common to both *Macbeth* and *Antony and Cleopatra*. And they are as unruly in the one play as they are still and harmonious in the other. My analysis of *Antony and Cleopatra* has already explored this elemental suggestion, and the correspondence, together with the obvious divergences, will be clear. Sea imagery, so vivid in *Antony and Cleopatra*, also occurs in *Macbeth;* but its preponderance is not sufficient in view of its Shakespearian universality to justify our stressing it in this connexion, except to note the same contrast of calm and chaos already observed. Moreover, the *Macbeth*-vision, being so essentially a vision of "spirit" or "nothing," lends itself rather to imagery of vast emptiness and rushing winds (like those of Claudio's hell), and evil birds a-wing on the impenetrable dark. It is a play of "flighty purpose" (IV. i. 145)—or purposeless flight. It is all spiritual, dizzying, swift, insecurely poised and immaterial. The solidity of the "sure and firm-set earth" (II. i. 56) must not hear and repeat the steps of wraithly murder whose Tarquin strides fall echoless at the hour when "nature" itself "seems dead" (II. i. 50).

Speed and intangibility peculiarize *Macbeth*. Miss Spurgeon notes here "the action of rapid riding which contributes and emphasizes a certain sense of rushing, relentless, and goaded motion, of which we are very conscious in the play," and quotes examples of such "riding" action in the imagery. Elsewhere I show in detail that "speed" is a recurrent thought in Shakespeare in connexion with the heightened awareness of poetry, love, and, we may add, lunacy.[1] "The lunatic, the lover, and the poet" are thus, in respect of swift consciousness, to be related to each other. And the extreme of lunacy is to be associated with the idiot-apprehension of the *Macbeth*-evil:

> I'll haunt thee like a wicked conscience still,
> That mouldeth goblins swift as frenzy's thoughts.
>
> (*Troilus and Cressida* V. x. 28)

[1] I quote from my letter to the *Times Literary Supplement*, Thursday, January 17, 1929:

". . . Shakespeare continually refers to the swiftness of abstract thought or 'meditation.' . . . This pure mental activity is compared in point of swiftness with 'thoughts of love' or love in many passages of Shakespeare: e.g., *Hamlet*, I. v. 29–30; *Love's Labour's Lost*, IV. iii. 330; *Troilus and Cressida*, IV. ii. 13–14; *Romeo and Juliet*, II. v. 4–8; and, in a negative sense pointing the comparison most clearly, *Othello*, III. iv. 174–9. The swiftness of thought is referred to in *Henry V*, Prologue to Act III, 1–3; and in the Prologue to Act V, at lines 8, 15, 23; in *Antony and Cleopatra*, IV. vi. 35–6; in *King Lear*, III. ii. 4. And the swiftness of love is referred to in *The Two Gentlemen of Verona*, II. vi. 42; in *Romeo and Juliet*, II. ii. 118–19; in *A Midsummer Night's Dream*, I. i. 143–9. The poetic image is 'lightning.' So much for the swiftness of meditation and love. Now the imaginative connexion of love and poetry in Shakespeare is apparent. The lover, like the poet, is 'of imagination all compact' (*A Midsummer Night's Dream*, V. i. 8). Love sees with the eyes of art (*A Midsummer Night's Dream*, II. ii. 104–5). Creative literature is born of the erotic impulse—the statement is clear and vivid in *Love's Labour's Lost*, IV. iii. 291–365. Here the speed imagery is insistent:

> For when would you, my liege, or you, or you,
> In *leaden* contemplation have found out
> Such *fiery* numbers as the prompting eyes
> Of beauty's tutors have enriched you with?
> Other *slow* arts entirely keep the brain. . . .

See also *Antony and Cleopatra*, V. ii. 96–100. It is clear, then, that love and poetry may be said to induce a consciousness which 'apprehends' a swift reality beyond the lagging attempts of intellect to 'comprehend' (*A Midsummer Night's Dream*, V. i. 4–6)."

To which I might add that the "swift thought" of *Antony and Cleopatra* (IV. vi. 35–36), may be paraphrased "passion." Any passionate thinking is "swift." Words may be "winged swift" in "scorn" so that they "outfly apprehensions" (*Troilus and Cressida*, II. iii. 123). The drink-consciousness induces "swift" images. See *2 Henry IV*, IV. iii. 92–127.

In *The Wheel of Fire* I have written: "The states of extreme evil and supreme love have a definite imaginative similarity. They stand out from other modes in point of a certain supernormal intensity, a sudden crushing, conquering power, a vivid and heightened consciousness. In these respects they seem to transcend the hate mode, except where that touches madness. *Macbeth* and *Antony and Cleopatra* are thus supreme in point of imaginative transcendence." That comparison will now be more clear. Moreover, it is not surprising that the two poems written by Shakespeare in his youth, wherein clearly he had absolute freedom in choice of subject, should reflect the two most intense and powerful of his tragic visions. *Venus and Adonis* shows us *Antony and Cleopatra* in embryo. In both the feminine element dominates the action. Venus' prophecy about love at the close is a valuable commentary on Shakespearian love tragedy. In exactly the same way *The Rape of Lucrece* is a commentary on and foreshadows *Macbeth*. The two visions are similar. As I have observed, Macbeth's crime is, or may be considered, a kind of self-love like Tarquin's lust. Cleopatra is compared to Venus in Enobarbus' description; Macbeth compares himself to Tarquin. We are, in fact, here faced with the positive and negative extremes of Shakespearian vision.[2] Thus *Macbeth* and *Antony and Cleopatra* stand out from the other great tragedies by their excessive intensity, which is to be related to the idea of "speed." For the *Macbeth* "speed" is but a branch of Shakespeare's usual "speed" thought with respect to poetry, love, and madness. It is the whirling agony I have suggested, metaphorically, to point the quality of Lear's madness.[3] In *Macbeth* it is even swifter, more unbearably swift, like the gyroscopic spin of consciousness in certain forms of nightmare. And what, then, of *Antony and Cleopatra?* The play is still, not swift. But this is a stillness which encloses motion, a stillness growing out of motion, as a swiftly rotating and multicoloured top is abnormally and strangely still, its varied colourings whitened by speed. It is still, that is, to the spectator; not to an insect that tries to lodge thereon. So, too, in *Antony and Cleopatra*, we who watch observe a stillness overpowering, yet one with, speed; an eternity

[2] On the plane of popular fiction we find reflections of these two modes: the love story and the "thriller." We might also observe the themes of Greek tragedy. Murders and marriages have a lasting appeal—and meaning.

[3] *The Wheel of Fire*, pp. 177, 222.

enclosing, yet born from, time; an ethereal uncoloured beauty which is yet blended of the *Macbeth* red, black, and gold, and a shimmering sea-blue of its own. From the height of our vision, action becomes static like Wordsworth's cataract, "frozen by distance."

The frenzies and phantasms of *Macbeth* range a world itself void and insubstantial. Each play shows us a nature reptilian, volatile, airy. It is hard to find exact words for this common element of spirituality and supernatural strangeness. "Nature" in both plays is transcended. The dominant spirit quality in both forbids a pure naturalism such as we find in *King Lear*. In *Macbeth* what "nature" there is is mostly distorted, in *Antony and Cleopatra* it is outdistanced. Therefore both "natures" are "strange": the word is used in both plays. The one is strangely beautiful, the other strangely evil. Both are beyond the natural. *Macbeth* has its "air-drawn dagger"; a phrase clearly referring "air" to the spirit-forms of imagination. So the Weird Sisters vanish:

> BANQUO. The earth hath bubbles as the water has
> And these are of them: whither are they vanish'd?
> MACBETH. Into the air, and what seem'd corporal, melted
> As breath into the wind.
>
> (I. iii. 79)

Notice the "water" suggestion, which supports my understanding of the water element in *Antony and Cleopatra* as a spirit medium, element of life strange to man; and the word "melted"; and the "air" and "breath" ideas, which, with the "fog and filthy air," may remind us of "cloud" imagery in *Antony and Cleopatra*. In *Antony and Cleopatra* there is one powerful effect of supernaturalism, the mysterious music that preludes the final defeat of worldly things and the ascension of love:

> FOURTH SOLDIER. Peace! what noise?
> FIRST SOLDIER.   List, list!
> SECOND SOLDIER. Hark!
> FIRST SOLDIER.   Music i' the air.
> THIRD SOLDIER.   Under the earth.
>
> (IV. iii. 12)

Again, "earth" and "air." Different as they are in quality, in point of pure supernaturalism these two incidents are also strangely similar.

The two plays have this common element of the immaterial (in the one) and supermaterial (in the other). It may be called "spirit"—spirit rich, attractive, dangerous—with a nightmare fascination in the one and a fascinating beauty in the other. The "spirit" element also occurs in the prophecies. *Antony and Cleopatra* shows us a naturalism so expanded to infinite proportions that it just touches the supernatural; hence the one fine supernatural effect of unearthly music; whereas the *Macbeth*-evil is wholly supernatural. So, too, the prophecies in *Antony and Cleopatra* are only slightly supernatural. The soothsayer words his skill aptly: "In nature's infinite book of secrecy/A little I can read" (I. ii. 9). Nature's infinity, that is our vision here. As for the other prophecy, in Act II, the soothsayer tells Antony no more than he knows himself: that Caesar's luck and personality both dominate him. In *Macbeth* the future is crudely, suddenly, presented naked to the present moment. We are "transported" beyond "the ignorant present" and feel "the future in the instant" (I. v. 57). But both plays are powerfully "spiritual." And these two spirit-worlds are enclosed in the persons of Lady Macbeth and Cleopatra. Each woman is ultimate in her play: she is the whole play's universe, with its rich fascination and serpentine grace, as Macbeth and Antony are not. They are in it; their ladies are of it: "it" being "evil" and "love" respectively.

We may, then, observe a certain elusive similarity between the essences of these two plays. Next I shall attempt more clearly to show how exactly they may be considered opposites. In *Macbeth* we have noted life themes of imperial splendour, feasting, and nature's creative innocence. These are, in one way or another, ranged against the evil, the death-consciousness, the dark. They have but insecure place in the *Macbeth*-world. Now these life themes are vividly fulfilled and realized in *Antony and Cleopatra*. Imperial magnificence scintillates throughout the play, and receives a finer expression than elsewhere in Shakespeare. Nor is it here strongly opposed to the love force. It both blends and contrasts with it, as may be seen from the passage, of clear symbolic meaning, which describes Antony and Cleopatra throned together in imperial magnificence and princely love. The contrast with *Macbeth* is clear: these are the very things Macbeth cannot grasp; they appear only to vanish, elusive. Feasting, too, is a major theme, whether in the fine scene on Pompey's galley, Enobarbus' description of Alexandrian revelling, or Antony's speeches in Act IV. So, too, in *Macbeth*, is feasting vivid: in the entertainment of Duncan, the banquet scene, and the death banquet of the Weird Sisters. There feast is desecrated by evil: the contrast is again vivid. With nature, as I have observed, the same contrast persists. In *Macbeth* nature is deformed, dislocated: in *Antony and Cleopatra* it is fulfilled and transfigured. In *Macbeth* the lovely passage on the breeding martlet with his "procreant cradle" suggests nature's rich profusion of life; the thought is stressed again in Lady Macduff's words about the wren; and such ideas—blending with "baby" themes—are clearly the direct antagonists of the evil, suggesting life and birth as opposed to death. Macbeth is without children; and his "fruitless" crown is to be contrasted with Banquo's "issue," or Duncan's. We may observe the description of Antony and Cleopatra throned in glory with their "unlawful issue." In *Antony and Cleopatra* we have constant suggestion of the mating of element with element, Antony's description of the Nile harvesting, the crocodile bred out of the Nile ooze; these thoughts blend with the sex conversation of Cleopatra's girls, and harmonize with the main theme of love. Nature here is endued with splendour and happy success. The spirit of evil disorganizes and distorts life forms in *Macbeth;* the spirit of love illuminates and fulfils them in *Antony and Cleopatra*. In *Macbeth* the evil has two modes of appearance: (i) spirit realities, essentially outside natural law; and (ii) natural life distorted, derelict, without "form"; either without organic form, as the bits of bodies used for the cauldron ingredients, or without the form of obedience to laws of kind, as in the strange behaviour of Duncan's horses "beauteous and swift, the minions of their race" (II. iv. 15)—we should contrast this with the vivid "horse" themes in *Antony and Cleopatra*—or the inverted relation of falcon and owl. "Spirit" is, in both modes, seen to be rudely disjointed from "matter": "form" being the effect of "spirit" or "soul" in—to use the Shakespearian word—the "shapes" of matter. The evil in *Macbeth* is essentially formless, whether it appear as "spirit" or in shape of "nature." Exactly the reverse is true of *Antony and Cleopatra*. There, all life forms are vividly fulfilled and spiritualized, inflated by spirit to the extreme limits of nature, thence transcending nature and widening into infinity. In *Macbeth* the lights of heaven are "strangled"—star, moon, sun. In *Antony and Cleopatra*, the nights are "shiny" (IV. ix. 3); stars, moon, and sun bend their love-light on earth. The extreme of this especial vision wherein the finite is rendered infinite by spiritual apprehension is apparent in Cleopatra's description of the universal Antony. In *Antony and Cleopatra* the universe is full, packed full of life forms. But *Macbeth* is empty, void with a dread infinity, a ghastly vacuum which yet echoes "strange screams of death." In *Macbeth* all nature, all life forms of birth, feast, honour, and kingly glory are opposed by this nothingness, this death. In *Antony and Cleopatra* the universal fires blaze down on earth, and earth reflects that glory, flashes it back from its own imperial splendour. Here we encounter vastness in form of sea and land, empire, earth and air and fire: in *Macbeth* we encounter vastness, too; but only a vast abyss of a spiritual "nothing."

Antony and Cleopatra in reality contains and surpasses all that is in *Macbeth:* surpasses that vision by showing its elements not in disharmony but in harmony, spirit mated to forms of life. Hence, as I have observed, Cleopatra has in her something of the Lady Macbeth evil woven into the rich and strange loveliness of her "infinite variety." We may note further that in *Macbeth* the evil is opposed not only by natural life forms but by a wholly supernatural "grace," and thoughts of angels and divinity generally. In *Antony and Cleopatra* there is no exact correspondence here: any powerful divine suggestion is blended with things natural and human. The "gods" and "fortune" are more vague than in *King Lear*. The life vision is expressed in terms of life and death as we know them; it recognizes no supernatural divinity, except such as may be closely harmonized with life and death, as we know them. The divine blends with the human, the human becomes divine. And yet we must, of course, never forget that the persons, ultimately, are not human at all, but purely symbols of a poetic vision. Finally, we may observe two similar speeches that contrast our two visions neatly with reference to the life image of babyhood. Lady Macbeth speaks:

> I have given suck, and know
> How tender 'tis to love the babe that milks me:
> I would, while it was smiling in my face,
> Have pluck'd my nipple from his boneless gums,
> And dash'd the brains out, had I so sworn as you
> Have done to this.
>
> (I. vii. 54)

Macbeth and Antony and Cleopatra

Compare:

> Peace, peace!
> Dost thou not see my baby at my breast,
> That sucks the nurse asleep?
>
> (*Antony and Cleopatra* V. ii. 311)

In the one, a death force is conquering life instincts; in the other, a life instinct, love, conquers death. So, too, Cleopatra's paradisal dream contrasts exquisitely with Lady Macbeth's agonized sleep.

The bond between Antony and Cleopatra makes them rise above, and scorn, imperial sway; that between Macbeth and Lady Macbeth is servanted to ignominious desire for glory. The one pair are united first by imperial position and advance thence to love; the other, first by love, and advance thence to imperial position. For we should observe what is a too easily neglected effect in *Macbeth*, the fine love which binds the protagonists. The domestic note is powerful in the early action. "My dearest love," Macbeth addresses his wife on his first return. "My husband!" is her greeting to him after his hideous crime. Ironic in their beauty of thought, too, are Duncan's words on Macbeth's "love" for his wife:

> . . . but he rides well;
> And his great love, sharp as his spur, hath holp him
> To his home before us.
>
> (I. vi. 22)

This natural love they desecrate for world glory: Antony and Cleopatra spurn world glory for love. The one story illustrates crime, action unfitted to the universal purpose; the other play shows us a story which receives universal sanction. Humanity is distorted in the one story: hence Macduff enters with Macbeth's head, the protagonist hideously decapitated. In the other, Cleopatra dies crowned and beauteous in a death which is but an added glory to life.

I conclude with a few remarks on *King Lear*. *King Lear* is to be mentally set between *Macbeth* and *Antony and Cleopatra*. The sequence is clear with reference to "nature": (i) nature formless, (ii) pure naturalism in a limited sense, and (iii) nature infinite. Or again, as follows: (i) supernaturalism (we have observed how the supernatural evil necessitates a similar supernatural "grace"—as in the ghost scene in *Hamlet*), (ii) naturalism, and (iii) what I have termed "universalism." Now in *King Lear* nature is both cruel and sweet. Mr. Edmund Blunden[4] has observed how, toward the end, the wintry effects of the middle action give place to the more summery images of the fourth act. This movement is related to Lear's reunion with Cordelia: "nature" is fulfilled by love, and sweet, natural effects accompany love here and elsewhere in Shakespeare. Here, however cruel and violent nature may be—in tempest or animal references—it is never distorted: natural laws are not broken. Goneril, Regan, and Edmund are all naturally wicked, Lady Macbeth unnaturally wicked[5]—hence her own torment, the disease-agony of fevered sleep, the sleepwalking scene. In *King Lear* the bad persons endure no unrest, even: they are merely fulfilling their natural impulses, and though this may draw on them criticism of unnaturalness, and indeed often does do so, yet we never witness the motiveless and paradoxical subjection to evil that is at the heart of *Macbeth*. Only once does the *Macbeth*-nature directly touch the *Lear*-nature: the murderers in the one, and the captain in the other, both, in similar circumstances, regarding evil as natural (*Macbeth* III. i. 91–103; *King Lear* V. iii. 38). Elsewhere the divergence is fairly rigid. But, though *King Lear* shows us a more natural state than *Macbeth*, it falls short of *Antony and Cleopatra* in general optimism. It is a tragic vision, a sombre statement. Dr. Bradley has well called it "bleak" in comparison with the more vivid effects of *Macbeth*. *Macbeth*, like *Antony and Cleopatra*, has colour: the red of blood, the gold of kingship, fires and glaring spectres, white radiance of divinity. *Macbeth* and *Antony and Cleopatra* are both, in opposite ways, "spiritual"; *King Lear* is "realistic." *King Lear*'s naturalism in comparison with *Macbeth* can be seen from the fact that all within it blends harmoniously: there is no such striking positive-negative contrast as in *Macbeth*. Good and ill are spectral figures here, indecisive in comparison with

[4] In his Shakespeare Association lecture, "Shakespeare's Significances."

[5] Lady Macbeth has a streak of natural goodness in her even at the climax of her evil-possession; just as Cleopatra shows a streak of evil within her love. The "good" in *Macbeth* is always one of "nature," family affection, allegiance, and all social ties. Hence the point of Lady Macbeth's:

Had he not resembled
My father as he slept, I had done 't.

(II. ii. 13)

the "grace"-"evil" contrast. All is levelled under a single view regarding human existence as a tragic struggle in which the good finally conquers, but at appalling sacrifice. *King Lear* is, in fact, a symbolic pattern of human affairs exactly correspondent to any philosophy which is limited to a strict "naturalism" —pessimistic but stoic.[6] This is the exact quality of *King Lear:* bleak, colourless, limited, naturalistic. Hence it is pagan through and through. In *King Lear* our vision is constricted to the earth: this is exactly what I mean by a "limited naturalism." So here the world is conceived as great—"the thick rotundity o' the world" (III. ii. 7), "this great world" (IV. vi. 137). In the universalized vision of *Antony and Cleopatra*, the world is the plaything of princes. It is shown as their lawful property, the heritage of man, a toy bandied from one to another. Finally, it becomes "the little O, the earth" (V. ii. 81). Our vision is infinity itself. So in *Macbeth* the sun is blackened: in *Antony and Cleopatra* it is finely mated to earth's bounty. In *King Lear* it is blurred—associated with "fen-suck'd fogs" (II. iv. 169)—a doubtful blessing.

Now in the matters of love and empire we again find that *King Lear* is set midway. In this essay I have shown that the other two plays present, respectively, a love-empire rhythm and an empire-love rhythm. Here, where human nature endures, in its painful evolution, an uncertainty, a sight of grotesque incompatibility, we find a corresponding neither-one-thing-nor-the-other in the matter of love and empire. Lear is both king and not king, and both aspects are twined with love themes. He expects authority without office. Does he love any of his daughters, and if so, which? Do any of his daughters love him, and if so, which? Such questions torment Lear. He resigns his kingship for an old age of love, then destroys his love because his authority is questioned. Much of this is reflected in the Gloucester-Edgar-Edmund theme. All these sons and daughters either sacrifice filial love for ambition or suffer distress or degradation in the cause of true love. The France-Burgundy contrast in point of love and ambition is also apposite. Toward the close we watch Edmund all-out for ambition, and Goneril and

[6] The *Lear*-vision appears to me as a life-view corresponding closely to that expressed by Middleton Murry's "God." And yet Murry's remarks on *Antony and Cleopatra* (e.g., "The Nature of Poetry," *Discoveries* [1924]) did much to stimulate my understanding of the play.

Regan, to do them justice, all-out for love. The general effect of the whole play is, then, mostly indecisive, with a victory at the close for love. *Macbeth* shows us a world in chaos, existence itself tottering, the child of peace and life struggling to be born amid the ravages of active death. *King Lear* shows a disorder without chaos, a wrench from peace, a contest painful and labouring, and, at long last, victory; in *Antony and Cleopatra* contest and division, life and death, disorder itself, create together a whole of perfect harmony. Death is seen conquering in *Macbeth*. In *King Lear* death and life are correlative, interdependent; death is the sweet end of suffering, the completion of life: "Break, heart, I prithee break." The extreme beauty of love, in the Lear-Cordelia reunion, comes before the extreme tragic agony of the close: these two, love and death, are synchronized in *Antony and Cleopatra*. In *Antony and Cleopatra*, death is the consummation of life, itself "a better life," in truth no death at all, but life. Here life conquers death.

VIII

ELMER EDGAR STOLL

The Dramatic Texture in Shakespeare

I have elsewhere[1] remarked the lack of suspense in Shakespeare as compared with Ibsen and even with Corneille and Racine. Save now and then, for a scene or more, he produces little surprise, with climactic preparation. What does he then instead? I have there also answered the question, but insufficiently. He offers, like the Greeks before him, who likewise did not keep the secret from the audience, an effect of excited anticipation; and more than the Greeks, and Corneille, Racine, and Ibsen too, a realization of the thoughts, feelings, and circumstances which rightly belong to a dramatic moment and are necessary to the illusion. At their best these effects may hold the interest as well as do those of surprise. Anticipation is ordinarily required for the arbitrary and artificial situations of his theatre and the ancient—disguise or mistaken identity, deception or slander, feigning or overhearing, oracles or prophecies coming true. Suspense—a gradual yet surprising disclosure to the audience as well as to people on the stage—is ordinarily required when the situation is brought about less quickly and peremptorily, and involves past conditions or events, present motives or intentions. Shakespeare generally keeps no secret, present or past. The story is told from the beginning; the motives or purposes, the moral or immoral, attractive or unattractive natures of the characters appear at the outset; the charac-

Reprinted from the *Criterion*, July, 1935. This essay appeared in an expanded form in, and is here reprinted by permission of the publishers from, Elmer Edgar Stoll, *Shakespeare and Other Masters* (Cambridge, Mass.: Harvard University Press). Copyright 1940 by The President and Fellows of Harvard College.

[1] Particularly in the chapter "Shakespeare and the Moderns" in my *Poets and Playwrights* (1930), to which this essay is supplementary. I am there indebted to Mr. Lubbock's *Craft of Fiction*. In the present article there are some echoes from my *Art and Artifice in Shakespeare* (1933).

ters themselves are numerous, the incidents frequent and various; and if Ibsen produces the impression of depth and volume, Shakespeare produces that of extension and expanse.

How, then, does he also concentrate this extension, give it structure, force, a sort of volume too? He has a bolder, more striking fable than the Norwegian; and there lies a certain effect (in the sculptural sense) of "relief." He has, of course, a good narrative method—contrast between scene and scene, interlocking of incidents and interweaving of the threads of story, crescendo and climax, complication and denouement. But so has Ibsen, a method certainly thriftier though not so striking. And, like the ancients, he has (something that is structural too) a more frequent and a more poignant irony. But these matters have to do with what is, though fundamental, rather external. What finer and more imaginative means does he employ? He has, at command, the treasures and incalculable resources of poetry; and there is nothing more marvelous in drama than the style and tone of *Hamlet* as distinguished from that of *Othello, King Lear, Macbeth,* and *Antony and Cleopatra.* In each there is a different atmosphere—a characteristic diction, imagery and verse—for a different world. But this is rather vague and intangible. How is it that apart from the poetry and the realization of character and circumstance he achieves a finer unity to make amends for the force and point of an ultimate startling disclosure?

Anticipation itself, when well contrived, yields a kind of suspense; as when, in the *Oedipus Tyrannus,* the Messenger from Corinth, bringing the news of Polybus's death, thinks to allay the hero's remaining fears by telling him that, though heir to the throne, he is not the king's son. This news is less reassuring—is still more exciting—to the audience, who know what is coming, and see it coming, than to the hero; the hero's own excitement, indeed, does not now directly appear. At other times it does so appear, and that of the less important characters as well; and then there are expectations fearful or joyful, to be justified or not. This is exciting both on the stage and in the house. For though the audience are aware of the outcome they are so only in general terms; identifying themselves with the hero, they live mainly in the moment, notice mainly what the dramatist is actually presenting; and they are particularly affected by joyful expectations that in their hearts they know to be fallacious. So true is this that many critics, like Lessing, have hotly declared against the method of surprise, although Shakespeare himself has followed it for an act or a scene, as at the beginning of *Hamlet* and at the end of *Othello;* yet in the play as a whole we need not greatly concern ourselves for its virtues, seeing that we have the practice of Ibsen, Corneille, Racine, and Lope to support us, as well as the explicit doctrine of the Spaniard and even of Aristotle. "Such incidents have the very greatest effect on the mind," says the Stagirite, "when they occur unexpectedly and at the same time in consequence of one another."[2] Shakespeare's, for the most part, have such effect as those of Aeschylus and Sophocles, not those of Euripides.

Then there is the matter of emotional interrelations. In general, not only before but after the turns of fortune, the demonstration of feeling on the part of the characters is in Greek and Shakespearean tragedy far more open and pronounced than in Ibsen and the contemporary drama. Thus the audience receive their emotions by contagion. In Ibsen the characters' feelings are given less scope, and the audience receive their emotions in a sense directly, but by a process that is indirect. Contagion is replaced by suggestion. Not privy to the secret, they live and learn as do the hero and the other characters on the stage; and as they receive impressions and gather information they are moved and respond. Through the preparation and the surprise, the gradual but stimulating disclosure, the hero or another may, at the great moment, with the highest effect upon them, speak quietly and reticently. But when the audience are to participate less, are to be less thrown upon their own resources, the perceptions and the emotions of leading characters must, accordingly, be more amply displayed; and Oedipus and Cassandra, Macbeth and Othello, visibly shrink from the abyss before they fall. Oedipus descries it from afar:

> O Zeus, what hast thou decreed to do unto me?

> Unhappy that I am! Methinks I have been laying myself even now under a dread curse, and knew it not.

> Forbid, forbid, ye awful gods that I should see that day.

[2] *Poetics* ix.

So Macbeth faces the horror of treason and assassination; Lear cries, "O let me not be mad, not mad, sweet heaven!"; Othello bids farewell to the plumèd troop; and Iago, as the hero approaches, the poison already working in his veins, mutters and chuckles, "Not poppy nor mandragora, nor all the drowsy syrups of the world shall medicine thee to that sweet sleep which thou ow'dst yesterday." And in Shakespearean tragedy, as in the ancient, superstitious intimations—premonitions and forebodings—abound.

Now this frankness of the villain, whether in confidence or soliloquy, and this clairvoyance and unrestraint of the hero are, though they involve a loss in verisimilitude and simulation, essential to the method. Even that still more unplausible consciousness, on the villain's part of his own villainy, and on the hero's of his own virtue,[3] which is a vestige of an earlier technique, contributes to it. Is this not part of the secret, to be shared? And without such excitement before the event—and after it of course there is still more—the letting of the audience into the secret from the outset would be a failure. Suspense itself is a matter of arousing emotion in the audience; and by this method of anticipation, imaginative if not suggestive, emotions are aroused.

What is more, this demonstrativeness helps hold the play together. It is not merely a matter of before and after but of here and there and up and down its course. In both Elizabethan and ancient tragedy, but above all in the Shakespearean, the passions are not only more amply depicted but also more fully developed than in the modern, and in characters important or unimportant; and in their changes and relations lies as much of the structure as in those of the incidents. They rise and fall, swell and subside both in the individual and (as we shall see) in the scene and the play as a whole; they are not confined within the limits of natural conversation; but as Mr. Shaw says of Othello, "[The words] are streaming ensigns and tossing branches to make the tempest of passion visible." How pronouncedly, too, the characters react upon each other! Five times after he falls into the Ancient's clutches Othello en-

---

[3] As in Othello's speeches (I. ii. 19–24, 30–32), instances, even today, but slightly objectionable from the standpoint of realism. Brutus, in the quarrel scene, is a case much more pronounced—misunderstanding the technique, critics have taken him to task for his complacence.

counters Desdemona, and, though without changing his resolve, with continually more marked effect upon both himself and her. The relation of the chief characters to the numerous minor ones is emotional as well: they are loved or hated, praised or condemned, rather than analysed or understood. This again the audience receive by contagion; and by it, together with the justification for such feelings in the presentation of the characters in question, their sympathies are engaged and guided. How they are safeguarded—against the errors of the critics!—by the outpourings of admiration and affection upon Romeo and Juliet, Hamlet, Lear, Othello, Coriolanus, and Antony and Cleopatra, and, at the beginning, Macbeth! For in Shakespeare sympathy is the incentive of suspense, as curiosity is in Ibsen; and the response is immediate, not delayed. In every way imaginable the dramatist takes advantage of his method; and the whole play is a system and rhythm—what is this but unity?—a contrast and harmony, of passions.

Play and scene fluctuate as well as the character. Both end quietly; and there are *still* scenes like that before Glamis Castle, as there are normal or unexcitable characters like Horatio, Banquo, Kent, Cassio, and Ludovico. The art is essentially classical, and involves repose. The principle is that of rhythm and contrast, not unrelenting tension and continual high pressure, as today; and by points of repose the balance is kept and the effect of tension is heightened.[4]

So much at present for the matter of interrelation: there is another (insofar as the two are separable) of comprehension. Shakespeare's tragedies are mainly not tragedies of fate but intrigue, the villain partly or entirely taking the place of destiny; and generally the hero engages in an action to which he is by nature averse. It does not develop out of the character as it more nearly does in Ibsen. At heart Othello is not jealous; Macbeth, not dishonourable or murderous; and this contrast is kept before our eyes. In the murder scene of Macbeth there is no surprising disclosure of fact, motive, or trait. There is the realization of all the circumstances of murder, and of such thoughts and notions, feelings and reactions, as these circumstances would arouse—the misgivings and trepidations, the starting at

---

[4] Cf. Coventry Patmore's *Principle in Art,* chap. vi, to which I am here indebted. Cf. also my *Poets and Playwrights,* pp. 79–85.

sounds and imagining of sounds that are not, the questions asked but left unanswered, the fears present and to come. In this rounded intensity of realization itself there is unity; but there is more. Why does Lady Macbeth cry "My husband!" when the man staggers in with blood on his hands, as if she were not sure he was, or as if he were now more than ever? Why does Macbeth himself cry "What hands are these?" as if they were not his own? And, again, "Will all great Neptune's ocean wash this blood clean from my hand?" And again, "Wake *Duncan* with thy knocking! I would thou couldst." In these wide-ranging imaginings and heart-searching outcries the situation is seized and comprehended rather than (through curiosity) fashioned and projected; the essential dramatic contrast is caught up and signalized; and what has gone before and what is yet to come, what murderer and murderess were and what they at present are, all flash before them—and us as well. And this concentrated comprehension is to be found elsewhere in *Macbeth*, as, among other places, where Macduff on hearing of the killing of his wife and children groans, "He has no children"; and where Lady Macbeth sighs, "The thane of Fife had a wife; where is she now?" and, again, "All the perfumes of Arabia will not sweeten this little hand."

It is to be found as frequently in *Othello;* as when, having just killed her, the hero exclaims, in a recoil of realization, after saying, as a matter of fact, at the knock of Emilia, "She'll sure speak to my wife":

> My wife! my wife! what wife? I have no wife;

or when, defending himself to Emilia after she enters, he declares, too truly,

> O, I were damn'd beneath all depth in hell,
> But that I did proceed upon just grounds
> To this extremity. . . .

or when, with no vestiges of a doubt or suspicion naturally bred within him, he realizes his monstrous error,

> Cold, cold, my girl!
> Even like thy chastity!

It is to be found in *King Lear*, as when the hero cries out, on seeing both daughters set against him,

> O heavens,
> If you do love old men, if your sweet sway
> Allow obedience, if you yourselves are old,
> Make it your cause;

or, on blindly conceiving that the daughter whom he had cast off still breathes:

> This feather stirs; she lives! If it be so,
> It is a chance which does redeem all sorrows
> That ever I have felt;

or when Kent, before that, considers the tragedy proceeding round about him:

> It is the stars,
> The stars above us, govern our conditions;
> Else one self mate and make could not beget
> Such different issues.

Often, as in the murder scene of *Macbeth* and the sleepwalking scene, these great spotlight glimpses are taken from a height; and sometimes, as there, from above the spiritual elevation of the speaker. Here is the *moral* inverisimilitude in the convention of clairvoyance. The murderer's and murderess's sensitiveness of conscience is, except as their crime is the doing of fate, incompatible with the murder. The conscience is external, a nemesis, not the accurate expression of a red-handed murderer's own moral nature; when we stop to think of it (as we are not expected to do) what right or reason has Macbeth at such a moment to "say Amen" and expect a blessing. But, as Mr. Chapman has it, "The hypersensitiveness of Macbeth and Lady Macbeth is one of Shakespeare's greatest strokes of genius." Both early and late in their story it is part and parcel of the tragic situation.

From an equal height, but either not so dramatic or not so characteristic, come narrower glimpses, of a moment in the play rather than the central situation, or else wider views, of the course of human existence. Of the former sort is Othello's "Farewell the plumèd troop" and "It is the very error of the moon," and Iago's "Not poppy nor mandragora," Cleopatra's "Have I the aspic in my lips?" and Juliet's "O churl! drunk all, and left no friendly drop to help me after?" Of the latter are Edgar's

> Men must endure
> Their going hence even as their coming hither;
> Ripeness is all. . . .

and Gloster's

> As flies to wanton boys, are we to the gods:
> They kill us for their sport. . . .

as well as Macbeth's "Out, out brief candle," Antony's "The wise gods . . . seal our eyes," and Prospero's "And like the baseless fabric of this vision." This speech of Gloster's seems too lofty for his intelligence, though the figure is within his range and the irony fits his case; but whether that or not, these higher (or wider) views give to the tragedy, to the image of life in it, an effect of unity. We can look before and after; we see "the whole of it"; the sky arches over the earth.

Not merely in tragedy but even in comedy, and not merely at the greatest moments in either, there is, if a less elevated, an equally rounded and far-reaching vision. In tragedy, as we have already seen, it may be given to minor characters, and as often to the villain, Edmund or Iago. Edmund's recognition of the justice of the gods on his father and himself is sublime:

> The wheel is come full circle; I am here.

He is tolerant enough, and his father is involved enough, for him to see it. But more in his native vein is what he says after the death of the sisters:

> I was contracted to them both. All three
> Now marry in an instant;

and when their bodies are brought in:

> Yet Edmund was belov'd!
> The one the other poisoned for my sake,
> And after slew herself.

Who among the legitimate can say as much? And Iago, reviewing his day and night of deviltry, chuckles characteristically as he declares,

> By the mass, 'tis morning;
> Pleasure and action make the hours seem short.

So in comedy there are remarks like Sir Toby's to Malvolio:

Dost thou think, because thou art virtuous, there shall be no more cakes and ale?

Trinculo's to Stephano and Caliban as their faculties succumb to drink:

They say there's but five upon this isle: we are three of them; if the other two be brain'd like us, the state totters.

and Helen's to Pandarus:

Let thy song be love. This love will undo us all. O Cupid, Cupid, Cupid!

Any of these, but particularly the last, might almost serve as epigraph for the play—if Shakespeare had plays with central ideas, *drames à thèse*. And on separate occasions how the poet embodies and inspirits the scene! In *Much Ado,* when Don Pedro says, "Come, shall we hear this music?" the romantic Claudio replies:

> Yea, my good lord. How still the evening is,
> As hush'd on purpose to grace harmony!

So in *The Tempest,* when Miranda, seeing for the first time other men than her father and (of late) Ferdinand, bursts out, "O brave new world, that has such people in it," Prospero, who better knows them, answers, indulgently but comprehendingly:

> 'Tis new to thee!

As for the interrelations, there is, as we have seen, little explicit analysis such as in Jonson and Ibsen, though in the latter, directly, there is not much either. Shakespeare's plays are not "studies," neither in psychology, as they have long been considered, nor in Elizabethan "humours," as by some scholars they have been thought of late. The audience are expected not to detect and discover but to sympathize or to condemn; and therefore, according to their natures, people do this in the play, even the character in question. Otherwise the emotional development might waver, the harmony be broken. Only in comedy (and in that tragedy which Mr. Shaw has with a grain of truth called Shakespeare's greatest comedy, *Coriolanus*), where, as Aristotle says, the characters are not better but in some respects worse than the men of the present day,[5] is there a greater freedom of analysis; though for Coriolanus there is, to keep our emotions active, far more of praise and blame than analysis, and to engage our sympathies for him, far more of praise than blame. But in Shakespeare even the comic figures are for the most part not worse, are not, as in the ancients or Jonson and Molière, the objects of satire, but are witty or ridiculous; and in the presentation of them there is somewhat the same method as that already considered in tragedy—that of lyricism, as in the case of Mercutio, Beatrice, and Falstaff, when their wit effervesces in fantasy; and that of self-exposure, as when the corpulent coward descants upon honour and discretion, and Dogberry and Aguecheek show themselves to be asses even in saying that they are.[6] In Jonson and Molière the vicious or obsessed as well as the normal persons who have to do with them are generally too preoccupied for fun. In Shakespeare the comic effect, not arising out of the elaborate exhibition of a vice, as the tragic not out of that of a ruling passion, must be explicitly indicated and fully appreciated on the stage; and it is by contagion that laughter, like tears, breaks out in the house. In Ibsen, with whom the effect, comic or tragic, is more as in Jonson and Molière, the very action is a process of analysis; or rather, it prompts and provokes the spectator, by its varied method of suggestion, to analyse for himself.

But a bird in the hand is, even in art, worth two in the bush; and imaginative realization is better than ingenious suggestion. The Norwegian, it would seem, has, like most other modern dramatists, no such resources as the Elizabethan for the presentation of the impression the characters produce upon each other, and no such resources for justifying it. I know Ibsen only in English; but he ordinarily uses prose, not verse; and his

[5] *Poetics* ii, v. The Aristotelian statement applies, of course, rather to classical and Jonsonian comedy than to the Shakespearean, where the heroes are generally romantic figures; and in *Macbeth, Antony and Cleopatra,* and *Timon,* where the heroes have faults, there is more analysis than in Shakespeare's other great tragedies, though in the first two it is avoided, and Macbeth's downfall is attributed to the influence of fate and his wife.

[6] See my *Shakespeare Studies* (1927), chap. viii. There is the lyricism also of witlessness and nonsense, as not only in Dogberry and Aguecheek but in Shallow and Silence, the Athenian mechanicals, and Falstaff's story of the knaves in buckram and Kendal green.

characters, as James once said, are ill-mannered. To us, at least, they are seldom likable or fascinating as Shakespeare's very villains are. Now upon the direct presentation in speech and demeanour, rather than upon implication or suggestion, the effect of nobility or meanness, of virtue or villainy, of charm or hatefulness, chiefly depends. How numerous and various are the admirers of Hamlet and Ophelia, Othello and Desdemona, Lear and Cordelia, Antony and Cleopatra, Viola, Rosalind, Juliet, Beatrice, each in character as he expresses himself! And how manifestly these heroes and heroines deserve or warrant the admiration and devotion, as Rosmer and Rebecca, Allmers and Rita, Peer Gynt, Borkman, Helmer, and Solness do not! Shakespeare, raising the question, can answer it; incurring the debt, can pay it.

Indeed, interrelations apart, it is a question whether the direct and ample method of presentation is not generally superior in effect to the realistic and suggestive. By the latter more is meant than meets the ear, but too often it misses the audience. They are required to think, rather than prompted to feel. The great privilege and prerogative of art is to be simple, sensuous, and passionate; and that the modern method in a measure surrenders. By the Shakespearean the external reality and individuality, though not the internal, is made more immediately manifest; and that of itself lends credibility to the action. And there is a farther, finer reality, whether external or internal, the overtone of it, so to speak, that cannot be made manifest save by image and rhythm. When Macbeth murmurs or mutters

> Duncan is in his grave;
> After life's fitful fever he sleeps well . . .

it is only from the way he says it that we learn how he envies his victim. The metaphor of life as a fever, sinking into a sleep! The fitfulness, the "restless ecstasy," of the first measures of the verse, and the fathomless repose of the three final monosyllables! What more is meant thus meets the ear.

Poetry, indeed, is Shakespeare's chief but unlimited resource. Poetry, as Mr. Housman has lately said, produces emotion; and in order to do that, it, as Mr. Abercrombie, another fine poet, said before him, "does not give us a copy or picture or projection of its reality: it represents reality by actually and truly calling reality into existence: it creates reality over again." As we have seen, Shakespeare does both the one thing and the other, as well as something which Wordsworth designates as in the gift of the imagination, "consolidating numbers into unity." And this he does not only by his focusing vision but also by bold simplifying conventions and an (as it were) musical repetition.

To these we turn. *Othello* is the perfect example of interrelation and interplay. As I have elsewhere shown, the very plot and the whole illusion depend upon them. By a convention or fiction Iago can make Othello jealous, without making him a dupe in the process, because he himself is impenetrably honest and sagacious not only in the hero's eyes but in those of everybody else about him, including his own wife. Everybody respects and trusts Iago; everybody admires Othello and wonders and grieves at his change. The initial premise, that a free and open nature "thinks men honest that but seem to be so," releases great emotional energy as it permits Othello, without a base suspiciousness and still loving his wife, to become frightfully jealous; and the unanimity of feeling at the change (like the unanimity of impression produced by Iago's imposture) both reduces the improbability of it and heightens its effect.

There is a musical method, that is a poetical—in music are not the emotions played upon more directly?—both in such bold manipulation and accentuation and also as the hero, passing at the end from under the cloud of delusion, becomes, though not altogether, himself again. Even in his rage his love is ever before us and of his old self we are continually reminded; and here in the finale, when the black cloud has passed over, this effect of rhythm and recurrence is appropriately heightened and intensified as, without psychological impropriety and with also a dramatic suspense, thoughts of the sword, the past, the future, come and go, or rise and fall, by a sort of undulation, in his consciousness.

And the musical method serves not only for structure but for emphasis. The climax is thus dwelt upon, and is signalized. This is advantageous to the emotional scheme and to the whole. What is important must thus or otherwise seem important; and that, again, is a matter of relations. Elsewhere the dramatist has, for such a purpose, had recourse at great moments to repeti-

tion; as when, before this, Othello appeals to his pitiless adviser
—"But yet the pity of it, Iago! O Iago, the pity of it, Iago";
when Antony moans, "I am dying, Egypt, dying"; when Volumnia supplicates her son,

> for how can we,
> Alas, how can we for our country pray,
> Whereto we are bound, together with thy victory,
> Whereto we are bound?

and when her son then turns to the Volscian for approval:

> Aufidius, though I cannot make true wars,
> I'll frame convenient peace. Now, good Aufidius,
> Were you in my stead, would you have heard
> A mother less, or granted less, Aufidius?[7]

The device here serves a purpose similar to that of the variation in the force and volume of the language—another musical
resource which, with both prose and verse, high style and low,
at his disposal, the Elizabethan employs in far greater abun-
dance than the modern. At the important moments he may be
quiet and simple like Ibsen or J. J. Bernard; but so as a com-
poser may be, not the dramatist who, with a breath-suspending
word, sets the seal upon his disclosure.

So far, for the most part, I have traced the musical development elsewhere. But there is more. Three epithets, on the lips
of various people, continually recur as applied to Othello, Desdemona, and Iago—"noble," "gentle," and "honest." And three
facts are fundamental to the fable—that Othello should be noble
(lofty and magnanimous), Desdemona be gentle (sweet and
amiable), as they are, and Iago seem honest (sincere and up-
right), as he does. Again the question raised is answered: the
epithet wholly fits. "Honest" in another Elizabethan sense,
moreover, that of chastity, is, after the temptation, frequently
applied to the heroine also, positively or negatively, by the hero
and villain, Emilia and Desdemona herself. That is the problem (if we may so call it) of the play—though not in the mind
of anyone, really, but the hero when in the toils. Moreover, to
Iago the three established epithets mean, dramatically, something different. Noble—"The better shall my purpose work on

[7] To Mr. Rylands I owe some of these examples, who has brought them
together for a somewhat different purpose (*Words and Poetry*, p. 215).

him"; gentle—"Ay," rejoins the Ancient to the General, "too gentle"; honest—"But I'll set down the pegs that make this music, as honest as I am."

Now this various and appropriate repetition is both a simplifying and a unifying device,[8] that is—for is not music the art in which structure and substance are inseparable?—a musical one. It both serves a purpose like that of Jonsonian or Restoration ticket names such as "Careless" or "Pliant," signalizing and emphasizing one quality, though without the disillusioning taint of allegory or personified abstraction; and also it furnishes, as uttered anew by a different person or in different circumstances, one more instance of a relation between character and character and reminds us of the others. Iago's remark, "Ay, too gentle," not only is quite in his own humorous-devilish vein but also (echoing Othello's, "And then, of so gentle a condition" [IV. i. 204][9]) again epitomizes the situation. There lies the whole tragic contrast: her sweetness is her undoing; her virtue is turned to pitch. Likewise the hero's desperate, doubt-stifling assertion,

> I do not think but Desdemona's honest,
>
> (III. iii. 225)

is countered by the still more insidious and unsettling reply,

> Long live she so! and long live you to think so!

And the same epithet serving for Desdemona and Iago is really an advantage. Every time the title is denied to her, or reclaimed for her, we remember him who bears it so equably and indisputably, and who alone has raised the doubt.

This use of repetition—a structural, musical use, I mean, as above, not that (in various fashion) for purposes of characterization, as in Hamlet, Lear, and Gloster, Shylock, Falstaff, Rosalind, and Cleopatra—is employed by Shakespeare almost wholly in tragedy; by Italian, French, and Spanish dramatic art it is employed mainly in comedy. For the difference there are several reasons: that Shakespeare's genius is prevailingly synthetic rather than analytic, tolerant rather than critical, tragic

---

[8] As is the stock epithet in Homer and Virgil; see Lessing and Mr. Lascelles Abercrombie's fine lecture *Progress in Literature* (1929), pp. 39 f. But its structural function is simpler.

[9] "Condition" means, of course, "disposition," "nature."

rather than comic. Few (if any) of his comedies are comic all
through; the others are fantastic, sentimental or romantic, even
pathetic or tragic, as well; and often several of these qualities
may reside in a scene, situation, or character at once and together. Repetition for the purposes of laughter would then be
fairly out of place. And in the comedies it is employed mainly
in the serious or (still in the good sense of the word) sentimental portions, as in the *Merchant of Venice* at the beginning and
the end, where Antonio and the others dwell on his sadness and
where Lorenzo and Jessica sing to each other (as it were) in
the moonlight, and in *Twelfth Night*, where, as Professor
Mackail has beautifully shown, the "dying fall," delighted in at
the beginning, is realized in the action itself at the close. In the
tragedies the comic element is episodic, is blended or subdued,
as in the scene of the Gravediggers in *Hamlet*, of the Porter in
Macbeth and of the Country Fellow in *Antony and Cleopatra*.
Here are repetitions, but no one in the audience has the heart
or any encouragement to laugh at them; uttered in ignorance
of the inner truth, they recall the death of Ophelia, the circumstances of the murder, the present despairing purpose of the
Queen. They, too, link and gather things together; they height-
en even as they relieve the tragic effect.

The only play that can vie with *Othello* in approaching the
condition of music is also the only one where the dramatist had
fairly a free hand, with no preceding play or well-known history to hamper him, that is, *Macbeth*. Here, as in the Venetian
tragedy, there is repetition both on the large scale and the small.
The appearances of the Weird Sisters are of the one sort, as is
Othello emerging from his delusion; the details of their prophecies as they are fulfilled and the reminders of the initial murder on the lips of the ignorant Porter at the gate, and of all
three murders on the lips of the Lady while sleepwalking, are
of the other sort, as are the epithets "noble," "gentle," and
"honest" in *Othello* and that of "gracious" applied to Duncan.
It is not the same method, but, again, it is musical, structural:
in another dramatist the two methods would have been more
nearly the same. Three times the Weird Sisters come upon the
stage, for the appearance before the last, Act III, scene v, is
certainly an interpolation; and when the fourth act begins,

Thrice the brindled cat hath mew'd . . .

the lines of incantation profit by all those which have been uttered before, the effect being cumulative, as at the third sounding of the trumpet. Fate still has her eyes on him, the Thane of Glamis; and her voice breaks upon us again (with no preparation save "I will to the Weird Sisters," two scenes earlier) like a faraway yet not forgotten theme or leitmotiv, now recurring, in an opera or symphony.

And the repetition involved in the piecemeal, alarming but continually reassuring, fulfilment of the prophecies produces a sort of suspense, but again that of anticipation rather than of a prepared surprise; and, if from anywhere, it would seem to derive from the Greeks. The *Oedipus*, where the method involves not only oracles but prophecies and imprecations, is the finest example. In both this tragedy and *Macbeth* some, indeed, of the repetitions are essential to the story as they come true, and to mere dramatic effect as the hero takes fright at a partial fulfilment of the prophecy and comfort from that which remains. But some of them are not, as when, after the full disclosure, the hero cries out in apostrophe to Cithaeron, place of the exposure, and the three roads and secret glen, place of the parricide. The cumulative effect of these and the other fateful words is greater than in *Macbeth;* but it is part of the same emotional method as there and in the *Agamemnon*, with its "net" or "robe" of ruin.

There is, however, in *Macbeth* a repetition less verbal and noticeable but perhaps still more structural, which resembles another sort that there is in *Othello*. I mean that whereby the fatal influence, of which the Weird Sisters are the voices, asserts itself and permeates the action. As on his first appearance in the third scene the hero echoes their last words in the first,

> So foul and fair a day I have not seen,

the relation is established even before (in keeping with their purpose) they have met him. And when they do, he responds to their suggestion, as instantaneously as the Moor to Iago's, and afterwards recalls it. The dagger is a "fatal vision," not the product of a diseased imagination, but sent to tempt him, as are the voice crying "Sleep no more," and the ghost appearing at the banquet, to plague him. Nature is here no mere background, but, in league with evil, plays a double role, like that of the Devil in the Christian system, "the tempter ere the accuser of mankind." As in *Julius Caesar* and *King Lear* she undergoes an upheaval, both portending and accompanying, according to a superstition not then extinct, the fall of the monarch. Night, thrice invoked to hide and warrant the murderers, hangs like a pall over them afterwards, with alarming noises and apparitions; the Lady has light by her continually, and in her sleep carries a taper. Sleep, whose sanctuary they have violated as they assassinated Duncan and incriminated his grooms, forsakes the one and brings down memories upon the other. In no play is there more of irony. What was a temptation becomes forthwith a torment. Indeed, by the unpsychological but dramatic fiction of supernatural and conjugal influence (instead, as in *Othello*, of the villainous) the temptation really is none—is no attraction—and the crime, once committed, is no satisfaction but a horror. And by the logic of circumstances as well as of superstition, "blood will have blood," and thus other horrors come in the trail of this. Blood, which, by the violence done to the hero's nature and, through her invocation of the spirits that tend on mortal thoughts, to the heroine's own, they are seeking and craving, sticks to them throughout their course, with its colour and its smell. "A little water clears us of this deed," she whispers; but it never does. The symbolism is, again, only that of superstition or folklore, as with the blood of Abel; and the vindictive recoil of nemesis is still more marked when Banquo comes to the feast as a ghost, and re-enters when his health is drunk. In these and other ways fate as continually and relentlessly presides over the Caledonian tragedy as over the Venetian.

The verbal repetition in Shakespeare is rather like that in Ibsen, who, with all his suspense, has this resource as well; and to him Ibsen is probably indebted. At any rate, ironical, seriocomic incidents before the catastrophe, such as Dr. Rank's last appearance in *The Doll's House* and Ulric Brendel's in *Rosmersholm*, owe something to the Gravediggers' scene in *Hamlet* and the Country Fellow scene in *Antony and Cleopatra*. In Ibsen the device, being less episodic, is, so far, more structural and rhythmical, the repetition involved having to do with the central motive of the play. But there is less of a contrast, the comic character being less of an outsider; he is aware, and is also serious, and in Shakespeare he is (in himself) wholly comic

and unconscious; there is less of the effect of volume, there being, as in general, less breadth of emotion to comprehend. And
the distant repetition of pregnant and pivotal phrases, like
"coming to the rescue," "claims of the ideal," "one cock in the
basket," "castles in the air," in such plays as *Ghosts, The Wild
Duck, Hedda Gabler,* and the *Master-Builder* has something in
common with *Othello.* It is more pronounced and elaborate,
has less to do with story and more with matters internal—
moods, motives, central ideas; it is more suggestive, again, but
less lyrical, making the spectator think rather than feel; yet it
performs the same simplifying and unifying, serious or ironic,
not comic, function. It also there sometimes serves the ulterior
purpose of symbolism. But in Ibsen, Shakespeare, and Sophocles alike, it is the use at succeeding important and significant
moments of an expression charged already with associations,
and now by further use charged anew. And thus are secured
concentration and rhythm in the play, both "economy of attention" and "heightening of consciousness" in the spectator.

Shakespeare, whether in the use of repetition or otherwise,
provides less for economy of attention, more for heightening
of consciousness, of emotion; but the merits of either dramatist, or of the method employed, are not now in question. What
is in question is whether in adopting the inherited and established method of anticipation—the popular Elizabethan dramatist, of course, had little choice—he made amends for its shortcomings; and this, as I hope to have shown, he did by manifold
interrelating and vivid comprehension of the widespread material, and by the fatal influence flowing through it. He made the
most of what suspense is by the method attainable. He took
advantage of the convention of clairvoyance and self-descrip-
tion as a means of impressing the issues of the play upon us, and
of harmoniously developing and varying the appropriate emotions of the characters, to arouse our own. Emotions, indeed,
in their fluctuations and relations, their clash and harmony,
make up the finer substance of the play; and the structure, as
well as the effect, is that of poetry, is like that of music. The
characters arouse emotions in other characters, and they are so
presented that they justify the emotions they arouse. And this
finer web and texture is made firmer and more perceptible by
a simplifying, rhythmical repetition of important themes and
phrases.

Above all, the emotions have the dimensions and the stature of passions, and in Shakespeare's greatest work the chief unifying force is to be detected not so much in the product as in what produced it. A great imagination fully aroused does not wander. Since writing the above I have happened upon Henley's essay on *Othello*, first printed in 1903, in which, though like a poet, the critic presents a conception of the tragedy similar even in phrasing and figure, to mine as expressed above and elsewhere. I quote only such sentences as here seem relevant:

The staple of drama is Emotion . . . *Dumas père* . . . all *he* wanted was "four trestles, four boards, two actors, and a passion." 'Tis the briefest, the most comprehensive, the most luminous statement of the essential of drama that ever, I believe, was made; and it fits the *Othello* of Shakespeare as it fits the Aeschylean Oresteia like a glove . . . Iago apart, the interest of *Othello* is entirely and unalterably emotional. You might play it in a barn, and it would still fulfil itself. The actors change: are now Othello and Iago, now Desdemona and Emila, now Othello and Desdemona, now Emilia and Othello, now Othello and Fate, the tremendous, the inevitable: even Death. But the passion persists; it shifts its quality as the Master wills, takes on the hues, speaks with the voice, dares with furiousness of love and hate and jealousy and misery and murder and despair. But once evoked, it never lets go of your throat; and this is what makes Othello the play of plays it is. . . . 'Tis as it were a soul in earthquake and eclipse;[10] and there is never a detail, never a touch of the cataclysm, however variable and minute, but is realized and recorded with so consummate an artistry, an intelligence so abounding, so complete and so assured, that the issue savours of inspiration.

[10] Cf. my *Art and Artifice in Shakespeare*, p. 22.

IX

J. I. M. STEWART

"Steep Tragic Contrast": *Macbeth*

It was the owl that shriek'd, the fatal bellman
Which gives the stern'st good-night.

MACBETH II. ii. 4

What I tell you three times is true.

THE BELLMAN

The leading exponent of the new realism in Shakespeare studies is Professor Elmer Edgar Stoll. No one has ever been more pertinacious in enforcing a critical theory of the plays. His erudition is noble and a little daunting; as I turn over his numerous monographs and volumes of collected essays I am alarmed by the length to which he has contrived to expand his thesis, by this and even by the mere foot-pounds of physical energy which the providing of the cross references must have entailed. Matthew Arnold was persuaded that one cannot always be studying one's own works, but I do not know that Mr. Stoll feels this: in his recent *From Shakespeare to Joyce* he gives more than a hundred invitations to consult previous writings of his own. And I am reminded as I read of something else which Arnold said in the same place:

It is not in my nature,—some of my critics would rather say, not in my power,—to dispute on behalf of any opinion, even my own, very obstinately. To try and approach truth on one side

From *Character and Motive in Shakespeare: Some Recent Appraisals Examined*, by J. I. M. Stewart (London, 1949), pp. 79–97. Reprinted by permission of the author and Longmans, Green & Co.

The quotations from *Collected Essays Papers &c. of Robert Bridges* and *The Poems of Gerard Manley Hopkins* are included by permission of the Oxford University Press; those from E. E. Stoll's article in *The Review of English Studies* by kind permission of the Clarendon Press; and that from Theodore Reik's *The Unknown Murderer* by kind permission of the Hogarth Press, Ltd.

after another, not to strive or cry, nor to persist in pressing forward, on any one side, with violence and self-will,—it is only thus, it seems to me, that mortals may hope to gain any vision of the mysterious Goddess, whom we shall never see except in outline, but only thus even in outline. He who will do nothing but fight impetuously towards her on his own, one, favourite, particular line, is inevitably destined to run his head into the folds of the black robe in which she is wrapped.[1]

For many years Mr. Stoll has had his particular line, and he is a very good fighter, although handicapped by a style obscuring what proves, in fact, a reassuringly simple and compassable stock of ideas. I consider here a paper in which these ideas are fairly fully expressed. It is called "Source and Motive in *Macbeth* and *Othello*."[2] If what is there propounded proves unacceptable, then Mr. Stoll, while remaining a learned and acute commentator on drama in general, cannot, I judge, be accepted with much confidence as a new guide to Shakespeare. But at least he is a more interesting writer than numerous Bradley-and-water critics who have largely ignored him. Had Mr. Stoll been attended to as he deserved he might have said less alarmingly often what it has been his to say.

Stoll begins by observing that Shakespeare is himself artistically responsible for what is represented in *Othello* and *Macbeth*, since he is constrained neither by his audience's sense of historical fact nor by expectations based on previous dramatisings of the stories. If he departs from Cinthio and Holinshed the impulsion must lie in his own sense of what is dramatic. And he does depart from them widely and similarly in point of motivation. What then is the dramatic principle at work?

In *Macbeth*, the argument continues, Shakespeare would seem to put the hero much further beyond the reach of our sympathy than Holinshed does. For Holinshed explains that the Scottish monarchy was not strictly hereditary and that Macbeth had some reasonable hope of the crown until thwarted by Duncan's declaring for Malcolm; that Duncan's administration had been "feeble and slouthfull"; and that Macbeth, after slaying him without treachery or violating the laws of hospitality, "set his whole intention to maintaine justice and to punish

---

[1] M. Arnold, *Essays in Criticism* (1865), Preface.

[2] This paper is printed in *Review of English Studies*, XIX (1943), 25.

all enormities and abuses which had chanced" and ruled justly
and efficiently for ten years. All this, which might serve to extenuate his hero's criminality, Shakespeare discards. And he
makes Duncan a trusting and gracious figure; the scene of his
foul assassination Macbeth's own castle; the issue for Scotland
an immediate and ever-rising bath of blood; the fatal deed itself neither preluded by any substantial aspiring to the royal
power and envisaging of its attractions, nor succeeded by any
satisfaction, however fleeting in its attainment. "As Mr. Firkins
and even Mr. Bradley have observed," Macbeth seems to be
more aware of deterrents than incentives. Massively built up in
terms of bravery or virtue at the beginning (and these qualities, with a large poetry, create sympathy and constitute a sort
of goodness on the stage), he goes in horror to his crime and
with horror remembers it. "The conscience in him, before and
after, is that of a good man." And so, after Shakespeare has
manipulated his source, the situation yields "a contrast big and
sharp enough." But it is what we may call a stagy contrast.
For any verisimilitude in Macbeth's fall from virtue to criminality fails as soon as we "pause to take notice how unpsychological the change . . . is."

Shakespeare, then, at once enlarges the wickedness of Macbeth's deed and diminishes its sober credibility. And if we are
inclined to any reaching out after fact and reason in point of
motivation he seems content to bring us up against the impon-
derable factor of the supernatural prompting by the prescient
women. We cannot, since they are out of nature, set a limit to
the power of their solicitations; and the odds against Macbeth,
being thus incalculable, permit of the impression that his nobility is, after all, in some sort unimpaired.

In *Macbeth* there are witches; in *Othello,* Stoll says, there is
a devil in the flesh. And Iago's function too is that of con-
fronting the hero with a soliciting to evil so supernaturally potent as virtually to absolve. This devil's malignity is invisible
and invulnerable, so Othello could not do other than succumb.
And the point is emphasised by relieving the devil of any substantial human occasion for his ill-doing; he acts not from motives but from a constituting principle and thus stands outside
the bounds of a realistic psychology.

Now, just this Iago, Stoll goes on, is Shakespeare's invention, not Cinthio's. For Cinthio's Ensign has provocation enough for his villainy, which he aims not directly at the Moor but at Desdemona, who has rejected his advances, and at the Captain (Cassio), whom he believes that she loves. In this there is a substantial internal motive for his wickedness. But Shakespeare's Ancient has only the grudge of a man who has missed promotion; with him any powerful prompting from sexual jealousy is reduced to the dimensions of excuse and afterthought.

And it is not only Cinthio's Ensign who is modified, it is also his Moor:

> Moreover, though Cinthio's Moor is given some noble and attractive traits, especially at the outset, Shakespeare's is both there and throughout on a far higher level of intelligence and feeling. He is not a stupid dupe or a vulgarly vindictive cuckold. He is not the man to call the informer in to do the killing, or the concealing of it afterwards. For his own safety Shakespeare's, unlike Cinthio's Moor, shows no concern. Nor is there, for that matter, the slightest evidence in his conduct or his utterance, nor in the woman's either, of the love Iago suspects between him and Emilia. . . . On the contrary, the black man is made the grandest and noblest of Shakespeare's lovers; and it is only through Iago's overwhelming reputation for honesty and sagacity, the impenetrableness of his mask together with the potency of his seductive arts, that he is led astray and succumbs.

Thus in both *Macbeth* and *Othello*, we are told, the sources are wrested to give the same essential spectacle, that of "the brave and honourable man suddenly and squarely—and fatally—turned against the moral order," and this contrary to all psychological prediction, so we are required to accept as a power setting the drama in motion evil forces which are independent of and more irresistible than any common and explicable human malevolence. Thus of realistic motive we must say that "the omission is deliberate and intentional, and the contravention of psychological probability is so as well." For when we dispassionately look at the tragedy, or fall, of Macbeth and Othello we are constrained to admit that

> neither change is probable. In neither is there much of what can be called psychology. In life neither person would really have done what he did. . . . The hero's conduct, at the heart of the action, is . . . not in keeping with his essential nature but in contrast with it.

And Shakespeare is responsible for deliberately contriving this. The stories as told in his sources have much more of sober likelihood.

But why, Stoll asks, in *Macbeth* and *Othello* does Shakespeare exhibit this spectacle of one inexplicably violating "his essential nature"? Because the excellence of the drama depends on the width of the gap between conduct and essential nature that the artifice of the playwright can persuade us—while still in the theatre—to accept. The thrill (and what the playwright is after is a thrill) comes from "the *good* man doing the deed of horror"—and the biggest thrill (we may legitimately infer from Stoll's thesis) will come from the best man doing the worst deed that we will at all swallow for the time. Thus Shakespeare chiefly seeks a kind of "emotional effect, with which psychology or even simple narrative coherence often considerably interferes." For anything making the deed less unlikely will necessarily make it, in this sense, less effective too.

Manifestly—and, if not forthwith, certainly upon a moment's consideration—by all the motives prompting or circumstances attending the murder of Duncan that have been omitted, the big, sharply outlined, highly emotional contrast in the situation of a good man doing the deed of horror would be broken or obscured. If Macbeth had been thwarted or (to use Holinshed's word) "defrauded," as having, at this juncture, a better title to the throne than Malcolm, or had thought himself better fitted to rule; or, again, if Duncan had not borne his faculties so meek and been so clear in his great office, as in the tragedy but not the chronicle he is; why, then, Macbeth's conduct in killing him would have been more reasonable and more psychologically in keeping, to be sure, but less terrible, less truly tragic.

The dramatist seeks primarily what is surprising and so productive of vivid sensation. It is to provide vivid sensation that the playhouses open their doors—"life must be, as it has ever been, piled on life, or we have visited the theatre in vain." That Othello should do what he does is (though Stoll does not use the word in this sense) "sensational" and in this there is satisfaction provided the illusion for the moment holds. That our emotion is one with which "psychology" would "interfere" need in no way disturb us. For "the object of poetry is to enthral," Longinus says, and the business of the drama is to o'erstep the modesty of nature, or at least to give us "what from life we do not get—enlargement, excitement, another world, not a copy of this."

But lest we should think plainness the special ornament of this contention (which might stand as an unaffected plea for *Tarzan of the Apes*) Stoll immediately conjures about it that darkness with which he still labours to be shadowed:

> In both *Macbeth* and *Othello,* then, it is the whole situation that is mainly important, not the character; it is the reciprocal matter of motivation (whether present or missing), of defects or qualities in both victim and victimizer together. . . . And that airy edifice, an imaginative structure, is the emotionally consistent action or situation as a whole—the conduct of characters both active and passive, perhaps also a motivation both external and internal, but in any case a combination of interrelations or circumstances as important as the motives themselves; not to mention the apportionment of emphasis or relief whether in the framework or the expression, the poetry which informs both, and the individuality of the speech, which, real, though poetical, leads one to accept and delight in the improbable things said or done.

What are we to say of the simplified Shakespeare who thus naïvely peers at us from amid the jungle of Mr. Stoll's complicated prose?

It is perhaps fair to pause here and remark that Mr. Stoll is by no means to be charged with the absolute innovation of the ideas to which he gives currency in this paper and elsewhere. Gustav Rümelin, writing three-quarters of a century earlier, presents a markedly similar theory of *Macbeth:*

> The dramatic treatment in *Macbeth* offers but small scope for realistic criticism, since . . . supernatural powers are employed, against which there can be no pragmatic criticism. . . . More serious difficulties occur in the character of Lady Macbeth. Her demeanour before the deed and after it appears to violate that psychological law of essential unity and consistency of character to which Shakespeare in general, although with some exceptions, adheres. The workings of conscience in her case are magical and demoniacal, and not psychologically conceivable. . . . In the character of Macbeth, wonderfully and strikingly as he is depicted, we miss something also. Before he falls into temptation he is represented by the poet as of a noble nature, as we gather not only from

his own deportment, but more clearly from the esteem in which he is held by the king and others. We have a right to expect that this better nature would reappear; after his glowing ambition had attained its end he ought to have made at least one attempt, or manifested the desire, to wear his ill-gotten crown with glory, to expiate or extenuate his crime by sovereign virtues. We could then be made to see that it by no means follows that evil must breed evil, and that Macbeth must wade on in blood in order not to fall. But . . . the nobler impulses of former days never for one moment influence him. Here too, as frequently elsewhere, Shakespeare exaggerates the contrast, and the effect, at the expense of psychological truth [*Auch hier überspannt Shakespeare den Contrast und den Effekt auf Kosten der psychologischen Wahrheit*]. . . . And yet all such criticisms cannot keep us from pronouncing Shakespeare's *Macbeth* the mightiest and most powerful of all tragedies.[3]

It is at once clear that Rümelin is very close to Stoll's

This, of course, is not what we call motivation, not psychology. . . . But the contrast is kept clear and distinct; and the emotional effect—that the whole world has acknowledged.

Nevertheless there is a radical difference between these two verdicts. In Rümelin's view the psychological incoherence frequently found in Shakespeare is a defect and chargeable (as by Schücking) upon the primitive and popular character of his art. But for Stoll the psychological incoherence turns out to be an aesthetic and dramatic virtue of the most classical and orthodox sort.

We may pause to note too another earlier examination of *Macbeth* which advances considerations similar to Stoll's— though like Rümelin's rather by way of stricture than of apology and revelation. It is to be found in an essay of Robert Bridges'. . . . And Bridges, it seems to me, presses somewhat further than either Stoll or Rümelin into the heart of the play, and by giving a deeper view of matters for which we must account, better prepares the ground for an adequate conclusion. In *Measure for Measure*—Bridges will be recalled as arguing —a coherent psychology is sacrificed to the exigencies of a striking story, pleasing to an unsophisticated audience. So too with *Macbeth*. But whereas in *Measure for Measure* the psy-

[3] I take the translation from the New Variorum edition of *Macbeth*.

chological incoherence is patent, in *Macbeth* Shakespeare devises means to conceal it.

How comes it that such a man as Macbeth commits such crimes? Shakespeare has no real answer, no "plain psychological conception," and his method of dealing with the point is not so much to reveal as to confuse. "Judging from the text, he does not wish us to be clearly determined as to whether Macbeth's ambition had preconceived and decided on the murder of Duncan; or whether the idea was chiefly imposed upon him by a supernatural devilry; or whether he was mainly urged to it by his wife, and was infected and led by her." Thus the effects obtained, although magnificent, are procured by a deception. And of the tragedies in general it may be said that Shakespeare is perpetually obliged to surprise his audience; to attain this he will risk, or even sacrifice, the logical and consistent; but in the theatre the inconsistency must not appear, and so Shakespeare develops a technique for obscuring it. For example, for some cardinal action in a play various possible motives will be hinted at and prominence given now to one possibility and now to another as is convenient. Thus through shifts of conduct inconsistent with any one motive we always have some congruous motive in focus, and we are seduced from the attempt at any final elucidation by Shakespeare's convincing verisimilitude and richness of detail.

Having found a story the actions of which were suitable, Shakespeare adopted them very much as they were, but remade the character of the actor. In the original story the actor would be known and judged by his actions: this Shakespeare reverses by first introducing his hero as a man superior to his actions; his art being to create a kind of contrast between the two, which has, of course, no existence in the original tale; and his success depends on the power and skill with which this character is chosen and enforced upon the audience; for it is when their minds are preoccupied with his personality that the actions follow as unquestionable realities, and, in the *Macbeth*, even preordained and prophesied.

This use of contrast, Bridges continues, holds nothing illegitimate or even peculiar in itself; and art here only calls for moderation. But Shakespeare, in the hunt for surprise that shall border on sensation, pushes the technique beyond discretion. *Some* element of the unexpected in a man's actions, *some* disparity between these and his character, is natural in drama. But "it cannot be conceded that any character is capable of any action: there is a limit, and Shakespeare seems to delight in raiding across it." The murder of Duncan is such a raid. In the history Macbeth kills Duncan in a soldierlike manner; in the play the circumstances are such as to entail the most dastardly violation of honor. For the sake of theatrical excitement the gap between character and action has been widened beyond credibility.

With this we may say that Stoll agrees. But for Stoll Shakespeare in all this is pursuing the legitimate aims of drama, and his artifices to this end are a virtuosity to be rejoiced in. Bridges regards them as a "dishonesty."

The problem is now tolerably distinct. In Shakespeare—and typically in *Macbeth* and *Othello*—there is something like a deliberate omitting of clear and sufficient motives for action; there is a lack of discernible correspondence between the man and his deed. And in place of such an unimpeachable "psychology" we are offered the "steep tragic contrast" afforded by men arbitrarily precipitated into situations to which they could by no means bring themselves; we are offered this and behind it—lest we should begin inconveniently to use our wits before we are out in the street again—now external forces of irresistible evil and now a sort of finessing technique in which motives are advanced and then withdrawn before their weight can be estimated. And this we are offered in the interest of *sensation*, which Bridges condemns and Stoll approves—declaring that "it is not primarily to present characters in their convincing reality that Shakespeare and the Greeks have written . . . but to set them in a state of high commotion."

Now, if this be how the matter stands with Shakespeare there can be little doubt (it appears to me) that Bridges' is the juster verdict on his art. For it is surely no good setting characters in commotion, however high, that is simply commotion per se; the commotion must be a specific commotion, and the character—at some level of his being—apt to it, or the effect will not be truly tragic. There is high commotion in Webster, but we could reassort the masks and the emotions without much loss. There is high commotion in the heroic plays of Dryden, but we may doubt whether any man came from that theatre feeling rapt to the heights of art.

It is true, of course, that the theory of drama as an impos-

sible, and for that very reason piquant, medley or concatena-
tion of emotions has its own aesthetic behind it, one expressed
compendiously enough by Francis Bacon when he declared that

Imagination . . . may at pleasure join that which nature hath
severed, and sever that which nature hath joined; and so make
unlawful matches and divorces of things.[4]

And it is true that there is support for this reading in the fact
that dramatic poetry demonstrably presents the mechanisms of
the mind and passions not always as we familiarly hold them
to be. But this reading, when pursued, degrades dramatic poetry against our deeper sense of it, leaving us (as Bridges discerns) nothing but *poetry*—and poetry basely or fatuously
used. We are left, indeed, with no more than an arbitrary fiction such as might be arrived at with one of those devices sold
to aspiring authors, in which a dial inscribed with numerous
characters and their attributes is spun upon a card giving a
variety of plots, and as the arrow falls so must the story be
framed. With such a machine a trained writer might contrive
piquant fictions enough, but not genius could make them last.
For artifices such as Stoll describes have surely not the life or
enduringness of representative fictions, and to view Shakespeare's plays as transcendentally clever constructions of this
kind is really to give the sternest good night of all to the reputation of the dramatist. And against Bacon here, and Mr. Stoll
after him, we may wonder whether we may not set the words
of a more catholic critic:

The irregular combinations of fanciful invention may delight
for a while, by that novelty of which the common satiety of life
sends us all in quest; but the pleasures of sudden wonder are soon
exhausted, and the mind can only repose on the stability of truth.

I must now try to show that "the stability of truth" does,
after all, underlie the motivation in *Macbeth*.

Macbeth is set (as Rümelin has it) in a "region of hoary eld"
[*auf den . . . Boden einer grauen Vorzeit*]; it is a drama filled
with darkness, the supernatural, sleep and dreams. And by
means of these, Bradley says,

[4] Francis Bacon, *Of the Proficience and Advancement of Learning*
(1605), Book II, iv, 1.

Shakespeare has concentrated attention on the obscurer regions of man's being, on phenomena which make it seem that he is in the power of secret forces lurking below, and independent of his consciousness and will.

The treatment of motive in the play will be found, I think, to follow from this. Macbeth's rational motives are made insufficient, elusive, contradictory, in order to bring home to us not the mere thrill of evil but its tortuousness and terrifying reach; its beckoning presence just over the threshold of certain more than common natures.

"In *Macbeth*," writes Sir Edmund Chambers, "the central idea or theme seems to be this: A noble character, noble alike in potentiality and fruition, may yet be completely overmastered by mysterious, inexplicable temptation."[5] Now, whether this is indeed, as Stoll would maintain, "not what we call motivation, not psychology," or is tantamount, in Bridges' words, to making "any character capable of any action," depends on whether the inexplicability is felt as absolute or contingent. For the mysterious and the inexplicable—matter to the springs of which we can only very uncertainly grope our way—are part of our experience of nature; and the dramatist is not confined to what he can make thoroughly lucid. Macbeth, certainly, must not be inexplicable as real people are never inexplicable. But he may, and that very effectively, be inexplicable after the fashion in which his sort of person is often inexplicable. If we can say as we watch, "Were I such a man, and my circumstances these, then—terrible as is the thought and mysterious though it be to our small knowledge of the human soul—it might well be thus that I should act": if we can say this, the inexplicability is of that contingent kind found in nature and allowable in tragedy.

And when Bridges admits as allowable in tragedy "*some* element of the unexpected in a man's actions, *some* disparity between these and his character," he shows himself aware of all this; much more aware than Stoll. But he contends that since Macbeth's crime is great, and by Shakespeare exacerbated, the gap between Macbeth and his deed is inordinate. Macbeth is not *remotely* the kind of man to kill Duncan as he does, and thus the element of the inexplicable here is no perception and

[5] E. K. Chambers, in the "Warwick" edition of *Macbeth*, p. 19.

acknowledgment of the inexplicable in nature, but a mere violation of nature.

But we must wonder whether behind this conception of the moral character of Macbeth, as behind Stoll's, there be not an undue influence from the classical theory of drama. For it appears to me that both critics view Macbeth through the spectacles of the *Poetics* and thereby burden themselves with a steeper "tragic contrast" than did Shakespeare, who did not use the spectacles of any books. Aristotle judged it necessary that a tragic hero should be better than ordinary men, and that any fatal flaw which his character held should be such as yet to leave him superior to depravity or vice. Implicit in this view is the opinion that moral character is simple and measurable; just as today we may say that the most suitable man for a given task will be one with an intelligence quotient within such and such a range so does the classical theory of drama say that the most suitable man for the task of hero in a tragedy will be one with a morality quotient analogously definable. Bridges, when he feels that the nobility of Macbeth must be such as to preclude his committing—under any circumstances—an atrocious crime, is conceivably swayed by this all-of-a-piece conception of character. But in life, as we know, every personality is in some degree dissociated; and this fact of universal significance, which is given gross expression in certain pathological states, often finds a species of covert (and perhaps obscurely cathartic or therapeutic) release in art. There are, in a sense, two Macbeths; and the dichotomy is rendered to us both directly and in terms of the poetic structure. Macbeth commits crime upon crime: first, as he supposes, a crime of ambition and then, as we know, crimes of fear and spite; his reputation crumbles and the man who had won "golden opinions" is known for avariciousness and as a lecher. In this he is as the imagery of the play represents him: too small for his robes; he shrivels at their touch; they are envenomed, as we might suppose. Macbeth clips to himself the virtues of the Sagas and exhibits more than the power of the men who composed them; and here he is titanic, as the imagery also represents him, and abounds in qualities which we envy as we watch. Perhaps this particular contrast—the contrast between the criminal who murders Duncan and the man whose "magnificent qualities of mind, extreme courage, and poetic imagination" call for our admiration—

ought not to exist in nature. But assuredly it does—being thereby not the less mysterious and awful (for the divine Abun-
dance is often that), but only the more proper for dramatic
representation.

And so Shakespeare did not, I suspect, conceive of Macbeth
as good or bad *simpliciter;* the "obscurer regions" of the man
held some antilogy too radical to make that a profitable approach. But Shakespeare did conceive of Macbeth as *imaginative* in all but the highest degree. And here indeed—in what
Bradley calls his "excitable and intense, but narrow" imagination, with its extreme sensibility to sinister and morbid impressions—appears to me to be one of the cardinal facts of the play.
Others are (1) his poetic genius and histrionic talent, inclin-
ing him to view his own conduct as a dramatic spectacle, (2)
that archaic quality of the play whereby Shakespeare thrusts
the action with an uncharacteristic obtrusiveness into a rude
past, (3) the pervasiveness of images of bloodshed, so that the
whole is seen, again in Bradley's words, "as through an ensan-
guined mist," (4) the speed with which the play hurries to an
unusually early crisis. In all these we have, as it appears to me,
the conditions for making the "inexplicable" element in the
tragedy of that kind which beckons us towards an actual mystery in things, rather than of the kind which merely occasions
a "sudden wonder" arresting for a day.

Perhaps much of all this is covered by the simple statement
that in everybody there is some lurking force of evil ready to
strike in a weak or unguarded hour. Sometimes this force hints
its strength as we sleep:

> Mercifull Powers,
> Restraine in me the cursed thoughts that Nature
> Gives way to in repose. . . .
>
>   wicked Dreames abuse
> The Curtain'd sleepe.

Sometimes it invades the waking mind in sinister fantasy:

> where's that Palace, whereinto foule things
> Sometimes intrude not? Who ha's that breast so pure,
> But some uncleanly Apprehensions
> Keepe Leetes, and Law-dayes, and in Sessions sit
> With meditations lawfull?

It can be potent in men of unimpaired moral perception; so inexplicably potent as to suggest mysterious solicitation exercised by an external malignant power (the witches, Iago, Iachimo). And, since this evil rises up in the form of horrible imaginings, it may be most overwhelming, and so, at a time of emotional stress, sweep on to action, in the most imaginative men—particularly in the man who is imaginative without the release of being creative. Macbeth is such a man. He and his wife are immensely potent, but their tragedy is a tragedy of sterility. Macbeth is such a man, exposed to exceptional emotional stresses.

The play opens upon rumour of battle, upon the assertion, as by a malevolent power, that

> Faire is foule, and foule is faire,

and then upon descriptions of war, rebellion, treachery and bloodshed in a semibarbarous and disordered society. Bloodshed has brought Macbeth fair report: "Brave Macbeth," says the Captain, recounting the fight with the merciless Macdonwald,

> unseam'd him from the Nave to th' Chaps
> And fix'd his Head upon our Battlements. . . .

And King Duncan exclaims

> O valiant Cousin! worthy Gentleman!

With the Norwegian army Macbeth and Banquo have fought as if

> they meant to bathe in reeking Wounds,
> Or memorize another *Golgotha,*

and this report too smacks of honour to the king. Presently Macbeth himself steps on the stage as if straight from this bloodbath, dazed by it, and unconsciously echoing the words of the witches:

> So foule and faire a day I have not seene.

"*Foul* with regard to the weather," the commentators say, "and *fair* with reference to his victory." But it is also the victory alone, the snatching honour by unseaming people from the nave to the chaps, that is both foul and fair—a monstrous confusion from which Macbeth, imaginative and highly organised as well as a soldier, now emerges, battle-shocked. That night he kills a man for a kingdom.

Macbeth's castle was not really a politic place in which to murder the king, a fact observed by Bridges:

Shakespeare, choosing that Duncan shall be secretly murdered, makes Lady Macbeth represent the advent of Duncan to their castle as a favourable opportunity; and he knows that the audience, blinded by the material juxtaposition, will regard it as such. Now to propose this dastardly violation of honour to Macbeth would, most probably, have stimulated his nobility and scared him from the crime however fully he might have been predetermined on it.

Why does Lady Macbeth insist that "time and place" have made themselves *now* and *here* at Inverness? It is partly because she sees that Macbeth's almost hypnoidal state is favourable; he is like a man moving in a blood-drenched trance, subject to visual and auditory hallucinations, uncertain of the boundaries of actuality and dream. And no doubt it is only another of the many ironies in this play that Lady Macbeth, exploiting a disorder akin to somnambulism in her husband now, herself falls a victim to the actual malady later on—when Macbeth himself has come horribly awake and will sleep no more. But chiefly it is because Lady Macbeth has a better understanding of the recesses of her husband's character than Stoll or Bridges succeeds in arriving at, and knows that the deeper criminality involved in violating a "double trust" will indeed scare him, but will compel more than it scares.

The abyss of evil is very real to Macbeth, and the deeper it is, the more luridly lit from below, the more it fascinates him as a dramatic spectacle in which he is obscurely called to engulf himself. The thought of murdering Duncan, first or new glimpsed in the recesses of his mind at the prompting of the witches, produces violent somatic disturbance, as the prospect of a ritual act of cannibalism may do in a Kwakiutl Indian. Nor is the parallel so outlandish as it may appear. For it is veritably the crime and not the crown that compels Macbeth, as it is the virtue that lies in the terrible and forbidden, and not the flavour of human flesh, that compels the savage. And Macbeth's mind is darkened and groping. For what effects the commission of a crime—criminology declares—is less a motive than a confluence of motives, the more potent of which may be only confusedly, if at all, within the conscious awareness of the perpetrator. And when Macbeth momentarily fights his way from the "obscurer regions" of his soul, when he would vindicate his action in other terms than of "secret forces lurking below, and independent of his consciousness and will," he knows that he has returned to a region in which there is no effective spur to his intent; and he knows when his crime is committed that it is absolutely futile. He has been betrayed by his intensely realising imagination—in itself a splendid thing—which, in a period of weakened rationality, has exhibited himself to himself as the central figure in a drama colossally evil. He has vividly seen not his true self but a treacherous criminal persona risen from its lurking place below the threshold of the diurnal Macbeth; it stalks before him, a gigantic shadow, into Duncan's chamber; it plays its part in a nightmarish festival of blood; and then it deserts him. He goes to the deed on the wings of a vast self-dramatising rhetoric. " 'Twas a rough night," he mutters, tight-lipped and appalled, when the deed is done.

The "gap," then, which Stoll distinguishes between the man and his deed does, in a sense, exist. But that it is a matter of psychological fact and not merely of theatrical fancy the following citation from a textbook of criminology may serve to enforce:

It is still not sufficiently realised that the criminal at the moment of the act is a different man from what he is after it—so much so that one would sometimes think them different beings. . . . Our psychological judgment, our instinct as well as our experience, seem to tell us sometimes that the deed does not belong to the doer nor the doer to the deed. Nevertheless the act must be an expression of the criminal's mental tension, must spring from his mental condition, must have promised gratification to his psychological needs. We are faced by a riddle as long as we do not know what motive actuated him. In many cases, and especially in the most serious crimes, he can, with the best will in the world, give us but inadequate information; he is unable to establish a connection between the deed and his personality.[6]

[6] T. Reik, *The Unknown Murderer* (International Psycho-Analytical Library, 1936), pp. 42–43. I am indebted in this section to Mr. Michael Innes's *Strange Intelligence,* an imaginary conversation included in a volume shortly to be published by Messrs. Secker and Warburg.

One could scarcely find a better commentary than this on the problem of Macbeth's crime. As has been said in an admirable place:

> Our unknown selves in life are sometimes more potent than our known. And that also should be a principle, among many others, of the art of Shakespeare interpretation.[7]

We cannot, I think, get away in tragedy from the strange fact of the interplay of conscious and unconscious motive and from the species of release which the exhibition of that interplay brings to an audience keyed to poetic apprehension. And yet a Macbeth mysteriously prompted from archaic strata of the mind will appear to many as something improper to dramatic poetry—as constituting, in fact, what Bridges, in another connection, calls "a pathological study which cannot hold our respect." And Stoll, who will have no psychology at all in *Macbeth*, expressly excludes this kind:

> The only psychology possible for Macbeth is a morbid or abnormal sort, which would have him tempted by the sight of cold steel to plunge it into you, or by an abyss to jump into it; but that, not clearly indicated, is out of the question for a popular tragic hero in the time of Elizabeth.

But at least we may suspect that any view of tragedy which chiefly canvasses what is "clearly indicated" will be in danger of being a superficial view, and will take us no further with Attic drama than with Elizabethan. And, indeed, I repeat that it is Aristotle's grand rationalising of Attic drama (epic, he says, will tolerate more of the "irrational" than drama) rather than the direct experience of Shakespeare that discernibly sways the critics, and sets them seeking for the plausible ἁμαρτία in the known and ponderable character to the neglect of those terrifying, surprising, but authentic shadows of our unknown selves which the penetrating rays of the poetic drama cast upon the boards before us. And if it still be urged that this line of argument substitutes a clinical for a tragic Macbeth I can only reply that the fascination and horror of bloodshed, particularly the fascination and horror of bloodshed in certain localities, are counterpoised forces not in the merely diseased mind but in

---

[7] The observation on "our unknown selves" occurs in a leading article in the *Times Literary Supplement*, 1931, p. 554.

the primitive, which is now the underlying mind; and as such they are always potentially eruptive in traumatic situations. Here is the fundamental mechanism or motive beneath the superficial incentives prompting Macbeth, and it is to bring the former sufficiently near the surface of the complex whole that Shakespeare disburdens the fable of much of the weight of the latter.

But Shakespeare not only neglects conscious motives; he blurs them—as Bridges, going deeper, discerns. And the explanation must lie, I think, in the fact that an intellectual as well as emotional confusion attends such a deed as the killing of Duncan. The "veiled confusion of motive" to which Bridges points, the indefiniteness as to when and in whose mind the idea of the crime first started up, echoes this. The blurring is indeed deliberately put into the play, and is achieved by devices that would be impossible in a naturalistic drama. Thus when Shakespeare secures the effect of there having been, and not been, a previous plot between Macbeth and his wife, he is certainly deserting nature for artifice. Why? In order to secure, I would suppose, by a non-realistic device such as he is always prepared to use, a dramatic correlative to the confusion in Macbeth's mind. If the audience can be made to grope among motives which are insubstantial, phantasmagoric, and contradictory, they will be approximating to the condition of the protagonist. There is no "dishonesty" here; there is only a subtle and powerful art. And it is an art constantly used in the interest of realising a *man*—an individual at once unique and representative, caught, as all men may be, in some giant's grasp from the infrapersonal levels of his own being.

I conclude, then, that before *Macbeth* we ought not to abandon the conception of a "psychology" (as Mr. Stoll would have us do) but deepen it. The "steep tragic contrast" of which we are indeed made powerfully aware results not from arbitrary contrivance but from the acknowledgment, lucid to our active imagination, that

> O the mind, mind has mountains; cliffs of fall
> Frightful, sheer, no-man-fathomed.

And—as Hopkins adds—

> Hold them cheap
> May who ne'er hung there.

In the theatre we do not hold them cheap; it is only in the study, or before a blackboard, that it occurs to us to believe that we have been cozened by a fiction. And to insist that we are wiser men when delivering lectures, or when annotating some new dissertation out of one written in 1915, than we are when actually subject to the experience that Shakespeare created for us, is an assumption which, in a critic however comprehensively read, cannot but suggest a somewhat narrow or insulated sensibility.

Much of what I have said here holds, too, of *Othello*. Only in *Othello* Shakespeare's anatomy of the soul, his exposure of the "hidden man," is accomplished by a bolder technique of dissection than that employed in *Macbeth*, a technique which must considerably modify—although not at all in Stoll's direction—our notion of the relationship that his art posits between some of his dramatis personae and individual human beings.

X

WILLARD FARNHAM

Timon of Athens

Coleridge calls *Timon of Athens* "an after vibration" of *King Lear*, "a *Lear* of domestic or ordinary life—a local eddy of passion on the high road of society."[1] In substance *Timon* has a special relationship with *Lear*. In form it has a special relationship with *Lear* and also with *Othello*, the tragedy that Shakespeare in all probability wrote immediately before *Lear*. Nevertheless, the tragic world of *Timon* is that of *Macbeth*, *Antony and Cleopatra*, and *Coriolanus*.

We should look at *Timon* as it is related to *Lear* and *Othello* before looking at it as one of the plays that constitute Shakespeare's last tragic world. The bond of substance between *Timon* and *Lear* is remarkable, and its existence is well recognized. The reader needs only to be reminded of its character. Each of these plays is a tragedy of atrocious human ingratitude in which repeated comparisons are made between men and beasts, and in which the idea is expressed that man is declining to a beastly state where

> Humanity must perforce prey on itself,
> Like monsters of the deep.
>
> (*Lear* IV. ii. 49–50)

In each play the hero gives away large worldly possessions, finds himself dependent upon those he has benefited, trusts blindly that in their gratitude these will show generosity to him, receives cruelty from them instead of generosity, lays

From *Shakespeare's Tragic Frontier: The World of His Final Tragedies*, by Willard Farnham (Berkeley and Los Angeles, 1950), pp. 39–50, 67–77. Reprinted by permission of the author and the University of California Press.

[1] *Coleridge's Shakespearean Criticism*, ed. T. M. Raysor (London, 1930), I, 238, 108–9.

curses upon the human nature in which he once placed his trust, and falls into madness or insensate fury.[2]

The bond of form between *Timon, Lear,* and *Othello* is perhaps less remarkable but is no less real than the bond of substance between *Timon* and *Lear.* Structurally, *Timon, Lear,* and *Othello* are in a class by themselves among Shakespeare's tragedies.

Before the writing of *Othello,* Shakespeare had usually conceived tragedy as a pyramid of rising and falling action corresponding more or less to the full turn of Fortune's wheel in medieval tragical storytelling,[3] and for several years he had conceived tragedy in no other form. This pyramidal form of tragedy tends to make half of the action the hero's rise and half his decline and fall. In *Richard III* the rise of Richard to kingship has a dramatic development which is about equal to that of his fall from kingship. In *Romeo and Juliet* the action in which Romeo wins Juliet is of about the same length as that in which he loses Juliet. In *Julius Caesar* and *Hamlet* such pyramids of rise and fall are constructed for Brutus and Hamlet with a marked advance in skill. Steps on the slopes are delicately marked, and the slopes are almost exactly balanced. Both Brutus and Hamlet rise to a height of successful achievement which is placed by the dramatist in the third act. At this height Brutus frees Rome from Caesar, and Hamlet demonstrates the King's guilt by means of the play within the play and steels himself to take revenge upon the King. The success is of the briefest and the turning point is a knife edge. Almost immediately the hero makes a misstep, which has been prepared for by the development of his character during the rising action, and his course turns downward. The crucial misstep, Brutus's refusal to forbid Antony's oration to the mob, or Hamlet's refusal to kill the praying king, is shown in its full significance only after the descending action is developed from it and after the pyramid is made a whole. It was in the use of this py-

[2] For what A. C. Bradley has to say about the bond of substance between *Timon* and *Lear,* see his *Shakespearean Tragedy* (2d ed.; London, 1920), pp. 246, 443.

[3] I have commented upon Shakespeare's use of the pyramidal tragic form in *The Medieval Heritage of Elizabethan Tragedy* (Berkeley: University of California Press, 1936), pp. 99 ff., 329 ff., 414 ff., 446 ff.

ramidal form that Shakespeare found himself as a writer of tragedy.

When he came to write *Othello*, he turned to a new form, which may be regarded as a development from that which he had given to *Richard II*, an early tragedy. *Richard II* shows the fall of its hero as beginning at the opening of the play and undergoing acceleration near the middle, at a point marked by an agony of realization on the hero's part that ruin and death press upon him. It also shows the rise of a rival as concurrent: as Richard falls from the kingship, Bolingbroke mounts toward it, and when Richard is murdered, Bolingbroke establishes himself on the throne. We thus see a man whirled down from the top of Fortune's wheel at the same time that another is whirled up to the top. We see actions of rise and fall, but not both for the hero. Richard himself characterizes the drama by means of the conventional figure of "Fortune's buckets," one bucket descending in a well while another, its counterpoise, rises (IV. i. 181–89). *Othello*, like *Richard II*, shows the fall of its hero as beginning at the opening of the play and undergoing acceleration near the middle, at a point marked by a crisis in the hero's emotions, but it does not show the concurrent rise of a rival to the position of prosperity from which the hero falls. Of *Lear* the same can be said, and also of *Timon*. But *Macbeth*, *Antony and Cleopatra*, and *Coriolanus* are built on the pyramidal scheme of rise and fall for the hero. In these three plays Shakespeare used the tragic form he had favored before he wrote *Othello*.

Let us consider the long slope of tragic decline as it appears in *Othello* and *Lear*. In each of these plays the hero is at first placed for a brief moment in prosperity. Even at this point forces are shown which are to bring about his ruin. Then, in the generous space allotted to the working of his fall, catastrophe is brought to pass by subtle gradations. The dramatic form used may be called that of a half-pyramid, for the second half of the pyramid of rise and fall is taken alone to fill out a play. But the half-pyramid is distorted. In the middle the line of descent is made to change its slope and become steeper than at first. The breaking of the line of descent to make its slope more precipitous is emphasized by a climactic storm of passion in the hero. This turning point midway in the tragedy corresponds to the change from rising to falling action in plays built upon the scheme of the full pyramid. In both *Othello* and *Lear* a climactic storm of passion at the turning point arises from the hero's first true realization of his tragic destiny and brings a derangement of his faculties. Just before the turning point of *Othello* the hero is still vigorously resisting his tragic fate; he looks upon Desdemona and says:

> If she be false, O! then heaven mocks itself.
> I'll not believe it.

(III. iii. 278–79)

But his resistance is finally destroyed by increased pressure from Iago, and he breaks forth with a wild vow of vengeance. Othello and his tempter kneel and thus mark the occasion as the vow is made. At their first meeting thereafter, still more pressure from the tempter draws from Othello a mad froth of words and sends him into a trance. The turning point of *Lear* follows exactly the same dramatic pattern but is developed with even greater imaginative power. To the end of Act II Lear resists and refuses to realize the fate that is to be his. At the beginning of Act III he opens his mind and heart to it. His denunciations, his subjection to the storm on the heath which is the physical accompaniment of his emotional crisis, and the onset of his madness make a grander version of the central cataclysm found in Othello.

There is a distorted half-pyramid in *Timon* which is very plainly the same in principle as that just traced for *Othello* and *Lear*. Timon is first shown in prosperity. Already the forces to bring about his downfall are in existence. Before the end of Act I we are told by his steward, Flavius, that his coffer is empty and that his lands are all mortgaged. Timon begins his descent but refuses to realize what is in store for him. He persists in holding a pitiful faith in the friends to whom he has given his wealth which is very similar to Lear's faith that Goneril and Regan cannot both fail him, and somewhat similar to Othello's faith in Desdemona. (The fact that Othello struggles to keep faith in an utterly innocent person makes some difference in the dramatic quality of his tragedy.) At last Timon accepts his fate. The mock-banquet scene in Act III is the stormy turning point of the action. It brings on a more abrupt descent and is marked by Timon's eloquent curses and his physical assault upon his guests. True madness does not follow, but the hero's fanatical dedication of himself to misanthropy and his taking on of the hermit's character show derangement in a less specific form. Alcibiades, the tough-fibered opposite of Timon, says of him after the alteration that

> his wits
> Are drown'd and lost in his calamities.
>
> (IV. iii. 88–89)

Apparently *Othello, Lear,* and *Timon* link the plays that make up Shakespeare's middle tragic world and those that make up his last. It appears that as Shakespeare turned, in *Timon,* to the presentation of his last tragic world, he concluded an exploration of human ingratitude which he had begun just before, in *Lear,* and made final use of a tragic form which he had worked with twice in succession just before, in *Othello* and *Lear,* and had devised for *Othello.*

Timon has his place in a tragic world that also includes Macbeth, Antony, and Coriolanus because he is so deeply flawed that his faults reach to the very center of his being and give a paradoxical quality to whatever is noble in his nature. Like Macbeth, Antony, and Coriolanus, and unlike Brutus, Hamlet, Othello, and Lear, he does not win sympathy easily and may even arouse great antipathy. The tragedy of Timon is that of a man who has an all-consuming love for humanity but, when he finds that he himself is not loved, lets this love turn to all-consuming hate. His love is so little a true forgetfulness of self, and thus so grossly imperfect, that it can change into its very opposite. Thinking to do good by scattering his great wealth prodigally, Timon blindly lets his substance and himself be devoured by selfish flattering companions. Reduced to poverty and cast aside by those whom he has benefited, he flees to a cave in the forest and dwells there like a beast for the rest of his life. He prays that all mankind may be confounded in beastliness and gives away new-found gold in ways that can help to bring such ruin of humanity to pass. He gladly looks forward to death, and achieves, in accord with his desires, a burial upon the seashore, away from the haunts of men, in a place where the waves can beat upon his tombstone.

Under the impact of human beastliness Lear does not himself become a beast, but Timon does. Lear has in him that

which allows regeneration through suffering, but Timon has
not. Here we find a profound difference between the two
Shakespearean tragedies that are built upon monstrous human
ingratitude. It seems that as Shakespeare goes from *Lear* to
Timon he continues to be obsessed by the vision of a protagonist preyed upon by devouring associates who out of gratitude should love and protect him—by the vision that has made
him think of Lear's daughters as "tigers," "she-foxes," or other
ravenous creatures, tearing at their father's flesh. But he finds
in that vision a new alignment of dramatic forces and a new
tragic meaning. The evil that works against Lear is presented
by Shakespeare's imagination in the guise not only of the beast
but also of the fiend. It is evil on the grand scale. It has a
backing of perverted spiritual greatness and at times fills us
with awe because its doers reach the level of the satanic.
Gloucester pictures Goneril as sticking "boarish fangs" in the
flesh of Lear. But to Albany she is devilish, nay, worse than
devilish, when he says to her:

> See thyself, devil!
> Proper deformity seems not in the fiend
> So horrid as in woman.
>
> (IV. ii. 59–61)

On the other hand, the evil that works against Timon is presented only in the guise of the beast. It is thoroughly petty. In
its army there are no great schemers or leaders, and its qualities
are merely insensibility to good and baseness lacking perception of good. Thus in *Timon* the associates of the hero who
prey upon him become much less important in the tragic
scheme of things and much less awe-inspiring than they are in
Lear. The hero makes up for this by turning into something
more fearsome than they—something devil-like as well as beastlike—and by preying bitterly on himself. All of this shows
Shakespeare at work upon the creation of a new tragic world.

In Timon there is a folly that can be highly irritating, even
to one who sympathizes with him. His folly reminds us of
Lear's but has much deeper attachment to its possessor than
Lear's. Lear has ever but slenderly known both himself and
the nature of humanity in general; yet we feel that his tragic
misjudgment of his daughters comes partly from the dotage of
old age. We get glimpses of the man he has been—a man ca-

pable of error certainly, but kingly in the highest sense. Timon, however, makes his tragic misjudgment of human nature not when he is in his dotage, but when he is in the prime of life and in the fullest possession of his powers. He is so completely lacking in wisdom that one wonders how he could ever have been useful to Athens in a responsible position. Moreover, Timon does not even have Othello's excuse for being blind. He is not taken in by any appearance so skilfully constructed as Iago's handiwork. Shakespeare has not made those who deceive Timon into masters of pretense, but has left them very ordinary hypocrites.

How, then, may we find paradoxical nobility in Timon? It is only after he sees mankind as evil and has burning hatred instead of glowing love for it that his paradox takes full form. For Timon is truly heroic only when he pours the lava of his hate upon the evils of the world. It is Timon the man-hater that has the finest poetry of the play, and it is in this Timon, obviously, that Shakespeare found most inspiration as he shaped the tragedy. The paradox of Timon's nobility of spirit really lies in the fact that as a lover of good he lacks grandeur, but is magnificent as a hater of evil, and he becomes a magnificent hater of evil only by becoming evil. For by the Christian standard Timon's terrible wrath is evil, not righteous, and Shakespeare's age was Christian enough to assume that the possessor of such wrath makes in gross form the error of confusing the sin with the sinner and hating the wrongdoer instead of the wrong done. In his fanatical change of spirit Timon hates not only those who have wronged him but the whole race of humanity. A man could go no farther in putting charity out of his heart. Many pre-Shakespearean writers of the Renaissance condemn the Timon of legend for his sinful and unnatural hatred of mankind. In Shakespeare's Timon there is all that these writers condemn, and it is given a new awfulness; but it is also given nobility.

Shakespeare's Timon is so deeply flawed that Professor O. J. Campbell, in a revealing examination of his character and the dramatic methods used for its presentation, finds him to be the hero of a tragical satire which in form and temper owes much to Ben Jonson's *Sejanus* and *Volpone*.[4] What one sees in Timon

---

[4] *Shakespeare's Satire* (New York, 1943), pp. 168 ff.

that is not in Sejanus and Volpone is the capacity to arouse great admiration as well as great aversion. In the comments of critics there is a violent conflict of aversion and admiration for Timon, and this conflict may be taken as a measure of the paradox in his character.

A few examples will serve to show the kind of comment that can be made by thoroughgoing scorners of Timon. William Maginn reveals detestation of him. Maginn's judgment is that "gold, and the pomps and vanities which it procures, had been to him everything"; that "when the purse was lost, he lost his senses too"; that "Apemantus was wrong when he told him he was long a madman, and then a fool. . . . Timon was first a fool and then a madman"; and that with or without gold the man showed his true character in his attitude toward women. "In his prosperity we do not find any traces of affection, honorable or otherwise, for women. In his curses, disrespect for the female sex is remarkably conspicuous." In short, as Maginn will have it, "Insanity arising from pride, is the key of the whole character."[5] Sir John Squire ticks Timon off with a pair of devastating phrases: "Timon is an ass in his faith and an ass in his disillusionment."[6] Mr. John Bailey thinks it impossible that we should care about him: "We see only the old spectacle of the quick parting between a fool and his money: one which never has greatly moved spectators and never will. . . . Such a figure cannot be the central figure of a great tragedy."[7]

After listening to these scorners of Timon, we are amazed to see how far some of their opponents can go. Mr. G. Wilson Knight sees in Timon not merely a great and estimable man, but a godlike creature "who aspires only to the infinite" and "chafes at the limitations of the physical." His very hate, thinks Mr. Knight, is not mere man's hate. "Apemantus and Timon hate with a difference: one, because he is less than mankind—the other because he is greater." It is even not too much for Mr. Knight to say: "We are here judging the chances of the spirit of perfected man [i.e., Timon] to embrace Fortune and

[5] *The Shakespeare Papers of the Late William Maginn,* ed. Shelton Mackenzie (New York, 1856), pp. 132, 134.

[6] *Shakespeare as a Dramatist* (London: Cassell & Co., 1935), p. 82.

[7] *Shakespeare* (London, 1929), p. 179.

find Love truly interfused in this 'beneath world': to build his soul's paradise on 'the bosom of this sphere.' Thus Timon is the archetype and norm of all tragedy."[8] Mr. Ralph Roeder and Mr. Peter Alexander have no less emphatic admiration for a divinely idealistic Timon. Mr. Roeder finds that Timon perishes of "immoderate virtues" and "the unanswerable disillusionment that attends the frustration of the most admirable human ambitions, the recognition of the cramping meanness of his mortal tether," and he adds that "tragedy can be refined no farther."[9] Mr. Alexander finds that the tragedy of Timon is the casting down of a "godlike image of man in his heart" by ordinary self-seeking men and his wakening from a "dream of restoring the golden age and all its charities in such a nest of vipers." Moreover, warns Mr. Alexander, to talk of Timon's tragedy as resulting from "kindly self-indulgence" or "easy generosity" is to talk in the vein of the legalistic and moralistic senators of Athens who, because of "their love of personal security," condemn the soldier for whom Alcibiades pleads.[10]

Though the beast theme of *Lear* is remarkable for its general dramatic effect, it is nothing so remarkable in this way as the beast theme of *Timon*.[11] In the beast theme of *Timon* one may perhaps find the essence of the tragedy. Shakespeare obviously put much of himself into its development, whatever portion of it he took from the Timon legend. It is of some significance that in no other of Shakespeare's plays does the word "beast" occur so often as in *Timon*.

[8] *The Wheel of Fire* (London: Oxford University Press, 1930), pp. 250, 248, 241.

[9] "Timon of Athens," *Theatre Arts Monthly*, X (1926), 455.

[10] *Shakespeare's Life and Art* (London: James Nisbet & Co., 1939), pp. 184, 185, 183.

[11] This section of the chapter has been published, substantially in its present form, as part of *The Beast Theme in Shakespeare's "Timon"* ("University of California Publications in English," Vol. XIV [Berkeley: University of California Press, 1943]), pp. 49 ff. For representative twentieth-century comments on the beast theme in *Lear* and *Timon*, see Bradley, pp. 246, 443; Theodore Spencer, *Shakespeare and the Nature of Man* (New York, 1942), pp. 142, 148, 182; G. C. Taylor, "Shakespeare's Use of the Idea of the Beast in Man," *Studies in Philology*, XLII (1945), 532 ff.; and R. B. Heilman, *This Great Stage: Image and Structure in "King Lear"* (Baton Rouge, La.: Louisiana State University Press, 1948), pp. 93 ff., 105 ff.

In *Timon*, Shakespeare is mastered by the conception of a human society whose more important members either reveal themselves to have more of beasthood than of manhood in them or else turn away from manhood in disgust and embrace beasthood. After the hero of the tragedy has become a misanthrope he offers the conventional fig tree of the Timon legend to the Athenians to hang themselves upon, but he is most himself, most truly the thwarted idealist, as he addresses a distinctively Shakespearean prayer to the spirit of his new-found gold, asking it to bring mankind to complete ruin so that beasts "may have the world in empire" (IV. iii. 395). When he prays for such confounding of mankind, he himself having retreated to the forest and given up manhood for beasthood, all his company in Athens except his faithful servants are already beastlike. Apemantus, the savage cynic, has not needed to retreat to the forest to embrace beasthood and rejoice in it. The others have exposed their natural beasthood while acting the part of men—the crew of flatterers, the senators, the whores, even Alcibiades. The most that one can say for Alcibiades is that his animal quality, which makes bloodshed and promiscuous mating his natural occupations, is not treacherous and is at times amiable.

In the first scene of the play Apemantus, cursing Timon's flattering friends, introduces the beast theme:

> The strain of man's bred out
> Into baboon and monkey.
>
> (I. i. 260–61)

Toward the end of the play Timon serves notice, when Alcibiades and the whores visit him in the forest, that he and his former friends are now beasts together:

> ALCIBIADES. What art thou there? speak.
> TIMON. A beast, as thou art.
>
> (IV. iii. 48–49)

Throughout the play, men call each other beasts or themselves beasts, or talk of humanity grown beastly. The commonwealth of Athens is said to have become a "forest of beasts," the underling of Alcibiades for whom he pleads before the senate is said to have committed outrages in his "beastly fury," and the warfare of which Alcibiades makes an occupation is said to be "contumelious, beastly, mad-brain'd" (IV. iii. 354; III. v. 72; V. i. 179).

In the climactic mock-banquet scene (III. vi) we find some of Shakespeare's most effective ringing of changes upon the beast theme. The author of the academic play on Timon which is apparently earlier than Shakespeare's tragedy builds a scene around the conception of a mock banquet of stones offered fittingly to false friends who are "a stony generation." He brings in no reference to beasts. At the banquet his Timon serves stones painted like artichokes and throws them at the guests. Shakespeare has at the center of his corresponding scene the conception of a mock banquet of lukewarm water offered fittingly to lukewarm friends, who are to be thought of as fawning beasts with lapping tongues ("Uncover, dogs, and lap"). The magnificent passage of verse in which Timon denounces his "trencher-friends" as beastlike parasites, calling them "affable wolves" and "meek bears," has the sign manual of Shakespeare.

The beastliness pictured in *Timon* is worse than that of beasts, for it walks in the shape of man and is a constant insult to a sense of decorum. The beastliness of beasts is attractive by comparison. In *Timon* men are condemned as beasts and yet we are given to understand that they would be better if they were actually beasts. Shakespeare puts a strain of animalitarianism into the dialogue, a strain of admiration for the natural and the primitive below the level of civilized human reason. But it is an animalitarianism that does not go very far. The true beast, even the "unkind" beast, is thought of as better than the depraved man of this tragic world, but he is only a beast after all, a subject of admiration *faute de mieux*. There is no turning to unreasoning nature for healing and uplifting of the spirit that has been overwhelmed by the spectacle of man's perversion. Timon flees to the forest not to find his soul in the solitude of nature, but to escape the "wolves" that he has found within the walls of Athens, wolves even worse than those that he will find outside. He cries:

> Timon will to the woods; where he shall find
> The unkindest beast more kinder than mankind.
>
> (IV. i. 35–36)

His liking for the natural beast is liking at all only because of what he feels for man. As he says to Alcibiades after calling him a beast:

> For thy part, I do wish thou wert a dog,
> That I might love thee something.
>
> (IV. iii. 54–55)

The implication, of course, is that the dog is a low creature but still better than Alcibiades. Certainly this passage does not show Timon, or Shakespeare, as a dog-lover in any ordinary sense. It has its place beside other passages in *Timon* and in Shakespeare generally which make the dog something less attractive than dog-fanciers find him.[12]

The beastlike men in *Timon* are often ravening devourers of each other. Much is made of this. Early in the play we find that flatterers eat lords, lords similar to Timon:

> TIMON. Wilt dine with me, Apemantus?
> APEMANTUS. No; I eat not lords.
>
> (I. i. 207–8)

Flatterers sauce their food with Timon's blood:

> APEMANTUS [*to Timon*]. I scorn thy meat; 'twould choke
> me, for I should
> Ne'er flatter thee. O you gods! what a number
> Of men eat Timon, and he sees them not.
> It grieves me to see so many dip their meat
> In one man's blood.
>
> (I. ii. 39–43)

The figure of devouring beastliness in cannibal man spreads to cover others than flatterers. Timon as host guesses that Alcibiades would rather be at a breakfast of enemies than a dinner of friends. And Alcibiades agrees that "so they were bleeding-new, my lord, there's no meat like 'em" (I. ii. 81–82). The thieves who come to Timon in the forest for some of the treasure he has found justify themselves by their want of meat. They say they cannot live like beasts, on grass, berries, and water. No, says Timon, nor on the beasts themselves: "You must eat men" (IV. iii. 431).

Some of this picture of men eating men seems to have been

[12] See Caroline F. E. Spurgeon, *Shakespeare's Imagery and What It Tells Us* (New York, 1935), pp. 194 ff.

developed from a comparison of Timon's flatterers to birds of prey or beasts of prey that had been made in the Timon legend. As we have seen, such a comparison appears in Lucian and in the academic *Timon*. But also in other places than the Timon legend a reader of the sixteenth century could find the concept of flatterers eating the flattered. Shakespeare doubtless had met with it in one or more of the collections of "sayings of the wise" that were popular in his day. A saying was credited to Alphonsus that "flatterers are not vnlyke Wolues: for euen as Wolues by tickling and clawing are wont to deuour Asses: so flatterers vse their flatterye and lyes, to the destruction of Princes."[13] On the authority of the *Lives of Eminent Philosophers*, by Diogenes Laertius, a saying was credited to the cynic Antisthenes that "he had rather haue Rauens in house with him, than flatterers: for Rauens . . . deuoure but the carkasse being deade, but the flatterer eateth vp the body and soule aliue"; and on the same authority a saying was credited to the cynic Diogenes that the beast "that bitte most greuously" was "emonge beastes, sauage, & furious, he that sclaunderously, and ill reporteth; but emong tame beastes, euermore ye Flatterer."[14] For the Elizabethan the evils of flattery were an attractive subject. He collected much about them from the books that he read, and he wrote much about them.

The beastliness of Apemantus in *Timon* is also backed by more than the Timon legend. Shakespeare's Apemantus is a cynic bearing some relation to the traditional Diogenes, whose reported sayings and doings were current among sixteenth- and seventeenth-century English writers and were often collected. Like Diogenes, Apemantus is called a dog, and like Diogenes he admits that he is a biting dog. And when he is called an "unpeaceable dog" by one of Timon's flatterers, his retort that he would "fly, like a dog, the heels of an ass" (I. i.

[13] James Sanforde, *The Garden of Pleasure . . . Done out of Italian into English* (1573), fol. 99^r.

[14] Ludovic Lloyd, *The Pilgrimage of Princes, Penned out of Sundry Greeke and Latine Aucthours* (1573?), fol. 183^v; Thomas Fortescue, *The Foreste or Collection of Histories . . . Dooen out of Frenche into Englishe* (1571, a partial translation of Mexía's *Silva*), fol. 29^v. Both of these sayings are given, with somewhat different wording, by William Baldwin in *A Treatise of Morall Philosophie* (1547), sigs. H 2 and G 8^v. See *Diogenes Laertius*, trans. R. D. Hicks ("Loeb Classical Library" [London and New York: Harvard University Press, 1925]), II, 7, 53.

283) is in the vein of Diogenes, who supposedly knew always how to discomfit those he disliked by witty reference to his title of dog, as when he said "to two infamous persons stealing away from him: Fear not . . . , doggs eat not thistles."[15] The condemnation of flatterers as devouring beasts which is attributed to Diogenes and which has just been quoted might have served as a model for Apemantus' bitter criticism of Timon's flatterers.

Moreover, the asceticism of the Diogenes of tradition seems to be Apemantus' rule of life. There was thought to be justification for saying that Diogenes "ledde a bestly lyfe," using the good things of the earth "no more than bestes" and drinking water as beasts do.[16] Apemantus at Timon's feast, eating root and drinking "honest water" while "rich men sin," is the same mixture of beastliness and moral fervor that Diogenes had the reputation of being.

One must not yield to a temptation to give Apemantus less than his due, to think that he is a snarling cur no better than Thersites in *Troilus and Cressida*. Like Thersites he is a privileged critic of the life and manners he observes, and like Thersites he plays a vulgar part very near to that of an allowed fool, though he is licensed to make himself even more obnoxious than a fool.[17] But unlike Thersites he has consistent philosophy in him, in addition to mere scurrilousness, and he distinctly does not gloat over the existence of the evil and folly that he scourges. It was possible in Shakespeare's age to praise Diogenes as a "heavenly dog."[18] Probably it was also possible to think that Apemantus in *Timon* was a beast for whom something good could be said.

It is upon a note of pity for Timon, for Timon with all his faults, that Shakespeare ends the tragedy. He makes Alcibiades

[15] Thomas Stanley, *The History of Philosophy* (1655), Part VII, p. 24.

[16] *A Dialogue betwene Lucian and Diogenes of the Life Harde and Sharpe, and of the Lyfe Tendre and Delicate*, tr. Sir Thomas Eliot (n.d.), fols. 7ᵛ and 5ʳ.

[17] O. J. Campbell observes that both Thersites and Apemantus are buffoonish commentators who display some of the characteristics of Jonson's Carlo Buffone (*Shakespeare's Satire* [New York, 1943], pp. 106, 187).

[18] See Antony Stafford, *Staffords Heavenly Dogge: Or the Life, and Death of That Great Cynicke Diogenes* (1615).

sound the note. Alcibiades, the warrior-politician, is of much grosser grain than Timon and is much inferior to him in spiritual worth, but nevertheless he has the ability to meet and overcome hostile forces in the world whereas Timon can only let himself be crushed by them. The contrast between the success of Alcibiades and the failure of Timon is somewhat like that between the success of Fortinbras and the failure of Hamlet. It contains one of Shakespeare's notable tragic ironies. In the last speech of the play, Alcibiades makes a comment upon Timon. This comment has the choral quality often given by Shakespeare to words of some prominent character in a tragedy which pass judgment upon the hero at the close of the action. After reading a copy of Timon's misanthropic epitaph, taken from his tomb on the seashore, the normally insensitive Alcibiades is moved to say something that we might not think him capable of saying.

> These well express in thee thy latter spirits:
> Though thou abhorr'dst in us our human griefs,
> Scorn'dst our brain's flow and those our droplets which
> From niggard nature fall, yet rich conceit
> Taught thee to make vast Neptune weep for aye
> On thy low grave, on faults forgiven. Dead
> Is noble Timon; of whose memory
> Hereafter more.
>
> (V. iv. 74–81)

Alcibiades does not find in Timon what Antony in a similar choral comment finds in Brutus, a gentle mixture of elements such that

> Nature might stand up
> And say to all the world, "This was a man!"
>
> (*Julius Caesar* V. v. 74–75)

But though Nature might not offer Timon as another paragon of her gentler workmanship, there was material in his violent being to make it proper that she should weep for and forgive his faults. It is proper that she should shed tears on his grave and forgive even those profound faults that led him finally to have unnatural scorn for the tears of suffering humanity. We are reminded that Timon's good steward, when he pities his fallen master, meditates on the way "noblest minds" can be brought by vile friends to "basest ends" (IV. iii. 464).

The "rich conceit" through which Timon's faults are wept for and forgiven seems to have been contrived by Shakespeare out of conventional matter concerning the burial of Timon. It is prepared for in two passages of the play, in which Timon speaks of wanting a grave on the shore of the sea. He speaks once of lying "where the light foam of the sea may beat" his gravestone daily (IV. iii. 381–82), and again of making his everlasting mansion where once a day "the turbulent surge shall cover" him (V. i. 220–23). The grave on the seashore is in various versions of Timon's legend. Plutarch, it will be remembered, says that Timon was buried on the shore and that the sea chanced to surround his tomb and make it inaccessible. Later tellers of the Timon legend embroidered this matter of burial. According to one account, the unsociable Timon left orders that he should be buried at the brink of the sea and that care should be taken to place his grave where the waves would make approach to it difficult or impossible. This account appears in English in the stories of Alday and Barckley. But Painter, following another account, has it that Timon wished to be buried near the sea because of a desire even more perverse than a desire for privacy in death. Says Painter: "By his last will he ordeined hymself to bee interred vpon the sea shore, that the waues and surges mighte beate, and vexe his dead carcas."[19] Shakespeare is close to Painter when he deals with Timon's burial. His Timon, like Painter's, wishes to have the sea beat upon his body. Yet in Shakespeare's Timon there is not so much a spirit of surliness when he plans to have his grave placed near the sea as there is a spirit of sad weariness. After he has written his epitaph, he can say of himself:

> My long sickness
> Of health and living now begins to mend,
> And nothing brings me all things.
>
> (V. i. 191–93)

And when we find that the waves shed tears upon his body instead of vexing it, we see fully Shakespeare's intention of leaving in our minds a man-hater worthy of sympathy, instead of one worthy of detestation.

In putting Timon to dramatic use Shakespeare apparently chooses for the first time to present a deeply flawed hero such

[19] *The Palace of Pleasure* (1566), fol. 58ᵛ.

as we have found to be characteristic of his last tragic world. He chooses for his hero a man who in the Renaissance has generally had a bad reputation as a hater of mankind and has generally been thought unworthy of mankind's sympathy. He lets him have all the faults that have been credited to him by unsympathetic tellers of his story. He tries to make us see these faults in the light of sympathy, but does not try to minimize them. In conclusion he suggests that we should forgive them, as Nature herself seems to forgive them.

The faults of Timon thus offered as forgivable go so deep that he himself is incapable of recognizing their existence. Timon is a remarkable contrast to the conscientious self-critics who are the heroes of Shakespeare's middle tragic world. Unlike Lear, for example, he never achieves by his separation from the vanities of the world a sympathy for the "loop'd and window'd raggedness" of poverty, and if we feel compassion for him after he has turned man-hater we find ourselves in the strange position of having sympathy for a would-be destroyer of sympathy among men. Yet, when he is without pity, he is most capable of winning pity.

In the same way, Timon is most capable of winning admiration when he might seem to be least deserving of it. But his paradoxical nobility of spirit is never that of an effective leader of men. Like Macbeth, Antony, or Coriolanus, he is a rare spirit deeply flawed, but unlike those heroes he does not belong among the rare spirits who "steer humanity."

XI

WOLFGANG H. CLEMEN

The Development of Imagery in Shakespeare's Great Tragedies

We cannot speak of the development of Shakespeare's imagery without keeping before us the general development of his art and mind. For the changes and the advance perceptible in his use of imagery result from this more comprehensive evolution. Some aspects of this interrelationship are to be dealt with in these remarks.

The tragedies display Shakespeare's dramatic technique at its best. This means that every element of style, in fact every single line, now becomes dramatically relevant. The same applies to the imagery, the images becoming an inherent part of the dramatic structure. They become effective instruments in the hand of the dramatist. We saw how they helped him to prepare the audience for coming events. But the imagery may also emphasize and accompany the dramatic action, repeating its themes; it often even resembles a second line of action running parallel to the real plot, and providing a "counterpoint" to the events on the stage.

The function of the images to forebode and anticipate, noticeable . . . in such plays as *The Merchant of Venice* and *King John*, becomes more important and more subtle in the tragedies. The imagery unobtrusively reflects coming events, it turns the imagination of the audience in a certain direction and helps to prepare the atmosphere so that the state of expectation and feeling necessary for the full realization of the dramatic effect is reached.

From *The Development of Shakespeare's Imagery,* by Wolfgang H. Clemen (London, 1951), pp. 89–105. Reprinted by permission of the author and Methuen & Co.

The fact that imagery plays such an important part in the tragedies indicates a fundamental change in Shakespeare's manner of presentation. In the early plays, it was his aim to make everything as obvious and plain as possible. Hence the programmatic expositions, the explanatory monologues, which acquaint us with the intentions of the characters. This direct and outspoken style is replaced in the work of the mature Shakespeare by a more subtle and indirect method. Things are suggested, intimated, hinted at; they are seldom expressly stated. And for this manner of suggestive and veiled presentation imagery is most suitable.

Ambiguity[1] plays an important role in this connection, as is obvious where Shakespeare makes his characters say something, the significance of which they cannot possibly grasp at the time of utterance. For what they say may have two meanings. The one meaning which the speaker has in mind refers to the momentary situation, but the other meaning may point beyond this moment to other issues of the play. Imagery may serve this purpose better than plain language and may lend itself more easily to ambiguity. An image is altogether a more complex form of statement than plain diction. Consider this passage from *Julius Caesar:*

> O setting sun,
> As in thy red rays thou dost sink to-night,
> So in his red blood Cassius' day is set;
> The sun of Rome is set! Our day is gone;
> Clouds, dews, and dangers come; our deeds are done!
>
> (V. iii. 61)

The increasingly complex significance of the rest of the passage develops from the simple meaning of the first words of the sentence. The sun has doubly set, for the "sun of Rome" is both the sun of that day, and Cassius himself. But the words "Our day is gone" have a threefold meaning: first, "Our day" is the real day, which has just passed, then again it means Cassius (in the preceding line it was said that "Cassius' day is set"), and finally, it denotes the period of life which all the persons concerned have passed through. Something new is about to begin for all of them now. The past day may also

---

[1] For ambiguity in poetry and drama cf. William Empson, *Seven Types of Ambiguity* (London, 1930).

refer to the approaching end of the play itself, because the
play will be at an end after two more brief scenes.

Another passage, from *Coriolanus* this time, may further
illustrate this ambiguity. Menenius says to the tribunes:

> This tiger-footed rage, when it shall find
> The harm of unscann'd swiftness, will too late
> Tie leaden pounds to's heels.

(III. i. 312)

The tribunes to whom these words are said apply "tiger-footed
rage" as well as "unscann'd swiftness" to Coriolanus. But, on
the other hand, in harmony with the underlying thought of the
play, both these epithets apply to the tribunes and to their
senseless agitation against Coriolanus, which is perceived and
tempered "too late." By means of this ambiguity, then, Menenius, Coriolanus' friend, is able to speak with the tribunes as
if he were on their side—whereas in fact he says precisely the
opposite.

This double meaning of images is also of importance for the
development of the dialogue in the tragedies. In interpreting
the tragedies, we must continually ask whether one character
has fully understood what the other said, or whether he or
she understood it in a secondary or false sense. This is of great
importance for the further course of the action. Shakespeare
seems to employ quite consciously this mutual misunderstanding of the characters as an instrument of dramatic technique.
In his early work, to be sure, we also find misunderstandings
as a result of ambiguities; but there it appears only in the form
of wit and punning. Whereas Shakespeare there employs the
pun, the play upon words, merely as a form of witty entertainment, an opportunity for clever repartee, he develops it in
his later work to a fine instrument of characterization and a
means of double interpretation of a situation. By means of the
multiplicity of meanings characteristic of the pun, Shakespeare
is able to let his characters understand each other in different
degrees. The characters may talk with each other and really
believe that they understand each other. But the true (hidden)
meaning of the one is not grasped by the other. The audience,
however, may well understand it. Out of this situation significant tensions grow between what the audience already knows
and what the characters on the stage are saying. Thus a play
on words may become the key to what is to follow. It is no

longer mere arabesque and unessential decoration, but rather a necessary, if tiny, link in the chain of the dramatic structure—for much now depends upon the comprehension of this quibble or pun at this particular moment.

Naturally, it is impossible to generalize about the motifs and themes which find expression in the imagery of the great tragedies. There are, however, some recurring and especially characteristic features which may be considered.

In the early histories, the characters turned to images when they sought to lend expression to the magnitude and intensity of their emotions, desires and aims. Marlowe's *Tamburlaine* was the model for such a use of imagery; consequently, many of those images and comparisons were too hyperbolical, too exaggerated; they were seldom appropriate expression. But in the tragedies, that appropriateness which was lacking in the early histories is achieved. The images no longer impress us as rhetorical and pompous; they are borne by great passion and correspond to the depth and immensity of human emotion. Thus we often meet with images which are built upon gigantic conceptions. Othello would not give up Desdemona:

> If heaven would make me such another world
> Of one entire and perfect chrysolite,
> I'ld not have sold her for it.
>
> (V. ii. 144)

Macbeth asks if the ocean would wash his blood-stained hand clean, and replies:

> No, this my hand will rather
> The multitudinous seas incarnadine,
> Making the green one red.
>
> (II. ii. 61)

and Hamlet taunts Laertes:

> let them throw
> Millions of acres on us, till our ground,
> Singeing his pate against the burning zone,
> Make Ossa like a wart!
>
> (V. i. 304)

It is characteristic of this gigantic conception of life that Shakespeare's tragic heroes in their imagery repeatedly express the presumptuous desire for the destruction of the whole world:

ANTONY.   Let Rome in Tiber melt, and the wide arch
            Of the ranged empire fall!

                                                    (I. i. 33)

CLEOPATRA. O sun,
            Burn the great sphere thou movest in! darkling stand
            The varying shore o' the world.

                                                    (IV. xv. 10)[2]

Almost all the heroes of Shakespeare's tragedies stand in close relationship to the cosmos, the celestial bodies and the elements.[3] This is a characteristic feature of the tragedies, lacking in the histories. Not only do the cosmic forces accompany the action of the tragedies; the characters feel themselves to be closely related to them and to the elements. When in the histories, the people turned their eyes to the sun, taking its dull gleam for a foreboding of evil,[4] this was in the tradition of omen. But in the tragedies, the characters apostrophize the sun and stars directly.

                Stars, hide your fires;
        Let not light see my black and deep desires. . . .

                                                    (I. iv. 50)

Macbeth cries before his murderous deed. "Moon and stars!" we hear Antony say (III. xiii. 95), and Cleopatra: "O sun, burn the great sphere . . ." (IV. xv. 10). The heavens seem sympathetic to what is occurring here on earth. To Hamlet, thinking of his mother's hasty remarriage, "Heaven's face doth glow" (III. iv. 48); and Othello, convinced of Desdemona's faithless-

---

[2] Further instances:

MACBETH. But let the frame of things disjoint, both the worlds suffer,

                                                    (III. ii. 16)

OTHELLO. Methinks it should be now a huge eclipse
          Of sun and moon, and that the affrighted globe
          Should yawn at alteration.

                                                    (V. ii. 99)

LEAR.   And thou, all-shaking thunder,
          Smite flat the thick rotundity o' the world!

                                                    (III. ii. 7)

[3] Cf. Max Deutschbein, *Die Kosmischen Mächte bei Shakespeare* (Dortmund, 1947).

[4] Cf. my article "Shakespeare und das Königtum," *Shakespeare Jahrbuch* (1932).

ness, cries out: "Heaven stops the nose at it and the moon winks" (IV. ii. 77). Macduff says, after the bad news has come: "New sorrows strike heaven on the face that it resounds" (IV. iii. 6). Sorrow reaching even up to heaven and forcing entrance there is a motif frequently expressed in the imagery. Hamlet, referring to Laertes' lament, says:

> whose phrase of sorrow
> Conjures the wandering stars, and makes them stand
> Like wonder-wounded hearers?
>
> (V. i. 278)

In *King Lear* Kent

> bellow'd out
> As he'ld burst heaven; . . .
>
> (V. iii. 212)

And Lear himself cries out at the end:

> Had I your tongues and eyes, I'ld use them so
> That heaven's vault should crack.
>
> (V. iii. 258)

Moreover, in the dramatic structure of the individual tragedies the appeal to the elements makes its appearance at definite turning points. Not until they begin to despair of men and earth do the tragic heroes turn to the heavens. When their firmest beliefs have been shaken, when they stand alone and forsaken, they renounce the earth and call upon the cosmic powers.

It is by means of the imagery that all the wealth of nature enters into the plays. Apart from *Midsummer Night's Dream* and *The Tempest*, the tragedies are the plays richest in nature atmosphere. The world of animals and plants, the scenery itself are evoked by the imagery; they lend the play not only background and atmosphere but also a vital connection with earthly existence, scarcely to be found in the work of any other dramatist. The word "atmosphere" is not, however, sufficient to denote the importance of the role of this varied nature imagery. For nature, the animals and plants, are players, as it were; they are forces in the organism of the play and hence not dissociable. In *Shakespeare und kein Ende* Goethe noted this "co-operation" of nature and the elements: "Even the inanimate world takes part; all the subordinate things have their rôle, the elements, the phenomena of the heavens, the earth and the sea, thunder and lightning."

Man and nature stand in a continuous relationship in the tragedies, and the imagery serves to emphasize this kinship. In many cases it would be inappropriate to say that the characters "use nature imagery." For nature, like the cosmos, is often like a character on the stage to whom one appeals; it is then no longer a *tertium comparationis.*

There was indeed a certain relationship between the characters and the world of nature in *Romeo and Juliet.* But to perceive the difference, let us compare Juliet's call to night, "Come, civil night, thou sober-suited matron" (III. ii. 10 ff.) with Macbeth's appeal:

> Come, seeling night,
> Scarf up the tender eye of pitiful day;
> And with thy bloody and invisible hand
> Cancel and tear to pieces that great bond
> Which keeps me pale! Light thickens; and the crow
> Makes wing to the rooky wood:
> Good things of day begin to droop and drowse;
> Whiles night's black agents to their preys do rouse.

(III. ii. 46)

In Juliet's monologue the night is still personified in traditional manner: "sober-suited matron," "gentle," "civil." In contrast to this, Macbeth's "seeling night" is something entirely different. "Seeling" does not denote a quality of a person, as do the epithets "gentle" or "civil." In the monologue from *Romeo and Juliet* the relationship of the person to the night is expressly stated, whereas in *Macbeth* it is merely suggested. In the lines which follow the actual apostrophe, Macbeth utters much of what he sees—but he leaves its significance unexplained. What Macbeth perceives in the world about him pertains to himself as well. The twilight—"light thickens"—is at the same time the twilight of his own soul. The "bloody hand" of the night recalls his own blood-stained hand, and from the word "invisible" we may gather the wish to make his own hand equally invisible. The good things of the outer world which "begin to droop and drowse" represent a like change in him, and, finally, "night's black agents," turning to their prey, are equivalent to his own desires bent upon their victim.[5] Thus Macbeth in his description of nature reveals his own inner state

[5] Cf. Empson, p. 23.

of mind. Every feature of this picture is true of himself and his designs.

A comparison of two other passages may show how differently Shakespeare now employs nature imagery. The first passage is from the Second Part of *Henry VI*, the other is from *Othello;* the motif of both passages is the sea with its dangerous rocks, sparing man out of sympathy. In *Henry VI* the Queen relates to the King:

> The pretty-vaulting sea refused to drown me,
> Knowing that thou would'st have me drown'd on shore,
> With tears as salt as sea, through thy unkindness:
> The splitting rocks cower'd in the sinking sands
> And would not dash me with their ragged sides,
> Because thy flinty heart, more hard than they,
> Might in thy palace perish Margaret.
>
> (*2 Henry VI* III. ii. 94)

In *Othello* Cassio tells the story of Desdemona's miraculous rescue after the stormy voyage:

> Tempests themselves, high seas and howling winds,
> The gutter'd rocks and congregated sands,—
> Traitors ensteep'd to clog the guiltless keel,—
> As having sense of beauty, do omit
> Their mortal natures, letting go safely by
> The divine Desdemona.
>
> (II. i. 68)

The diction in the passage from *Othello*, with its unusual and suggestive epithets and metaphors, is finer than in the lines from *Henry VI*. But the difference in the attitude towards nature is far more important. In the first case we have to deal with a "conceit" artfully constructed upon antithesis and parallelism. The sympathetic sea, the splitting rocks, are very consciously inserted into the long speech of the Queen as a means of contrast. In *Othello*, however, the sea imagery grows immediately out of the experience of the voyage. In the words of the other characters of this scene, too, we can feel the sea air. In the whole play the sea has an important role—as scene, background, and as Othello's own vital element.

Shakespeare's art of personification, of endowing abstract realities with the breath of life, undergoes a noteworthy development in the tragedies. The personifications, such as we often meet with in *King John*, for example,[6] are still patterned after the medieval type of personification. They derive from the allegorical world of the Middle Ages, from the time when all abstract qualities were thought of as human figures having certain attributes. In his later work, Shakespeare frees himself more and more from this tradition of the Middle Ages, although it was still living on in his own day in allegorical interludes and pageants. Those abstract images, behind which a visible human figure stands, become fewer and fewer. Shakespeare's manner of personifying becomes freer and bolder. He creates images of astonishing peculiarity and incomparable originality. At the same time the range of abstractions expressed by imagery becomes wider. These abstractions play an important part in the tragedies. Just as man now stands in closer connection with nature and the cosmos, so, too, he appears in relationship to certain forces determining and guiding his very existence. Be they called "fate," "doom," "time," or "metaphysical powers," these occult forces have a hand in every tragedy; man appears to be surrounded by them. Their vivid reality often becomes perceptible in the imagery. Hence we must seriously consider the images which represent these abstract realities. It is not only that these images tell us what Shakespeare himself thought about certain subjects. Their appearance at a certain point in a play has a deep significance. Thus, for example, the frequent time images in *Troilus and Cressida* reveal that, in this play, Shakespeare wanted to show the changing and dissolving effect of the passing of time. Or again, in *Antony and Cleopatra*, the repeated appearance of fortune images reflects the role fortune plays in determining the action.

In the tragedies—more than in all the other plays—the imagery expresses the mutual relationship of the forces at work in human nature. Ideas such as honour, judgement, conscience, will, blood, reason, etc., frequently appear in metaphorical guise. Whoever undertakes to investigate Shakespeare's conception of the human character will be amazed to find how many of the passages with the mutual relationship of spiritual and mental qualities as their subject appear in metaphorical language or employ imagery.

This kind of imagery should warn us not to apply modern conceptions of human character to Shakespeare's plays; it gives

---

[6] Cf. Caroline Spurgeon, *Shakespeare's Imagery*, p. 246.

us hints as to how Shakespeare conceived of mental processes and conflicting qualities of character.[7] For it is certainly not true that Shakespeare consciously "translated" into the language of imagery what he had to say about human qualities and dispositions (for the sake of a more poetic mode of expression, for example). On the contrary, imagery is an integral component of the thought; it discloses to us the particular aspect under which Shakespeare viewed these things. Imagery here is a form of imaging and conceiving things. "Metaphor becomes almost a mode of apprehension," says Mr. Middleton Murry.[8]

A passage from *Macbeth* may show us clearly in what new manner Shakespeare now visualizes abstractions and human characteristics.

Macbeth says, speaking of Duncan:

> that his virtues
> Will plead like angels, trumpet-tongued, against
> The deep damnation of his taking-off;
> And pity, like a naked new-born babe,
> Striding the blast, or heaven's cherubim, horsed
> Upon the sightless couriers of the air,
> Shall blow the horrid deed in every eye,
> That tears shall drown the wind. I have no spur
> To prick the sides of my intent, but only
> Vaulting ambition, which o'erleaps itself
> And falls on the other.
>
> (I. vii. 19)

This is very different from the gorgeousness of Spenser's allegories; it is bolder, mightier, and more dynamic, and rather recalls the passionate sublimity of Milton. "Pity, like a naked new-born babe, striding the blast" may illustrate how far Shakespeare has moved from the conventional type of personification and how his imagery tends towards the strange and unique. It is notable, too, that these abstractions are now placed in enormous space, transferred to a world of clouds and winds, of boundless distance. "That tears shall drown the wind" is hyperbolical, recalling Elizabeth's phrase in *Richard III:* "That I . . . may send forth plenteous tears to drown the world"

[7] For the background of Renaissance theory of humors cf. John W. Draper, *The Humors and Shakespeare's Characters* (Durham, N.C., 1945).

[8] *The Problem of Style* (1923), p. 13.

(II. ii. 70). But whereas this phrase was a rhetorical exaggeration in the manner of Marlowe, "That tears shall drown the wind" grows organically from the whole comprehensive image which is based on gigantic dimensions. Furthermore, Macbeth's whole world is determined by these tremendous and strange powers which find expression in several such images. The last lines betray the intricacy and boldness of Shakespeare's fully developed art of metaphorical association. The image of the rider, touched upon in "heaven's cherubim, horsed upon the sightless couriers of the air," is picked up again in "prick" and "spur," and is thus again used in another connection. "Intent" is conceived of as a horse, and "vaulting ambition" again as "rider." Thus an image, once set afire, as it were, seizes upon everything still to be said and creates bold and most extraordinary conceptions, like "vaulting ambition."[9]

This harmony between the given situation and the whole atmosphere of the play may also be traced in the imagery by which Shakespeare characterizes his men and women. A passage from *Julius Caesar* may serve as an example. In the third scene the conspirators meet in the streets of Rome at night during a terrific thunderstorm. By means of the imagery, the night and the thunderstorm are made very vivid, being also a suitable background for the dark conspiracy. The mood and situation naturally suggest the likening of Caesar to this fearful night.

> CASSIUS. Now could I, Casca, name to thee a man
> Most like this dreadful night,
> That thunders, lightens, opens graves, and roars
> As doth the lion in the Capitol. . . .
>
> (I. iii. 72)

The image fulfils two functions at one and the same time: it characterizes Caesar and adds to the nocturnal thunderstorm atmosphere. That imagery thus serves a double purpose is a characteristic of the tragedies.

This development does not necessarily imply that certain stylistic patterns of imagery which were characteristic of the

---

[9] Professor Spurgeon interprets this image as follows: "and finally, the vision of his 'intent,' his aim, as a horse lacking sufficient spur to action, which melts into the picture of his ambition as a rider vaulting into the saddle with such energy that it 'o'erleaps itself,' and falls on the further side" (p. 334).

early plays now no longer appear. But if they are now used, they mean something different; they are purposely inserted to characterize the moment and the person concerned; they are employed at precisely this point with a dramatic intent. This may be illustrated by an example from *Troilus and Cressida*. On the occasion of his first undisturbed meeting with Cressida, Troilus avers the trueness of his love—later "swains in love," he says, will measure the fidelity of their love by Troilus:

> when their rhymes,
> Full of protest, of oath and big compare,
> Want similes, truth tired with iteration,
> As true as steel, as plantage to the moon,
> As sun to day, as turtle to her mate,
> As iron to adamant, as earth to the centre,
> Yet, after all comparisons of truth,
> As truth's authentic author to be cited,
> "As true as Troilus" shall crown up the verse,
> And sanctify the numbers.
>
> (III. ii. 181)

This sequence of pretty comparisons is continued by Cressida in the same manner. It is as if we had before us two courtly lovers from the early comedies, where such agglomeration of clever comparisons was the fashion. But these two passages have their special dramatic significance within the framework of the whole play. Before the course of the play brings the tragic termination of their love, Shakespeare shows the two lovers in a mood of lyric ardour which stands in greatest contrast to the sceptical coolness and the bitter disillusionment of the following scenes. In order to enhance this effect, and to emphasize the unsuspecting, unconcerned and almost playful mood of the lovers, Shakespeare lets both speak here in a style which recalls the imagery of the early comedies. "The illusion must convince before it is pricked and shown to be a bubble," says Sir Edmund Chambers, referring to this passage.[10]

In the early plays, it was Shakespeare's habit to embellish certain general themes appearing in the conversation with metaphorical epithets and definitions. The resulting imagery was undramatic; it was rhetorical decoration and no integral part of the dramatic structure. But let us examine the famous words of Macbeth on sleep:

[10] *Shakespeare: A Survey*, p. 194.

> Methought I heard a voice cry "Sleep no more!
> Macbeth does murder sleep," the innocent sleep,
> Sleep that knits up the ravell'd sleave of care,
> The death of each day's life, sore labour's bath,
> Balm of hurt minds, great nature's second course,
> Chief nourisher in life's feast.
>
> (II. ii. 35)

Viewed from the outside, this series of metaphorical expressions for sleep is in no way different from the earlier type. Nevertheless, we scarcely need to say that the imagery of this passage is of the greatest dramatic suitability. For sleep is in this case no "theme of conversation," but a dramatic issue of first importance. That Macbeth has murdered Duncan while asleep is what is especially fearful in his deed. The wrong has been done, as it were, not only to Duncan but also to the sacred nature of sleep. And "wronged sleep" rises in the conscience of the murderer like a real power. The rich imagery therefore is no digression. It is no burst of fine-sounding words and names, no interruption of the action. It is a vital, throbbing expression of what is taking place at this moment in Macbeth's soul. Macbeth perceives again and again what he has done with a strange clarity, and expresses this in imagery (cf. I. vii. 19). "Sleep" runs like a key-word throughout the whole play and is the occasion of many metaphors, of which the above passage is the climax.

A comparison of this passage with the words of the sleepless King Henry IV appealing to sleep may show how Shakespeare's power of metaphorical expression has in the meantime grown in depth and concentration.

> O sleep, O gentle sleep,
> Nature's soft nurse, how have I frighted thee,
> That thou no more wilt weigh my eyelids down
> And steep my senses in forgetfulness?
> Why rather, sleep, liest thou in smoky cribs,
> Upon uneasy pallets stretching thee
> And hush'd with buzzing night-flies to thy slumber,
> Than in the perfumed chambers of the great,
> Under the canopies of costly state,
> And lull'd with sound of sweetest melody?
> O thou dull god, why liest thou with the vile
> In loathsome beds, and leavest the kingly couch
> A watch-case or a common 'larum-bell?
>
> (2 *Henry IV* III. i. 6)

In the earlier play, the King reviews in almost epic contemplation the effect of sleep among the different levels and classes of his subjects (the rich, the poor, the sailors on the high seas, and himself), but here in *Macbeth*, instead of a concrete picture executed in twenty-six lines (of which only the first half was quoted here), we have compressed into four lines a summary of the fundamental, timeless, eternally valid attributes of sleep.

The most important standard, accordingly, whereby to judge the imagery of the tragedies, is the degree of harmony existing between the image and the dramatic situation producing it. It may be that the dramatic situation admits of a richer expansion of the imagery; on the other hand, the speed of the play, or of the scene, may not permit the development of the whole image, so that as a result the image merely flashes up for a moment. This latter case is more frequent than the former, because the insertion of a wholly executed image would mean retarding and interrupting the rapid progress of the dramatic action. Shakespeare must bring in the image without making more words of it. "Shakespeare smuggles in the images" we might say of many passages of the tragedies in which the image is only touched upon and hinted at. In *Troilus and Cressida* Ulysses says of Achilles:

> the seeded pride
> That hath to this maturity blown up
> In rank Achilles must or now be cropp'd,
> Or, shedding, breed a nursery of like evil,
> To overbulk us all.
>
> (I. iii. 316)

This passage may serve as an example of how Shakespeare merely lets his diction take on the *colour* of the image in mind, the image being implicit, no longer expressly uttered. "Macbeth is ripe for shaking," says Malcolm at the end of the fourth act (IV. iii. 238), quite aware of the way things will end. This image, too, is suggestive, awakening the notion of the ripe fruit which must be shaken from the tree. At an earlier stage Shakespeare would have given us the whole image. Thus in *Richard II*, we read:

> The ripest fruit first falls, and so doth he;
> His time is spent,
>
> (II. i. 153)

or in the *Merchant of Venice:*

> The weakest kind of fruit
> Drops earliest to the ground; and so let me:

(IV. i. 115)

Thus the development towards dramatic imagery is a development towards condensation and suggestiveness. Shakespeare compresses into one short sentence an astonishing wealth of associations. No matter what he is writing, he is always accompanied by pictorial conceptions and associations. No longer is there purposeful "hunting" for suitable images, as in the early plays; the matter of which he wishes to speak has already appeared to him in a metaphorical form. If we see or read a tragedy for the first time, we scarcely notice to what unbelievable degree imagery is employed. This is in part due to the fact that much of it belongs to the type merely suggested, implied and concealed imagery that has unobtrusively melted into the language. But it is also because the imagery is so wholly adapted to the situation and the emotion of the speaker that we fail to feel anything unusual in it. Mr. Middleton Murry, discussing the poetic and dramatic value of the conceit, quotes a passage from *Antony and Cleopatra* (IV. ix. 15–18) and notes how little we are disturbed by this difficult and extravagant language; on the contrary, how much we are moved by it. He writes convincingly: "The dramatic intensity of the situation in which they [the words] are spoken is such that it seems to absorb the violence of the imagery, without need to modify the image itself. The conceit becomes the natural extravagance of a depth of emotion that would also go unuttered."[11] Shakespeare's use of the single metaphor calling forth a more comprehensive image has become much bolder in the tragedies in comparison with the earlier plays. A few examples only may be quoted. Coriolanus says:

> I mean to stride your steed, and at all times
> To *undercrest* your good addition
> To the fairness of my power.

(I. ix. 71)

Coriolanus is here expressing his thanks for the charger which has been presented to him. By "undercrest" Shakespeare makes

---

11 *Shakespeare*, p. 273.

Coriolanus say that he will wear this present as proudly as an embellishment of a helmet. A single metaphor suffices for what we needs must explain in many words. Hamlet bids Horatio:

> Observe mine uncle: if his occulted guilt
> Do not itself *unkennel* in one speech. . . .

> (III. ii. 85)

By association "occulted" leads to "unkennel," and thus a whole picture is lit up in our imagination. But ordinary words, too, if employed in a new and figurative sense, may have a surprising freshness. When Gloucester gives Edmund the order to sound Edgar, he simply says: "*wind* me into him," a phrase which with its vigorous simplicity remains unforgettable. By such unusual metaphors the audience are more startled than by an ordinary phrase which may pass unnoticed. We "prick up our ears" at such passages, the picture fastens on our imagination and we are less likely to skip such a line.

A study of the imagery in Shakespeare's tragedies helps us to appreciate them as an organism in which all the parts are interrelated and mutually attuned. Each tragedy has its own unmistakable individual nature, its own colour; it has its own landscape, its own atmosphere, its own diction. All details are closely connected, as in a finely meshed web; they are mutually dependent and point ahead or hark back. It is amazing to observe what part the imagery plays in helping to make the dramatic texture coherent as well as intricate. The same motif which was touched upon in the first act through the imagery is taken up again in the second; it undergoes a fuller execution and expansion, perhaps, in the third or fourth. As Professor Spurgeon has demonstrated, these leitmotivs of the imagery run through the play like a brightly coloured thread. Of *Macbeth* it has been noted with acumen that Shakespeare substitutes the unity of atmosphere for the dramatic unities of time and action.[12] This is true of many of the Shakespearian tragedies. This unity of atmosphere and mood is no less a "dramatic unity" than the classical dramatic unities. And the imagery of a tragedy plays an important part not only in creating a dramatic unity of the atmosphere but also in binding the separate elements of the play together into a real organic structure.

[12] Max Deutschbein, *Macbeth als Drama des Barock* (Leipzig, 1936).

XII

D. G. JAMES

The New Doubt

In trying to speak of *Hamlet*, I give myself some comfort by saying at once that I shall be content to play the role of a Teucer to the Ajax of Mr. Granville-Barker. Mr. Granville-Barker concluded his essay on *Hamlet* with these words:

> In England, for the best part of a century before *Hamlet* was written, and for sixty years after, the finer issues of the spiritual revolution which the Renaissance had begun were obscured by secular discord, persecution, and civil war; and the ensuing peace left them hardened into formula. To the popular mind thus distressed and coarsened, the finer issues implicit either in play or character might well make small appeal. Nor would they be likelier to touch the conscience of the positive eighteenth century. Not till it was waning, and many men had come to find their set creeds unsatisfying, till they began to ask the old essential questions once again, to have a better answer if they might, did the Hamlet of spiritual tragedy come by his own; then to become, indeed, the typical hero of a new "age of doubt." It was as if Shakespeare, so alive to the spirit of his own time, had been in this mysteriously attuned besides to some
>
> prophetic soul
Of the wide world dreaming on things to come.

While our age of doubt endures and men still cry despairingly "I do not know . . ." and must go on uncomforted, the play will keep, I should suppose, its hold on us. If a new age of faith or reason should succeed, or one for a while too crushed by brute reality to value either, Hamlet may then be seen again simply as the good Polonius saw him.[1]

From *The Dream of Learning: An Essay on the Advancement of Learning, Hamlet and King Lear*, by D. G. James (Oxford, 1951), pp. 33–57. Reprinted by permission of the author and the Clarendon Press. The quotation from Harley Granville-Barker's *Prefaces to Shakespeare* is included by kind permission of the owners of the copyright.

[1] *Prefaces to Shakespeare,* Third Series (London, 1944), pp. 328–29.

In these, as I believe, profound words, is the essence of what I have to say. I am not, I trust, unmindful of all the work which has gone into exhibiting to us the Elizabethan Hamlet; but those who have illuminated the play by historical research have not themselves been unmindful that Hamlet was not merely contemporary with his age; and the mind of Shakespeare is not, I take it, expressible as a function of a number of features of the age in which Shakespeare lived. The historian must accept the creativeness of the rare and great mind as itself a brute fact, and as a major brute fact; there is no resolving it away; it is peculiar, unique, and inexplicable; it is creative both of itself and of its civilization. The apparently simple category of cause and effect does not apply here; in such a mind, the facts and features of its age are material worked upon and transfigured into expressive symbols. Indeed, the symbol is not a statement or even a translation of the fact; instead, the fact emerges into clear light in the form of the symbol which alone is the full because significant fact. Thus, *Hamlet* better helps us to understand the Elizabethan uncertainty about ghosts than books written by lesser contemporaries of Shakespeare whose study of these things is far more partial and abstract than Shakespeare's treatment of them in his play.

I am not here chiefly concerned with these matters. I wish only to suggest that we may go too far in seeing Shakespeare as one *behind* whom we must look in order to understand him; we may rightly look to what came after. There is much, indeed, in Bacon which was of the Middle Ages and of the Renaissance; but the core of him was what we can only call modern; he was one of the first of the moderns; his vision of things was creative of, and is better understood in the light of, what came after him; and what makes Bacon important and gives to him his splendid literary powers is, I venture to say, his modernity. What was of the Middle Ages in him and of the Renaissance is, of course, of deep interest to us; but it is not this which makes him loom so large, which indeed gives him his peculiar greatness, and secures for him the attention and admiration of all succeeding generations. And so it is, I think, with Shakespeare. He was, in all truth, as Mr. Granville-Barker says, greatly alive to the spirit of his own time; but he, like Bacon, was prophetic, though of different things. The "finer issues of the spiritual revolution" of his time are still our issues; it is Hamlet as a figure expressive of modernity which holds our rapt contemplation; he, too, is one of the first, and is perhaps the greatest, of the moderns. The spirit of Bacon is still potently alive; so is Hamlet's. We read, in a nineteenth-century poet, that we are

> Light half-believers of our casual creeds,
>   Who never deeply felt, nor clearly will'd,
> Whose insight never has borne fruit in deeds,
>   Whose vague resolves never have been fulfill'd;
>   For whom each year we see
> Breeds new beginnings, disappointments new;
>   Who hesitate and falter life away,
>   And lose tomorrow the ground won today;

and it is natural to acknowledge that Arnold's description of us is true enough. But Arnold's lines, fine as they are, are a poetry of brief statement; Shakespeare's play is the detailed image, the elaborately wrought symbol, of this unresolved distress of modernity. Our modern world, at its outset, beheld itself here, defined, and in that measure created; here it has continued to behold itself; this play, far more than any other work of art or philosophy, has held our fascinated study. Bacon, I have said, was prophetic; and yet he looked to a conclusive event, an absolute achievement through knowledge which was also power. Shakespeare, in *Hamlet*, was also, I have said, prophetic; but he saw uncertainty, ignorance, failure, and defeat. I do not say he saw, even in *Hamlet*, only these things; but that he saw at least these things, we cannot deny. Bacon looked to unquestioning religious faith and to natural philosophy; but Hamlet certainly had no unquestioning faith; he had no philosophy, natural or other; and his problems were hardly to be resolved by the use of scientific method, or knowledge, or experiment.

I cannot, within my limits, proceed to a systematic study of the play of *Hamlet:* I must move discursively, but not, I trust, evasively.

I have suggested where, as it seems to me, the centre of the play lies. Some have seen Hamlet as congenitally indisposed to action: Goethe and Coleridge saw him largely in this way. But in fact, the play forbids this; and Ophelia's description of

Hamlet is no doubt intended to suggest to us a difference between the Hamlet we see now and the Hamlet of earlier days. He had been the courtier, the soldier, and the scholar:

> The expectancy and rose of the fair state,
> The glass of fashion, and the mould of form,
> The observed of all observers. . . .[2]

But now he is quite, quite down. New circumstances have arisen, and in them he is distracted, uncertain of his way, unable to resolve an intolerable state of things; and the play presents this man in this condition, what he does, and what happens to him. This indeed is not all it does; but this it does chiefly.

To see Hamlet as merely a perplexed mind, an uncertain intellect, would be grossly to simplify; no play could be enacted out of such abstracted matter. Hamlet is a man of strong passion, if he is also one of weak will; but the weakness of his will and the strength of his feelings, whether of contempt and disgust for Claudius or of admiration for Horatio, are of a piece with his intellectual condition; and if I appear to speak of Hamlet as of some ghostly and bloodless intellectual, it will not be in entire forgetfulness of the rest of him. Nor, if I appear to lift Hamlet out of the play and seem to offend against a canon of contemporary criticism, shall I forget the risks I am running. I must indeed ask forbearance for what cannot, within the scope at my disposal, be a full-length study of the play; I shall proceed with what I acknowledge to be a limited purpose in view; I only think that nothing that I say is in the last resort at odds with any full consideration of the play as a work of dramatic art.

Now we have, in the first place, to see Hamlet as a man uncertain of his duty in the circumstances in which he finds himself. Ought he to murder the murderer of his father and the seducer of his mother? That is the question:

> To be, or not to be: that is the question:
> Whether 'tis nobler in the mind to suffer
> The slings and arrows of outrageous fortune,
> Or to take arms against a sea of troubles,
> And by opposing end them? To die,—to sleep. . . .

[2] Quotations from Shakespeare are made from the Arden editions, Old Series.

I am not unaware that I am plunging into, to say the least, debated territory. But it is better, I think, for me to declare myself at once and make clear where, on this battlefield, I stand and fight; and Mr. Granville-Barker would, I am sure, forgive me if for the moment I make Dr. Johnson my Ajax; he stands foursquare, if shot at, in this as in his other battles. His interpretation of this soliloquy seems to me incomparably the best yet offered. The thought of the soliloquy is not, at the outset, of suicide at all, but of personal immortality: whether we are to be or not to be, to live or in truth to die; and in the context of this thought, which recurs at the conclusion of the lines I quoted ("And by opposing end them? To die,—to sleep . . ."), Hamlet asks whether it be nobler to suffer the slings of fortune or to take arms against troubles and end them. Hamlet's mind is moving fast: we may read the "that is the question" as referring both backwards and forwards; and the two questions, whether we shall live or die and whether it is nobler to suffer or to take arms against our troubles, are tied up with each other and are in Hamlet's mind quite inseparable. Certainly, the thought of suicide occurs later with the talk of a bare bodkin making a quietus for us; this is one way of taking arms against a sea of troubles; and then Hamlet's thought turns at once, again, to death and a life to come. He had spoken first of taking arms against others with the chance that he be killed; and his mind had passed at once to the thought of what might come in another world than this. Now he speaks of killing himself; and now, again, his mind turns to what would come in another world.

> For who would bear the whips and scorns of time . . .

> When he himself might his quietus make
> With a bare bodkin? who would fardels bear . . .

> But that the dread of something after death,
> The undiscover'd country from whose bourn
> No traveller returns, puzzles the will . . . ?

We do offence to the speech, or so it seems to me, unless we see Hamlet contemplating, first, the killing of others with perhaps, then, his own death, and second, a suicide; both are ways of taking arms against a sea of troubles, and the taking arms in either form is seen against the fearful background of a world to come in which condign punishment may be inflicted by a righteous God. What kind of an eternity will the taking up of arms, whether against others or oneself, bring one? Therefore the overriding question is, "Whether 'tis nobler . . . ?" This we must know, for God, if there be a God, may punish us through eternity for a wrong choice. There is the intrinsic ethical question—which is in itself nobler? But Hamlet ties up this question along with the thought of eternal sanctions imposed by God. If there were no afterlife it would not matter, or matter less, which line he took; but he cannot here, upon this bank and shoal of time, jump the thought of a life to come. There is, then, an ethical question; there is also a metaphysical and religious question; and to neither does he know the answer.

I only emphasize here, in passing, Hamlet's fearful imagination of a life after death. I venture to think we often underrate this. Here, indeed, we need to remember how close these Elizabethan days were to the Middle Ages; here we must hold our modernity in restraint. If we need to illustrate further that in this matter Hamlet was not fetching excuses for delay, we may look at lines Shakespeare wrote in another play a few years later. In *Measure for Measure* the Duke has urged Claudio to be absolute for death: the afflictions of life make death sweet. Later in the same scene, Isabella has told Claudio that "the sense of death is most in apprehension." But the reply of Claudio, given indeed to Isabella but coming in effect as a reply both to her and to the Duke, is dreadful in its imagination:

> Ay, but to die, and go we know not where;
> To lie in cold obstruction and to rot . . .
>
>   and the delighted spirit
> To bathe in fiery floods, or to reside
> In thrilling region of thick-ribbed ice;
> To be imprison'd in the viewless winds,
> And blown with restless violence round about
> The pendent world; or to be worse than worst
> Of those that lawless and incertain thought
> Imagine howling: 'tis too horrible!
> The weariest and most loathed worldly life
> That age, ache, penury and imprisonment
> Can lay on nature is a paradise
> To what we fear of death.

Hamlet too had "lawless and incertain thought," and it will not do to say that here, in the face of this, Hamlet is finding extravagant or recondite reasons for his hesitation. Since the days when these lines were written the eschatological imagination has fallen steadily back before the onset of naturalism. A. C. Bradley merits our gratitude, and I should be the last man to speak of him without deep respect; but an English Hegelian would be intelligibly disposed to underrate Hamlet's fear of other worlds and to say that his thought, if it moved on these lines, was a symptom merely of a morbid and diseased state. My own wish is frankly to elevate Hamlet's intellectual distresses to an equality in importance with his emotional state; the strength of the emotional shock he has suffered is equaled by the weakness of his mind in the face of difficult moral and metaphysical issues. Hamlet was, after all, an intellectual. We must bear in mind that Shakespeare was the first to make him a member of a university, and *Hamlet* was acted before the universities of Oxford and Cambridge. (We may also recall, with alarm, that Polonius had been a member of a university; some will further note, and with still greater alarm, that he had clearly, when at the university, been a member of the dramatic society.) But my point is that *Hamlet* is not a tragedy of excessive thought; so far as we are to see the cause of Hamlet's destiny in intellectual terms, it is a tragedy not of excessive thought but of defeated thought. Hamlet does not know, and he knows of no way of knowing. And then comes the line,

Thus conscience does make cowards of us all;

resolution is sicklied o'er, and enterprise loses the name of action. It is hard to know what it is right to do; and we do not know whether in fact we live after we die, and in a universe in which a moral order asserts itself. No doubt Shakespeare had to be careful how he expressed the issues which confronted Hamlet. But the plain issue was, Does God exist or not? What was at stake in Hamlet's mind was nothing less than the greatest issue which confronts our mortal minds.

"Conscience does make cowards of us." There has been, I am aware, much dispute as to what the word means here. For my part, I find not the least difficulty in believing that the word carries both its usual meaning and that of "reflection and anxious thought." It is a platitude of Shakespeare study that Shakespeare could, with wonderful ease, charge a word with two or three meanings at once; there is hardly a page of Shakespeare which does not illustrate this; and in any case, the word "conscience" means for us all both a command to do what is right and anxious reflection as to what is, in fact, the right thing to do. If I had to choose (what I feel under no compulsion whatever to do) between the two meanings proposed, I should unhesitatingly choose the former and usual meaning. A. C. Bradley was cross (in a footnote) with the *Oxford Dictionary* for giving its authority to construing "conscience" in this passage as meaning "moral sense or scrupulousness," and he declares that "in this soliloquy Hamlet is not thinking of the duty laid upon him at all." But how then can he begin to explain the lines:

> Whether 'tis nobler in the mind to suffer . . .
>
> Or to take arms . . . ?

It is precisely his duty Hamlet thinks of, and of his duty, which he finds it hard to decide, in relation to a possible world to come; and the difficulty of knowing what is right, and the uncertainty of our last destiny, together puzzle and arrest the will. Conscience requires that we do what is right; but then, what *is* right or wrong in these circumstances? Anxious reflection discloses no clear conviction; nor does it provide knowledge of a world to come. This is the moral and metaphysical uncertainty in which Hamlet finds himself. He does not know and cannot find out. Conscience makes demands, but it also provides no clear moral or metaphysical sense. Until he finds himself in this climacteric condition, life has gone on smoothly enough; but now, and suddenly, he knows that he lacks the insight, or the knowledge, or the faith, which will steady him and carry him forward in a single and continuous course of action. In this, Hamlet knows he is different from Horatio, whose calm and steadily appointed way of life we are expected to admire. Horatio is precisely one who in suffering all, suffers nothing; he has accepted the first alternative Hamlet had proposed to himself: "Whether 'tis nobler in the mind to suffer the slings and arrows. . . ." Horatio has, we are expected to understand, decided that it is nobler so to suffer, and he has taken the buffets and the rewards of fortune with equal thanks; he knows his line and he is steady in it. Hamlet has not decided, and hence his peculiar distress.

It is very important to observe the play here on the word "suffer." Horatio is one who suffers everything and suffers nothing. What does this mean? I take it to mean, in the first sense, that Horatio accepts equally the fortunes and misfortunes of life; he embraces his good fortune with restraint and he endures his misfortunes. Therefore, in the second sense, he suffers nothing; he is not put out or mastered by circumstance; he is master of himself and of circumstance; he sustains a steady and imperturbable calm. In the one sense of the word, he takes what comes, without rebellion against it; he does not oppose it to end it; he is thus passive. But in the other sense, he is precisely not passive, but pre-eminently active and creative in his life. Such a steadiness and even tenour, in a philosophy of "suffering," Hamlet does not possess. Horatio is one who, in suffering all, suffers nothing; Hamlet is one who, in suffering nothing, suffers everything. He is active where Horatio is passive, and passive where Horatio is active. His passivity is of the wrong sort; he is blown about by every gust of passion. But it is the same when he is active: his activity, like his passivity, is an affair of passion merely. Judgement is not in it. He is passion's slave, played on like a pipe, lapsed in time and circumstance, unaccountable, now listless, now violent.

But we must remark how Hamlet speaks of Horatio: he does so in words of passionate admiration. His election had sealed Horatio for himself because in suffering all, Horatio suffered nothing; and it is the man who is not passion's slave whom he would wear in his heart's core. How clearly he would be like Horatio! And yet, in the face of what has happened, ought he to be like Horatio? or ought he not to take up arms against his troubles, and violently end them and perhaps thereby himself? He did not know. The ghost had given Hamlet specific instructions to contrive nothing against his mother:

> leave her to heaven,
> And to those thorns that in her bosom lodge,
> To prick and sting her.

But ought he perhaps to leave Claudius to heaven also? When his guilt was proved beyond any doubt, Hamlet still did not

kill him; he left him alone, giving a reason, plausible enough
in Hamlet's eyes, in the eyes of his audience, and in our eyes,
and yet inhabiting a middle region between sincerity and in-
sincerity. We are told that in explaining why he does not there
kill the King, Hamlet was sincere; it was a belief of the time.
But it was certainly not universal. Claudius at least could have
told him it was nonsense; Claudius has just made clear to us
what was necessary if he, Claudius, was to win heaven. And
could a Hamlet who half his time believed neither in heaven
nor hell, sincerely and with a whole mind say these things?
He leaves Claudius, and goes off to rage at his mother.

Conscience, says Hamlet, makes cowards of us; we are made
afraid by it; and who of us does not know that this is true?
In the soliloquy in Act IV ("How all occasions do inform
against me") the same thought is uppermost. God has given
us capability and godlike reason; we may, Hamlet certainly
does not, live in a bestial oblivion of it. What he charges himself with is excess of scruple in employing it in his moral difficulties, thinking too precisely on the event; his scruples, he
says, are craven; or at least they are one part wisdom and
three-quarters cowardice:

> A thought which, quarter'd, hath but one part wisdom
> And ever three parts coward.

He is disposed to upbraid himself for letting all things sleep;
but he also acknowledges, even in his bitter reproachment of
himself, that he is at least one-quarter wise in thinking precisely on the event: he could not do other than think precisely
on such momentous issues. But then, if his precise thinking
issues in no results, no assured decision, no clear path of duty,
how can he be other than afraid of doing one thing rather
than the other? He has cause and will and strength and means
to do it; yes, all these he has; but has he the conscience to do
it? That is the question, and conscience makes cowards of us.
But where is a resolution of this distress to come from? From
thinking precisely on the event? Apparently not; Hamlet is a
thinker and has thought enough. Then let him plunge, and do
what no doubt most people would expect of him; he talks
fustian at himself about greatly finding quarrel in a straw
when honour's at the stake, and this in future will be his line.
But will it? Of course not. It is better to have three-quarters

cowardice and one-quarter wisdom than four-quarters of bravado and tomfoolery, and Hamlet knows this well enough. But where and how will he find escape from this proper and rightminded cowardice? This is his problem; and it is, I suppose, everybody's problem.

I am aware that I may well be manifesting a deplorable cocksureness in all this. But at least I shall make clear what I intend, and I confess to some impatience with what seems to me the present-day willingness to give up Hamlet for a mystery. Now it is true, no doubt, that we must not see the play as merely an affair of the character of its hero. But few of us will deny that Hamlet's procrastination is the major fact in the play and that it was intended by Shakespeare to be so. But are we really to find his procrastination a mystery and to leave it a mystery? Is there really anything mysterious about a man who has come to no clear and practised sense of life, and who, in the face of a shocking situation which quite peculiarly involves him, shuffles, deceives himself, procrastinates, and in his exasperation cruelly persecutes the person he loves best in the world? Is this beyond our understanding? If we fail to understand it, is it not only because it is all so near to us and not because it is far off in Elizabethan times? Conscience, Hamlet said, makes cowards *of us all*. He was thinking of himself not as the exception, but as the rule.

Even if what I have said is true, it may still be replied that I am building up too much from the great soliloquies of Acts III and IV. There is much before, between, and after these speeches; there is indeed, round about them, the play as a whole. But I trust I may be allowed to make a few observations in further defence of what I have been saying. A. C. Bradley declared that it was only late in the play that Shakespeare gives any ground for thinking that Hamlet doubted what his duty was. In Act V, scene ii, he has been speaking of his uncle, and he asks:

> is't not perfect conscience
> To quit him with this arm? and is't not to be damn'd
> To let this canker of our nature come
> In further evil?

Certainly, the question is asked; and here at least (as Bradley tacitly acknowledges) "conscience" means conscience and no

mistake; and with the thought of conscience comes again the
thought of a world after this one—"is't not to be damn'd . . . ?"
But certainly, if this were all we had to go on, it would not be
a great deal; it comes too late in the play. I have spoken of
two of the soliloquies, those of Acts III and IV. Of the soliloquy in Act IV ("How all occasions") and of that in Act II
("Oh, what a rogue and peasant slave am I") Bradley remarks
that in them Hamlet bitterly reproaches himself "for the neglect of his duty. When he reflects on the possible causes for
this neglect he never mentions among them a moral scruple."[3]
In fact I think, as I have suggested, that this, so far as it refers
to the soliloquy in Act IV, is not true: it is thinking too precisely on the event which is there put down for the cause of
the delay. But leaving that aside, we have to take account of
the circumstances in which these two speeches are made. The
first is made immediately after the players have shown him their
paces; the second after Fortinbras has marched through against
Poland. The player and the soldier come upon him—how could
they else?—as deep and bitter reproaches. Nothing could be
more natural than this: the player and the soldier move easily
and naturally into their appointed actions; they suffer no arrest
or inhibition; and Hamlet is filled with shame when he thinks
of himself. What then could be truer, in any delineation of
human nature, than that his mind should then, in face of those
whose inner lives get so little in the way of their duties, turn
to the second of his great alternatives, to taking arms against a
sea of troubles and, as Mr. Granville-Barker says, to "brute
capacity for deeds of blood"? These are not occasions of mere
reflection; the shame of his helplessness goads him towards the
more violent of the two choices. But in between these two
soliloquies comes, in Act III, the soliloquy which every school-
boy knows by heart and which the world has always put down
for the essence of Hamlet. Here he is under the stress of no
immediate instigation which would merely rouse his blood
and allay his judgement. Here he comes quietly on and speaks,
and that very night the play is to be performed at court. We
are in a part of the play where the time sequence of the action
is given with unmistakable clarity. Hamlet had agreed with the
player, when arranging to have *The Murder of Gonzago* per-

[3] *Shakespearean Tragedy* (2d ed.; London, 1920), p. 97.

formed, that it should be the following night; and early in the scene in which Hamlet speaks the great soliloquy it has been made clear that the play is to be performed that night. There has been previously, as Mr. Granville-Barker remarked, "a spell of timelessness," and now the carefully defined temporal sequence is "used," said Mr. Granville-Barker, "to validate the dramatic speed, even as was timelessness to help slow the action down" and give a vague impression of inaction and delay. The tension tightens; Hamlet may have no doubt in his heart of the King's guilt; but soon there will be proof; and then, if ever, Hamlet must make his decision. At this point, Hamlet comes on and speaks his speech; and the purpose of this speech must be above all to define the issues. If, after the play scene, he is not to act, we must be given fair reason: we must understand it, and the reason is as I have tried to expound it. This soliloquy is therefore central; on this, if on anything, the play turns. In the anguish of uncertainty which he here expresses he sees Ophelia and speaks his cruelest words to her. Then the play scene; then a lifting of the tension in a measure, as he talks to Rosencrantz and Guildenstern. Then he is summoned to his mother and it is of his mother he thinks. It is midnight and he could drink hot blood; but still it is of his mother he thinks, not of his uncle. He goes to his mother but alights upon the King as he goes. But he does not kill him; he shuffles out of it and talks off his exasperation to his mother. But all is over. Very soon he will be in effect a prisoner, on his way to England. It is indeed, as he goes, that he hears of Fortinbras; and he ends his long soliloquy with,

> Oh, from this time forth,
> My thoughts be bloody, or be nothing worth.

But he had said something like this after hearing the player; he had afterwards had his proof and his chance; and nothing had come of it. He may say what he likes about his thoughts being bloody; but this they will never be. "My thoughts be bloody, or be nothing worth," but was his thinking precisely on the event "worth nothing"? It was at least one-quarter wisdom; and Hamlet, storm as he will at himself, will not throw up that wisdom for mere thoughts and deeds of blood. As Mr. Granville-Barker said, here is the end of a movement—the second movement—of the play. A new movement will begin; but

Hamlet will not design and accomplish its ending. Someone else will do that.

I suggest, therefore, that it is not only what a careful inspection of the speech discloses that we have to take into account; there is also the crucial position of the speech in the action of the play as a whole. And to this I add that we must see this speech as close to, indeed as of a piece with, the conversation with Horatio in which Hamlet declares the quintessence of Horatio's mind and character which he so admires. This conversation occurs later in the third act and immediately before the play scene; the moral and intellectual confusion of Hamlet, and then the calm and impregnable bearing of Horatio, are driven hard home as the inner spiritual setting of the ensuing climax of the play.

But it is not only this. Everywhere in this play there is uncertainty and doubt; everywhere also there is incalculable and almost incredible conduct. In belief, as in conduct, nothing is firm and clear. If we look to belief: the ghost may be an honest ghost; he may be the Devil; he may be an illusion. Man has an immortal soul; he is also the quintessence of dust. Death may be a nothing, or a sleep, or its world may contain a heaven and a hell. It may be right to leave criminals to the action of heaven; it may also be right to find quarrel in a straw when honour (whatever that may be) is at the stake. There may be a God to point his canon at self-slaughter; but also there may not be, and only, in his place, a congregation of vapours. And if we look to the conduct of others: a brother can murder his brother whose wife he has seduced, and he can smile and be a villain. A loving wife will betray her husband and promptly marry again with no obvious compunction; and before these two a court will cringe and crawl. Ophelia will apparently play in with the others. Of clarity of belief and clarity of conduct there is nothing. The world has crumbled to shifting sand; there is nothing which is firm and no one on whom to rely. Except indeed Horatio, who in suffering all suffers nothing, who has made a choice; and him Hamlet wears in his heart's core, ay, in his heart of heart.

But can we, before we go further, say anything which is at all clear about the fundamental ethical issue which confronted

Hamlet? I think it is possible to do so; and to do so in the first place in terms of an opposition, with which Hamlet plays a good deal, between "blood" and "judgment." Hamlet has said to Horatio that he suffers nothing in suffering all; and he goes on to say that they are blessed

> Whose blood and judgment are so well commingled
> That they are not a pipe for fortune's finger
> To sound what stop she please. Give me that man
> That is not passion's slave. . . .

"Blood," here, is the same as "passion," and together are opposed to "judgment," a word which is frequent in Shakespeare's plays of this time. In the first act, Laertes tells Ophelia to regard Hamlet's favours as "a fashion, and a toy in blood"; Hamlet tells his mother that at her age

> The hey-day in the blood is tame, it's humble,
> And waits upon the judgment; and what judgment
> Would step from this to this?

And then again, he says of himself, in the soliloquy in the fourth act,

> How stand I then,
> That have . . .
> Excitements of my reason and my blood. . . .

The opposition of these two is frequent and clear. Besides, the King speaks of Ophelia in her madness as

> Divided from herself and her fair judgment,
> Without the which we are pictures, or mere beasts;

and this chimes in with Hamlet's

> What is a man,
> If the chief good and market of his time
> Be but to sleep and feed? a beast, no more.
> Sure he that made us with such large discourse,
> Looking before and after, gave us not
> That capability and god-like reason
> To fust in us unused.

It is clear that what is of the blood is animal and is opposed to judgement, which is reason; and Hamlet in one place declares that reason is from God and godlike.

Now we observe that Hamlet, in the soliloquy in the fourth act, speaks of "Excitements of my reason and my blood": both his reason and his blood are roused, he says; and in the mood in which he finds himself after hearing of Fortinbras, he implies that both his reason and his blood require that he takes arms. But in the speech to Horatio he speaks of blood and judgement, which are also passion and reason, being so well commingled in Horatio that he is neither a pipe for fortune to play upon nor a slave of passion; this is part and parcel, apparently, of Horatio's power to suffer all and to suffer nothing; and Horatio is also

> as just a man
> As e'er his conversation coped withal.

In order to try further to illumine this pair of terms, I turn for a moment from *Hamlet* to *Troilus and Cressida.* . . . I look now, without apology, to the scene in *Troilus* where Hector, Troilus, Helenus, and Paris discuss the whole matter of the cause and rightness of the Trojan War. Shall they return Helen to the Greeks? And Hector begins the debate by saying:

> modest doubt is call'd
> The beacon of the wise, the tent that searches
> To the bottom of the worst.

Modest doubt is the beacon of the wise and tents into the depths, and Hector denies that it can be reasonable to decline to give up Helen. It is Troilus who replies: he passionately denies that the "worth and honour" of a king can be weighed against "fears and reasons." What he calls "honour" and "greatness" are infinite; "reasons" are but so many miserable counters. Helenus comes out on the side of Hector; and Troilus turns on him to say:

> Nay, if we talk of reason,
> Let's shut our gates and sleep: manhood and honour
> Should have harehearts, would they but fat their thoughts
> With this cramm'd reason: reason and respect
> Makes livers pale and lustihood deject,

where "respect" means "anxious consideration."

Then, when Hector declares that Helen is not worth holding, and Troilus replies by asking

> What is aught but as 'tis valued?

Hector in turn replies:

> . . . value dwells not in particular will;
> It holds his estimate and dignity
> As well wherein 'tis precious of itself
> As in the prizer.

Value, that is to say, is not something arbitrarily placed by the individual or "particular will" upon an object or act; it is something there to be discovered, presumably by reason.

I cannot now follow in close sequence this remarkable debate; I quote again only Hector's words to Troilus which occur later in the scene:

> is your blood
> So madly hot that no discourse of reason,
> No fear of bad success in a bad cause,
> Can qualify the same?

and Troilus replies that the reasons of Hector and the ravings of Cassandra

> Cannot distaste the goodness of a quarrel
> Which hath our several honours all engag'd
> To make it gracious.

But the purpose and issue of this debate is clear: reasons, discourse of reason, modest doubt, "respect" are set over against honour, blood, dignity, glory; the one side proclaims reason and modest doubt, the other declares that these "Make livers pale and lustihood deject." I see here the fundamental issue which also agitates Hamlet. Fortinbras and Troilus hold, in these matters, the same role: when honour's at the stake they act against all considerations of reason and modest doubt. Hamlet does not do so; he cannot do so; and at the lowest estimate, his not doing so has one-quarter part of wisdom. He cannot forbear to place the check of reason and judgement upon passion, blood, and honour. He wants a just commingling of the two; the sheer mastery of himself by unreflecting blood will not serve. But no doubt

> reason and respect
> Makes livers pale and lustihood deject.

It is this which, I think, lies at the centre of the play; and with this great ethical issue is joined the questioning of last things of which I have spoken earlier.

XIII

D. A. TRAVERSI

Othello

Othello is, by common consent, one of Shakespeare's most completely "objective" plays. The internal conflict of *Hamlet*, the identification of the hero's tragedy with the effort to achieve self-definition, is now polarized into the more truly dramatic conflict between Othello and Iago. The substitution as vehicles of the tragic emotion of one complex and incoherent character by two more simple, sharply defined personalities in conflict carries with it an extension of the ability to present the dramatic implications of character. This ability had been partially obscured in the problem plays, where the conception of motive is often uncertain and where sentiment is commonly more profound than coherent. Hamlet unites a vast number of impulses and feelings in the utterances of a single man, but it cannot be said that his behaviour is always consistent or his motives fully comprehensible. Othello, on the other hand, is fully and continuously a person. His sentiments and actions are throughout perfectly intelligible, perfectly consistent with the character as defined; his emotions, unlike those of Hamlet, are always strictly related to their causes as dramatically presented. Othello is, indeed, the first of a series of Shakespearean heroes whose sufferings are explicitly related to their own failings, but who manage in spite of these failings to attain tragic dignity. Like Antony and Coriolanus after him, he dramatizes as "nobility" his own incapacity to cope with life; and as in their case, the very weakness which is obvious to all around him and by which Iago engineers his downfall is turned into true tragedy. The dramatic construction of the play, in short, turns upon the close, intricate analysis by which the two contrasted characters of the Moor and his Ancient are at every moment dove-

From *An Approach to Shakespeare*, by D. A. Traversi (2d ed.; London, 1956), pp. 128–50. Reprinted by permission of the author and Sands & Co. (Publishers) Ltd.

tailed, seen as opposed but strictly related conceptions. Scarcely since the First Part of *Henry IV* had Shakespeare presented character with such assurance, but the objectivity which had there illuminated a detached political study is now controlled by the presence of an intense tragic emotion.

It is obvious (and this is a convenient starting point) that the poetry of Othello is largely concentrated upon physical passion, but the peculiar way in which that passion is habitually expressed by him is highly significant. His poetry naturally dwells repeatedly upon love; but the feeling it expresses is one which, by revealing its own incompleteness, suggests an inability to attain adequate fulfilment. In his meditation, for instance, over the sleeping Desdemona before he stifles her (V. ii), we find intensity remarkably matched by coldness, sensuous feeling by a curious remoteness from the "blood." Beginning with an invocation to "you *chaste* stars," he goes on to speak of a skin "whiter than *snow*" and "*smooth as monumental alabaster*"; while there is something intense but distant in the apostrophe to "thy light," which follows, and in the almost studied reference to "Promethean heat." Collecting together these images, we come to feel that Othello's passion at this critical moment is as cold on the surface as it is intense just below; it combines a certain monumental frigidity in expression with a tremendous impression of the activity of the senses.

That the senses are present is clearly guaranteed—at this stage in the play—by Othello's own behaviour; and, indeed, the same speech proves that this is so. As he gazes upon his victim, his underlying sensuality is felt above all in the comparison of Desdemona to the rose and in the keenness with which the sense of smell appears in "balmy breath" and in "I'll smell it on the tree."[1] Even here, however, the sense of incompleteness

---

[1] It is useful to recall at this point the frequency with which the rose is associated, in the sonnets, with the "canker" of faithlessness:

> How sweet and lovely dost thou make the shame
> Which, like a canker in the fragrant rose,
> Doth spot the beauty of thy budding name!
>
> (Sonnet 95)

"Fragrant" here, incidentally, can usefully be associated in its effect with "balmy breath" in the speech under consideration. There are other parallels in the play; Othello, in accusing Desdemona, addresses her as "rose-lipp'd cherubin" and subsequently as a "weed" so lovely "that the sense aches at thee" (IV. ii).

persists. The impression is one of overwhelming passion unable to express itself otherwise than in cold and distant imagery: the imagery, never quite freed from the conventional, of the sonnets. One could not imagine Antony making love to Cleopatra in these terms. Antony's love, at its moments of unimpeded expression, has at its command a vast, rich, unambiguous range of imagery; Othello's, thwarted by the course of his tragedy, cannot really surpass the conventional in its expression. Even when he is stressing the full happiness he had hoped to find in his love, he chooses to see perfection, not in terms of overflowing vitality, but in the chill flawlessness of a precious stone:

> Nay, had she been true,
> If heaven would make me such another world
> Of one entire and perfect *chrysolite*,
> I'd not have sold her for it.
>
> (V. ii)

It is not, indeed, in devotion to Desdemona that Othello expresses most powerfully the full possibilities of his nature. The strength of his passionately emotional being finds adequate expression, not in love, but in triumphant soldiership, in his reference to the

> Pride, pomp, and circumstance of glorious war.
>
> (III. iii)

Here in the poetry of action, untrammeled by reference to objects and needs beyond itself, the egoism essential to the character realizes itself fully and without hindrance. In Othello's love poetry the same intensity fails to express itself completely towards another person; it remains apparently cold on the surface, with an intense fire beneath that makes it the more capable of corruption.

This corruption, the central theme of the play, is the work of Iago. The image of the rose already referred to implies that of the "canker" which destroys it; the simultaneous presence of these twin aspects of passion is here given tragic projection in a clash of opposed attitudes. To understand fully the inadequacy of Othello's passion and the fact that it precedes his tragedy, we have to turn to Iago, for the two characters, as I have said, are contrasted aspects of a single situation. At first

sight the Ancient is all that his general is not, cynical and
"intellectual" where Othello is passionate and trusting to the
point of folly. These qualities, however, are not merely opposed but complementary. If Othello's passion expresses itself
in a peculiar coldness, Iago's cynicism and belittlement of
natural emotion are full of the feeling of "blood." "Blood," or
sexual emotion, is the driving force of his intelligence, although
it is a force always controlled and criticized by that intelligence.
He tells Desdemona on her arrival at Cyprus that he is "nothing
if not critical" (II. i), and he shows Roderigo a passionate
(that is the only word for it) contempt for "blood"; but it is
"blood" which is at the root of the man, criticism and all.
Consider the temper of his remarks to Roderigo, when he is
advancing the claims of reason and control:

If the balance of our lives had not one scale of reason to poise
another of sensuality, the blood and baseness of our natures would
conduct us to most preposterous conclusions; but we have reason
to cool our raging motions, our carnal stings, our unbitted lusts.

(I. iii)

How intensely we feel "blood" at work in the very criticism
of passion! "Reason" balances—"poises," as Shakespeare so delicately puts it—the scale of sensuality, foreseeing in its un-
checked operation the "most preposterous conclusions"; but
the vigour of the references to "raging motions," "carnal stings,"
and "unbitted lusts" demonstrates unmistakably the source of
Iago's peculiar vitality in action. His is, in fact, the reason of
Hamlet, perverted from its "god-like" function of harmonizing
the various human faculties in the pursuit of a clearly understood end to a principle of negation and destruction. Although
Iago sees at once more clearly and more perversely than Hamlet, his destructive attitude proceeds from the same inversion
of normal human functions, and his superior clarity only produces a greater consistency in negation. Where Hamlet's motives for neglecting life (and it is only this aspect of his character that now concerns us) are confused, contradictory, those
of Iago are consistently cynical and degrading; but the same
negative attitude toward the flesh is behind the judgements of
both. Iago's intellect dwells from the first pungently, insistently, upon the bestiality which underlies human passion; but the
presence of the despised emotions is implied in the very in-

tensity with which they are contemplated. It is impossible not to feel the intense sexuality behind his feverish activity in the dark at the opening of the play. Revealing itself in the persistent animality with which he incites Roderigo to disturb the "fertile climate" in which Othello dwells and so to "poison his delight," it dominates both the man and the scene:

> Even now, now, very now, an old black ram
> Is tupping your white ewe. Arise, arise;
> Awake the snorting citizens with the bell,
> Or else the devil will make a grandsire of you.

> (I. i)

The grotesque tone of the last lines in itself reflects the source of the intensity behind Iago's every action. The "passionate" Othello never expresses himself in love with such physical intensity as the sceptical, controlled Iago; in this paradox lies a key to the whole play.

It is Shakespeare's achievement to have converted into a tragedy this intuition of opposed emotions simultaneously present in a single situation. Othello and Iago, for the duration of their tragedy, live the conflict active in Shakespeare's imagination. If Iago represents the "canker" in the "rose" of Othello's love, we must watch that canker gaining ground step by step in the development of the intrigue. The egoistic elements in Othello's love must not only be defined; we must watch it crumble into helplessness and incoherence. The process must be strictly dramatic. The defects by which Iago engineers the downfall of his victim must be those first stated, or at least implied, in his own utterance. Othello, the tragic hero in his weakness and nobility, stands at the centre of the play. In his self-imposed consistency he is the point upon which the whole action turns; the forces which dissolve his integrity operate through the hostility of Iago by bringing to the surface his own deficiencies. The fusion of dramatic purpose and poetic impulse sought by Shakespeare in the self-defining complexities of the problem plays is at last achieved in the full objectivity of his first completely realized and in some ways most disquieting tragedy.

Shakespeare loses no time in indicating beneath the appearance of consistency and strength the fundamental weakness of his hero. One can detect from the first in Othello's every asser-

tion a note of self-dramatization, as though each action beyond its intrinsic importance must also be regarded as a contribution to the rhetorical fiction whose justification is a main
purpose of his life. His first utterance (I. ii) is a round assertion
of his royal lineage and of his services to Venice:

> My services, which I have done the signiory,
> Shall out-tongue his complaints. . . .
>
>   I fetch my life and being
>   From men of royal siege.

One need not deny the power of his impulsive rhetoric, while
sensing a touch of irony in the too-facile gesture to his audience which follows: "When I know that boasting is an honour." Othello's rapt declarations are not boasting, because
boasting implies a self-consciousness which is far from the
essential simplicity of the character; but they show a certain
barbaric complacency which has already allowed Iago to allude
to his speeches as "bombast circumstance" (I. i) and will shortly induce him to caricature his description of his love-making
as so much "bragging" and "fantastical lies." The complement
of this complacency, the defect of "a free and open nature,"
is the simplicity which leads Othello to think "men honest
that but seem to be so" (I. iii), to misread the motives of those
around him in the light of his own naïve self-esteem.

This complacency directly affects his love. Othello, in spite
of himself, submits with a touch of unwillingness to love. He
feels it somehow incongruous with the "unhoused free condition" in which alone his rhetorical instincts can attain full
expression; and even the first appearance of Desdemona, whose
love can so easily become for him a condition of "circum-
scription and confine," merely underlines the possibility of
tragedy. For Othello is rarely able to get sufficiently far from
himself to love Desdemona fully. His happiness in the opening
scenes is, like everything else in his character, self-centred,
naïve, even egoistic; and his account of his wooing makes this
clear. It was, in fact, by his passionate, simple-minded delight
in his own magnificent career that he won her, and—we may
fairly add—it was in no small part because she ministered to
his self-esteem that he valued her:

> She lov'd me for the dangers I had passed
> And I lov'd her *that she did pity them.*
>
> (I. iii)

Othello's estimate of his situation is nothing if not simple; but his simplicity is terribly, tragically vulnerable.

For the subtleties in the knot of passion, though neglected by him, are by no means excluded. Their existence is confirmed by the atmosphere of doubt and foreboding which surrounds Othello's love. For the Venetians around Desdemona, her relations with the "lascivious" Moor are mysterious, unnatural, and deeply disturbing. For her own father, who holds to the last that his child has deceived him, Desdemona's action proceeds from a perversion of the judgement, and passion is a poison, in inexplicable contrast with his daughter's docility, which acts through the erring senses and enslaves the will:

> A maiden never bold;
> Of spirit so still and quiet that her motion
> Blush'd at herself; and she—in spite of nature,
> Of years, of country, credit, everything—
> To fall in love with what she fear'd to look on! ...
>
> I therefore vouch again,
> That with some mixtures powerful o'er the blood,
> Or with some dram conjured to this effect,
> He wrought upon her.
>
> (I. iii)

In his perplexity Brabantio lays exaggerated emphasis upon his daughter's submissiveness until simplicity itself becomes, in this world of sophistication and scepticism, faintly equivocal. The adjectives "still" and "quiet" and the suggestion, barely indicated, of shame in "blush'd at herself" stand in a peculiar relationship to the mixtures "powerful o'er the blood" which have overcome her judgement. One need not, of course, in making this point, accept Iago's account of Desdemona as a "supersubtle Venetian" who has moulded the ingenuous "erring barbarian" to her purposes. Iago invariably pushes his own interpretations of human motive to the extreme indicated by his own peculiar logic, and in so doing falsifies true experience. He represents only one possible attitude—the least flattering—towards love, but this attitude is palpably relevant to what we may call the Venetian atmosphere of the play; it springs from reservations actually present in Shakespeare's experience and is not new to *Othello*. Like Isabella and even Ophelia before her, Desdemona has the power to exercise upon men an influence of whose nature and strength she remains until the last moment very largely unaware; and this power, given a logical basis and a perverse interpretation in Iago's "philosophy" of "nature," becomes a principle of dissolution and destruction.

If Othello's "nobility" provides one of the main conceptions upon which the closely knit structure of the play rests, the "critical" scepticism of Iago is certainly the other. Through his plotting, the mysterious poison which had worked, according to Brabantio, upon Desdemona becomes an active and sinister reality. For Iago *is* that poison, no longer hinted at or obscurely present in minds never fully conscious of it, but turned to destructive activity. According to his "philosophy," there is nothing in the world of "nature" to prevent desire from passing easily—and meaninglessly—from one object to another. In the case of Desdemona he contends that it must so pass:

Mark me with what violence she first loved the Moor, but for bragging and telling her fantastical lies; and will she love him still for prating? Let not thy discreet heart think it. Her eye must be fed; and what delight shall she have to look on the devil? When the blood is made dull with the act of sport, there should be again to inflame it and to give satiety a fresh appetite, loveliness in favour, sympathy in years, manners and beauties; all of which the Moor is defective in; now, for want of these required conveniences, her delicate tenderness will find itself abused, begin to heave the gorge, disrelish and abhor the Moor; very nature will instruct her in it and compel her to some second choice.

(II. i)

Love, being merely a prompting of the senses to which the will gives assent, needs to be continually "inflamed" if the blood itself is not to be "made dull with the act of sport." For love, as in *Troilus*, is simply an "appetite," intense but impermanent, like all sensual experience, and in particular like the impressions of taste. In the moment of fulfilment, Iago tells us, it is full of relish, of "delicate tenderness"; but it must continually be "fed," lest it turn to abhorrence, "disrelish" and "heave the gorge" in nausea at the former object of its choice. The original impulse, once satisfied, fatally demands renewal; without this, it turns to indifference and even to loathing. In this way the doubts and reservations that from the first accompany Othello's love in the minds of those who surround him are given clear logical expression. Brabantio had thought that Desdemona's choice of Othello, because prompted by irrational passion, was against the rules of nature; Iago, on the contrary, believes not only that the choice was natural but that "nature," which had brought her to it, would inevitably drive her to change. It is the conflict between this attitude, at once rational and essentially destructive, and Othello's generous but uncritical acceptance of the promptings of passion that is the subject of the play.

By the beginning of the second act the position of the chief characters in the play has been sufficiently defined. Iago's, in particular, is the part played by the "canker" that destroys the rose in the sonnets; to him is due the "festering" of the lily that turns beauty to corruption. But this conviction, having attained intellectual definition and the will to convert it into action, calls for dramatic representation in the interplay of motive and character. The process of disintegration to which Othello is subjected begins almost as soon as he arrives at Cyprus on his mission of war. Before the canker begins to work, however, Shakespeare balances the contrasted forces of the play one against the other. The day which opens with Othello's fortunate landing and should have been marked by the peaceful consummation of his marriage ends in a night of darkness and strife in which Iago's plot is fast taking shape. But before the destructive process begins, we are given one short glimpse of Othello in his happiness. Separated by stormy seas during their voyage from Venice, he meets Desdemona once more and enjoys a brief moment of fulfilment which, it seems, nothing in life can equal. His one desire is to hold this moment, to make it eternal:

> If it were now to die,
> 'Twere now to be most happy; for I fear,
> My soul hath her content so absolute
> That not another comfort like to this
> Succeeds in unknown fate.

> (II. i)

179

But even here Othello *fears*. This precarious moment of happiness will never find its fellow, for the temporal process is, as we have repeatedly seen, one of dissolution and decay. Only death can come between this temporary communion and its eclipse; but death, of course, implies the annihilation of the personality and the end of love. As soon as the lovers have left the scene, Iago's destructive cynicism returns—in the critical tone of his dialogue with Roderigo—to become the driving force of the action. From this moment it never loses the initiative.

The transition from concord and fulfilment to passion-driven strife is handled by Shakespeare with considerable care. In the following scenes (II. ii, iii) the motives of felicity and disillusionment are simultaneously developed. It is night, the night in which Othello has announced "the celebration of his nuptial," but also the night in which Iago's activity turns rejoicing into savagery and drunkenness. His instrument to this end is Cassio, in whom all his unflattering conclusions with regard to love find their confirmation. We shall only understand Iago's part in this tragedy if we realize that he plays throughout upon the real weaknesses of his victims. These weaknesses he elevates, following his "philosophy," into consistent principles, turning what is largely infirmity, susceptibility, or indecision into a positive tendency to evil; but his observations, though they do not account fully for the behaviour of his victims, always pick on something really vulnerable in them. And that something is invariably connected with desire or "appetite." Cassio's imagination, stirred by Iago, lingers upon Desdemona with intense but passing sensuality. She is "exquisite," "a fresh and delicate creature," with an "inviting" though "right modest eye." He regards her, in short, as a choice morsel to be contemplated, tasted, and enjoyed, so Iago, in speaking of "provocation" and "an alarum to love" (II. iii), simply gives substance to an innermost thought. For Iago merely brings consistency to unrealized desires, which thereby become in his hands instruments all the more dangerous for being imperfectly understood by his victims. Having observed in Cassio just sufficient "loose affections" to make his accusations plausible, he uses him to bring out Othello's unconsidered sensuality, to ruin his judgement and destroy his peace.

By inflaming the fuddled Cassio to act, Iago releases the

forces of passion on the island. As the drunken revelry, prevailing, takes the mind prisoner, so jealousy creeps into Othello's mind through Iago's action upon the instability which makes his will—unknown to himself—the slave of passion. Othello, as we have seen, has neglected the part played by physical desire in his "free and bounteous" love for Desdemona; Iago, for whom all love is simply the reaching-out of such desire for gratification, gives a very different interpretation of the Moor's character:

> His soul is so enfetter'd to her love,
> That she may make, unmake, do what she list,
> Even as her appetite shall play the god
> With his weak function.
>
> (II. iii)

It was precisely this idea of being "enfettered" by his love that Othello had so confidently rejected in asking permission to bring Desdemona to Cyprus (I. iii); it offended his belief in himself as a warrior and as a man. But Iago's action, based as always on the rationalization of affection as "appetite," aims directly at the dissolution of this heroic simplicity and at subduing Othello by bringing out the animal beneath.

In this he succeeds with surprising ease: surprising, that is, unless we remember how Shakespeare has prepared the way by stressing the Moor's disastrous ingenuousness. Iago knows that his victim, once confused, is lost, so his primary aim is to involve him in uncertainty. For Othello is quite incapable of suspending judgement. Suspense offends his self-confidence, contrasts with the capacity for action upon which he prides himself. His nature demands an immediate resolution, which can in practice be nothing but an acceptance of Iago's insinuations:

> . . . to be once in doubt
> Is once to be resolved; exchange me for a goat,
> When I shall turn the business of my soul
> To such exsufflicate and blown surmises,
> Matching thy inference.
>
> (III. iii)

Few things in Othello are more damning than this continual tendency to protest rhetorically against the presence of the very weaknesses that are undoing him. He refers contemptuously to the "goat," the most notorious symbol of sensuality, just as Iago is poisoning his mind through his "blood"-inspired imagination; and the reference, strengthened by the sense in "exsufflicate" of the beast breathing heavily in the external manifestations of passion, is at once grotesque and significant.

Flattering his victim's "free and open nature," Iago proceeds to clip the wings of his freedom and to convert his frankness into suspicion. Having first deprived him of certainty, he plays upon his sensual fancy, describes Cassio's "dream" with a full insistence upon the grossness of physical contacts, and makes him visualize the sin by which Desdemona is offending his self-esteem. Othello responds to these insinuations with an intensity that proceeds from hitherto unsuspected aspects of his nature. He demands instant proof. The completeness of his fall is reflected in the gross irony implicit in his demand: "Villain, be sure thou prove my love a whore," and Iago leads him on with a sneer that now works like poison on his fantasy:

> . . . how satisfied, my lord?
> Would you, the supervisor, grossly gape on?
> Behold her tupp'd?
>
> (III. iii)

Here, besides rousing still further the sensual elements in his imagination, Iago touches Othello at his most vulnerable point; he offends him in his personal respect. His reaction is a characteristic mixture of pathetic bewilderment and defiant self-esteem. Conscious of the racial difference which separates him from the Venetians around him and vaguely aware of a mortifying social inferiority,

> Haply, for I am black,
> And have not those soft parts of conversation,
> That chamberers have . . .

he thrusts aside the doubt that assails him in the man of action's superior reference to "chamberers," only to fall at once into a further uncertainty of a more concrete and, perhaps, for him of a more mortifying kind:

> . . . or, for I am declined
> Into the vale of years.

The instinctive reaction—"yet that's not much"—is not sufficient to undo the final impression of failure, openly recognized in the conclusion,

> I am abused, and my relief
> Must be to loathe her . . .

in which misery and outraged self-respect compete for precedence. Iago's very boldness, in fact, has won its point. He must have been very sure of the Moor's blindness to work upon him with so gross a caricature, but his confidence has been justified by the event. For the caricature, for all its grossness, has roused not Othello's indignation, but his outraged self-esteem; and the grossness of the approach has brought to the surface the destructive forces of his neglected animal instincts.

The increasing insolence—one can call it nothing else—of Iago's comments as he comes to realize that his success is assured is most notable. Perhaps the irony reaches its climax when the plotter makes his victim stand aside and assist in silence at what he imagines to be Cassio's account of Desdemona's infidelity (IV. i). Every word is a mortal wound for Othello's pride. Iago sneers, and disclaims the sneer with a phrase that is itself an affirmation of contempt:

> OTHELLO. Dost thou mock me?
> IAGO.   I mock you! no, by heaven,
> Would you would bear your fortune *like a man.*

He roundly taxes the heroic Othello with lack of manliness:

> Whilst you were here o'erwhelmed with your grief—
> *A passion most unsuiting such a man—*
> Cassio came hither. . .

>   Marry, patience;
> Or I shall say you are all in all in spleen,
> *And nothing of a man.*

>   (IV. i)

Nothing could do more than this savage element of caricature in Iago's treatment of Othello to convey the degradation of the victim; no better foil to the Moor's earlier rhetoric—rhetoric which stands in the closest relationship to the subsequent tragedy—could be conceived.

A few ambiguous phrases, a trick almost infantile in its simplicity, and a persistent inflaming of the sensual imagination of his victim, and Iago has reduced Othello to an absolute slavery to passion. He himself, in a solitary moment, describes perfectly his own method and achievement:

> The Moor already changes with my poison:
> Dangerous conceits are in their nature poisons:
> Which at the first are scarce found to distaste,
> But with a little act upon the blood,
> Burn like the mines of sulphur.
>
> (III. iii)

The relation of poison to taste, and of both to the action of the "blood," is by now familiar. It describes the process which has reduced Othello's egoism to incoherence. He now sees himself, in his imagination, betrayed; and it is the knowledge, rather than the betrayal, which affects him:

> I had been happy, if the general camp,
> Pioners and all, had tasted her sweet body,
> *So I had nothing known.*
>
> (III. iii)

The form of this confession is highly revealing. The problem of *Othello* is the problem of consciousness, of the relationship of instinctive life to critical detachment. It is precisely because knowledge, reason, is in *Othello* a destructive faculty at war with heroic simplicity that the tragedy takes place. By the end of this scene Othello's new "knowledge" has had two consequences. It has destroyed the simplicity upon which his real nobility had been based, and it has roused his own sensual impulses to a destructive fury. Sensual passion and prowess in action are, in Othello, mutually exclusive; the entry of the one implies the dissolution of the coherence and self-confidence necessary to the other. The very man who had once declared that the "young affects" of sensuality were in him defunct (I. iii) now breaks out into the poignant physical intensity of the phrase "*tasted* her *sweet* body." But it is significant that when he becomes aware that his peace is undermined beyond hope, he refers to his loss, not first of Desdemona, but of his integrity as a warrior. On the one hand, the loss of his military prowess in action:

> Farewell, the tranquil mind, farewell, content!
> Farewell, the plumed troop, and the big wars
> That make ambition virtue;
>
> (III. iii)

on the other, that sense of Desdemona's supposed promiscuity which grows upon him till Iago can make the ironic comment,

"I see, sir, you are eaten up with passion!" Othello's further history is no more than the aggravation of the condition here defined.

The scene in which these developments take place forms a kind of pivot upon which the whole subsequent action turns. At the end of it Othello's fate is sealed, and we have only to trace the growth in him of destructive animal feeling and the crumbling into futility of his personal pride. As it closes, Othello abjures love and invokes vengeance in a speech which reveals the changing temper of his emotions:

> Like to the Pontic sea,
> Whose icy current and compulsive course
> Ne'er feels retiring ebb, but keeps due on
> To the Propontic and the Hellespont;
> Even so my bloody thoughts, with violent pace,
> Shall ne'er look back, ne'er ebb to humble love,
> Till that a capable and wide revenge
> Swallow them up. Now, by yond marble heaven,
> In the due reverence of a sacred vow,
> I here engage my words.
>
> (III. iii)

The full rhetoric so typical of the character is still present in the ample opening gesture of the speech; but the power by which Othello is brought to imagine the Pontic Sea in its irresistible course is the rising "violent" power of "blood," abjuring love—by a vital contradiction—and dedicating itself—but in the fulness of a passion frozen into an "*icy* current"—to revenge. Iago's preceding comment, "your mind perhaps may change," is, as usual, perfectly timed to rouse the opposite reaction in Othello. Thwarted in love, his egoism will be consistent in revenge, decisive, irresistible; all the intensity of sensual feeling which was never fully gratified in his relations with Desdemona is now to be exercised in exacting retribution for the ruin of his integrity. The type of passion so notably absent from his declarations of love (or at least so constrained in their expression) reveals itself in a craving for destruction which Iago's activity ceaselessly nourishes.

As the plot advances, and Iago's control over Othello grows, the element of "blood," which had been lacking in his expressions of love, makes a disturbing appearance—disturbing because it does not come to give warmth and embodiment to passion, but rather appears as an acute and terrible repulsion against all contacts of the body. We see and feel its effects when he falls into a fit and mumbles frenziedly, in the presence of the mocking and exultant Iago, about "noses, ears, and lips!" (IV. i) We feel them in those bestial phrases in which his outraged egoism gropes towards its revenge: "I'll tear her all to pieces" (III. iii); "I see that nose of yours, but not that dog I shall throw it to" (IV. i); and still more in the combination of affronted self-respect and rising savagery which prompts the exclamation, "I will chop her into messes; cuckold me!" (IV. i) But they appear most clearly of all, and in closer relation to the love they are corroding, in that terrible scene (IV. ii) in which the crazed Othello turns, with a mixture of intense physical attraction and open repulsion, upon Desdemona. The feeling in that scene, it is important to note, is very reminiscent of the sonnets. Desdemona is a *"rose*-lipp'd cherubin"—such imagery, a compound of poetic convention and deep emotion, is very characteristic—and Othello's loathing is expressed in typical sense imagery:

DESDEMONA. I hope my noble lord esteems me honest.
OTHELLO.　　O, ay; as summer flies are in the shambles,
　　　　　　That quicken even with blowing. O thou weed,
　　　　　　Who art so lovely fair and smell'st so sweet
　　　　　　That the sense aches at thee, would thou had'st ne'er
　　　　　　been born.

(IV. ii)

The mention of "weed," the reminiscence of convention behind "lovely fair," and the keen evocation—almost unnaturally sensitive—of the faculty of smell are all suggestive of the sonnets. Like "lilies that fester," their effect depends upon a sharp opposition of acute sense impressions. The intensity of desire implied in "sense aches at thee" and the feeling for life behind "quicken" are set against the loathing which produced "shambles" and the "blowing" of the flies. "Blowing" is especially subtle in that it speaks of the generation of flies out of corruption while using a word that suggests the opening of the rosebud into mature beauty. The reminiscence of the sonnets is not accidental, for *Othello* is precisely a dramatic representation of the inevitable degeneration, in a world where "value" has no foundation, of desire into selfish and destructive appetite.

This surrender to bestiality brings with it the collapse of Othello's integrity as a person. He expresses himself, as I have suggested, most confidently in the egoistic poetry of war; and it is significant that his acceptance of Iago's insinuations is regarded by him as tantamount to a renunciation of his prowess as a soldier. As his ruin proceeds, the egoism which had always been a part of his character comes more and more to the fore, not in connection with military glory, but rather in his attitude towards his own folly. In the last scene this folly is completely unmasked. Emilia addresses him as "dull Moor," and his own comment is as simple as it is true—"O fool, fool, fool!" Yet, in spite of all his folly, his egoism contains a considerable degree of tragic dignity. The weakness and the tragedy stand, in fact, in the closest relationship. The great speeches in which he attains tragic stature by expressing his "nobility," are, at the same time, merciless exposures of weakness. In the first of them, made to Desdemona, what emerges above all is the unpreparedness of the speaker to meet the situation in which he finds himself. Had life presented to Othello a problem which could have been met by the active creation of a nobility at once true and flattering to his self-esteem, all—we are told—would have been well.

> Had it pleased heaven
> To try me with affliction,

he begins, and in cataloguing the forms which that affliction might have taken we feel the speaker recovering confidence, assuring himself that in resistance too there is a kind of heroism, that the exercise of patience to the limit of endurance is not incompatible with his conception of his own moral dignity. It is only in the latter part of the speech that we are shown the true source of Othello's suffering:

> . . . but, alas, to make me
> A fixed figure for the time of scorn
> To point his slow, unmoving finger at!
>
> (IV. ii)

To become an object of ridicule without being able to react, to assert his own "nobility"—this is the shame from which Othello feels that there is no escape, and which accompanies him to his tragic end.

That end adds little that is new to our knowledge of his character. As T. S. Eliot has noted,[2] Othello's last speech is more than a piece of splendid self-centred poetry (though it is most certainly that); it is also the dupe's attempt at self-justification in an irrelevant pose:

> I have done the state some service and they know't. . . .
>
>   Then must you speak
> Of one that loved not wisely but too well;
> Of one not easily jealous, but, being wrought,
> Perplexed in the extreme.
>
>   (V. ii)

Who, in point of fact, has ever been more easily jealous than Othello? It is, we feel, splendid declamation, but it is also largely beside the point. For the real point lies in the presence of Desdemona's body, killed by the speaker himself in his own blindness, and the speech is not only "poetry" but the revelation of a character. "Perplexed," betrayed by emotions he has never really understood, Othello's last words are a pathetic return to his original simplicity of nature. Unable to cope effectively with the complicated business of living, he recalls his generous past and commits the simple act of suicide. But already the critical acid applied by Iago has destroyed the structure of his greatness.

I have attempted by analysis to bring out the advance in Shakespeare's dramatic power represented by *Othello*. His control of the intrigue is far more complete than it had ever been in the problem plays. In *Hamlet* and *Measure for Measure* plot and poetry are still comparatively separate entities; Hamlet's soliloquies are imperfectly fused with the rather disjointed action of the play, and the Duke's function vacillates between the engineering of the plot and the resolution of its problems in terms of poetic "symbolism." *Othello* is very different. The process by which Iago undermines Othello's confidence is perfectly reflected in the corrupting entry of his cynical, destructive "blood" imagery into his victim's noble but self-contained poetry. Plot and imagery, dramatic development and poetic expression are fused as never before. It is significant that this growth in control over material corresponds to a clearer

[2] In his essay on "Shakespeare and the Stoicism of Seneca" in *Selected Essays* (London: Faber & Faber, 1932), pp. 130–31.

distinction beween the conflicting emotions whose projection into opposed characters is the chief feature of the play. We might even say that there can be traced in *Othello* the beginnings of the process by which the contrasted attitudes towards experience simultaneously present in the sonnets and problem plays are eventually separated out into an opposition of "good" and "evil." The words "good" and "evil" are, of course, to be used with care. The most that we can securely say is that "evil" is connected with the elements of frustration, of disharmony, in the problem plays, and "good" with the full, balanced ordering of experience which eventually produced Shakespeare's latest comedies. *Othello*, of course, is still far from such ordering. The prevailing tenour of the play is still destructive—so much so, maybe, that it is lacking in proper moral balance and does not give complete satisfaction as a work of art. But, in spite of all the interrelation of imagery, Iago is felt to be definitely opposed to Othello in the dramatic scheme. In spite of all his shortcomings, Othello is felt to be connected with love and natural emotion; and there is nothing grudging about the nobility which Shakespeare confers upon him at his best moments. Iago, on the other hand, is felt, for all his superior "intelligence," to be at once limited and evil; in fact, he is Shakespeare's personal development of the conventional Machiavellian villain of the stage. Within the unity still (as always) imposed by related imagery and by a closely continued dramatic scheme, we are for the first time within reach of the decisive orientation of Shakespearean good and evil in *Macbeth*.

XIV

WILLIAM FROST

Shakespeare's Rituals and the Opening of *King Lear*

In a provocative article, "Shakespeare and the Use of Disguise in Elizabethan Drama,"[1] Miss M. C. Bradbrook calls attention to the pervasiveness in Shakespeare's plays of what she terms an "overlaying . . . of dramatic identity, whereby one character sustains two roles." Taken in her broad sense, which includes far more than mere matters of costuming, disguise strikes me as having at least two distinct potential advantages to the Elizabethan, if not to the modern, dramatist. In the first place, it is an obvious extension of the basic theatrical convention according to which a group of human beings, the actors, pretend to be other people for the purposes of the play. Thus disguise has its roots in the very nature of drama, as distinguished from other literary forms. In the second place, in respect to the theatre's relation to real life, disguise, or the understanding that a character in a play is assuming some other role than his "true" one, bypasses a problem of literal verisimilitude and liberates both actor and playwright for more imaginative uses of language, gesture, costume, and action. When Edgar plays poor Tom it is understood as a basic premise that he *is* "counterfeiting" ("My tears begin to take his part so much/They'll mar my counterfeiting"—III. vi. 63–64), so that for performer and script-writer alike the question of "realistic" or documentary presentation of a typical Bedlam beggar is less than urgent. Edgar the son of Gloucester, being neither a professional actor nor a professional social worker, will presumably be acceptable

Reprinted from the *Hudson Review* (Winter, 1957–58) by permission of the author and the editor.

[1] *Essays in Criticism* (1952), II, 159–68. The phrases quoted are on page 160.

if he plays the Tom o' Bedlam his imagination conceives. Similarly, the lines spoken by a character playing a "false" or secondary role—whether voluntary or involuntary, for Miss Bradbrook treats madness as one form of disguise—are obviously open to heightening, to special rhetorical effects, on the dramatist's part.

An analogous element in Elizabethan drama, it seems to me, is ritual, or what might be called the ceremonial situation. Like disguise, it is probably connected with the nature of dramatic art at its very core, if the theories of anthropologists and classical scholars be correct. And like disguise again, ritual can operate to free both actor and playwright from the demands of strict verisimilitude, for the participants in a rite are assumed a priori to act parts and to speak language not simply their own or natural to them as individuals, but traditional or appropriate in some way to a publicly acknowledged occasion. I should like to extend the term "ritual" here to include any speech or situation which will be felt by participants or spectators to be predictable in important respects. In this sense ritual would include not only marriages and funerals, like those in *Much Ado* or *Julius Caesar;* not only prayers, curses, and invocations, like those in *Hamlet* and *King Lear;* not only coronation processions and depositions; not only banquets, dances, masques, and such theatrical entertainments as plays-within-a-play; but also ceremonial arrivals and departures, like the splendid send-off given Antony by Cleopatra in Act I, the "further compliment of leave-taking" between France and Lear, or Cassio's welcome of Desdemona to Cyprus; trial scenes, whether in court, as in *Measure for Measure* and *The Merchant of Venice,* by combat, as in *Richard II* and *King Lear,* or by senatorial investigation, as in *Othello;* obituary announcements and their reception; kisses on the fourteenth lines of sonnets; the swearing of oaths, as in *Love's Labour's Lost* and *Hamlet;* acts of banishment; graveyard visits, such as the "obsequies and true love's rite" of County Paris; and finally scenes in which a ruler holds court, as at or near the beginning of *Richard II, Henry IV,* Part I, *Twelfth Night, Measure for Measure, Hamlet,* and *King Lear.* All such scenes are capable of greater or less formality on the stage, as the dramatist desires. The preparations for Bolingbroke's combat with Mowbray are extended and stately, the farewell of Hotspur to Kate so abrupt as to amount to an anti-ritual.

Ritual has these characteristics, at least: it is ordinarily public, it is deliberate, and it is presumed to be predictable, in outline if not in detail. When Richard is sent for it is known that he will give up the crown; when Claudius assembles his court he has already decided what action to take against Fortinbras. Such a scene as the opening of *Henry IV*, Part I, has some of the elements of a state-of-the-union message, and some of those of a presidential press conference. Like such throne-room scenes, trial scenes are normally intensely public, and while their outcome—as in *Measure for Measure*—may actually astonish participants and spectators alike, the fact that there will be an outcome, and of a certain kind, is well understood in advance. Since ritual is frequently felt to express simple appropriateness to an occasion at least as much as practical, purposive utility, the sort of language used in it can be heightened in various ways without appearing needlessly artificial; this fact no doubt partly accounts for its frequent appearance in verse-drama especially, whether of the seventeenth or the twentieth century.

The various advantages of ritual to drama, however, probably do not need stressing at the moment. Any one who has seen a good performance of the conjuring scene in *Doctor Faustus* or of the conclusion of the first act of *Heartbreak House* will be aware of its theatrical effectiveness. Furthermore, Western theatre has been for so long predominantly naturalistic and antiritualistic, and life in America today is so intent on discarding whatever vestigial rituals may still be about (we don't have speeches from the throne, we have fireside chats), that criticism is perhaps occasionally in danger of becoming hypnotized by idealized visions of a more largely ceremonial stagecraft. One particularly ritual-happy critic, for example, has observed of *Hamlet* that "on stage, the music and the drums and the marching of royal and military pageantry, are directly absorbing, and they assure us that something of great and general significance is going on."[2] If they only could, how easy to write a tragedy! Or how little eccentric would have appeared the man in the Broadway farce who *liked* to attend commencements! Against the strong intoxication of boom-boom, tramp-tramp dramaturgy perhaps it is time to

[2] Francis Fergusson, *The Idea of a Theater* (New York: Anchor Books), p. 124.

make the point that, like patriotism, ritual is not enough. In this essay I should like to comment on some of its drawbacks, and to conclude with an example of Shakespeare's power to transcend them.

"The trick of that voice I do well remember," says the blinded Gloucester, on being addressed as Goneril-with-a-white-beard; "Is't not the King?" "The trick of that voice"—for all the patterns of imagery, the ironic paradoxes, and the strong concatenated plots, it is still by the tricks of their voices that we remember the Shakespearean tribe, by Falstaff's "They hate us youth" or Regan's "What need one?" But a primary effect of much ritual is to damp down the oscillations of personality, subduing them to the exigencies of what is ceremonial, appropriate, and expected. For me the basic objection to Gertrude's obituary on Ophelia ("There is a willow grows aslant a brook/That shows his hoar leaves in the grassy stream") is not the standard naturalistic one that Gertrude, if she saw all this, should have jumped in and stopped it; but rather that the all-too-appropriate pastoral-cum-phallic imagery in her oration has an inevitably depersonalizing effect on Gertrude herself. There is the same sort of difficulty about the ritual insanity of Ophelia. In a play where the women theoretically account for so much of the motivation of protagonist and antagonist alike, ceremonial decoration may trespass too perilously on the narrow budget of lines allowed to female roles. Early in *Antony and Cleopatra*, on the other hand, the balanced formal appeals of Caesar to Antony and of Pompey to Cleopatra shortly afterwards—the set speeches beginning "Antony,/Leave thy lascivious wassails" and "But all the charms of love,/Salt Cleopatra, soften thy waned lip!"—these appeals seem to me vigorous and functional, for they strengthen one's awareness both of the situation's urgency and of the fissure in Antony's nature. For the moment, tricks of voice in Pompey and Octavius might well be merely diverting; these politicians are here part of a frame, not parts of the picture.

Besides its possible blotting-out effects on individuality of character, ritual also involves the danger of mechanizing action, of replacing possible real significance with an illusion of built-in significance. The very guarantee-in-advance of drama carried by a marriage or a trial may be disastrous; having one's initials engraved on an electric toaster does not essentially "personalize" the operations of the gadget. The more obviously ingenious the contrivance, the greater the danger of its developing into a marionette dance:

> Good shepherd, tell this youth what 'tis to love.
>
> It is to be made all of sighs and tears,
> And so am I for Phebe.
>
> And I for Ganymede.
>
> And I for Rosalind.
>
> And I for no woman.

What might have been an emotion becomes in effect a conundrum.

There is also the temptation for the dramatist to extract an added *frisson* from ritual by interrupting it, as when the King throws down his gage in *Richard II*, the bridegroom answers "No!" in *Much Ado About Nothing*, or an unexpected guest appears for dinner in *Macbeth*. As for the first of these three occasions, I do not know if it has been pointed out that John of Gaunt's get-in-there-and-fight-son speech to Bolingbroke ("God in thy good cause make thee prosperous!/Be swift like lightning in the execution. . . .") consorts somewhat oddly with the fact, made clear later in the scene, that Gaunt has known all along what Bolingbroke's real fate is to be: that is, banishment, not a chance of death at Mowbray's hands.[3] Nor can the weak staginess of the lists-at-Coventry scene be well defended, in my opinion, on the grounds that it adumbrates a fatal staginess in Richard's nature; it exists in the play all too clearly for its own theatrical sake, whatever the incidental advantages to characterization. I am inclined to make a similar point about the elaborate trial scene in *The Merchant of Venice*. If Portia has really discovered a law that any alien who plots against the life of a Venetian forfeits his own property, and if Shylock's original bond with Antonio really constituted such a plot in the meaning of this early Mundt-Nixon-like legislation, then all the previous manoeuvering that followed her appearance in the scene, including the "quality-of-mercy-is-not-strained" speech, the interchanges about "a Daniel come to judgement," and so forth—all this is in danger of remaining

---

[3] Kittredge, however, believes that the council meeting to decide on the banishment takes place on stage during a trumpet flourish, just after the king intervenes and prevents the fight.

manoeuvers, not war; and manoeuvers with cleverly painted wooden guns, at that. If Shylock has really walked into such a standing trap from the outset—though a trap mysteriously unapparent to the best legal minds in Venice, until Portia's arrival —where is the celebrated "mercy" in duping him into supposing that his bond with Antonio has been for one instant valid?

The standard answer to such logical objections is that the very order of events on the stage will prevent an audience, swept on from crisis to crisis, from ever raising them; and I agree that it is only when the reel is run through backwards, so to speak, that the patching becomes apparent. But even allowing that the two scenes I have just cited carry their own illusion with them, they still illustrate, in my opinion, ritual running away with a play for the moment and substituting its own kind of gaudy satisfaction for the deeper satisfactions of drama. The interlocking trial scenes that make up the last act of *Measure for Measure*, though more elaborate and far less naturalistic than the trial in the *Merchant*, seem relatively successful, being sustained by previous allegorical elements in the play's structure and theme. Furthermore (and I think the point a crucial one) we as audience do not discover only at the conclusion of the trial that the Duke has had the answers all in his pocket in advance; we know from the start of the act that he has them, and we know what they are. Compared to each other, the two trial scenes show a development away from merely sensational suspense and towards maturer irony.

Even in *Measure for Measure*, however, the kind of dramatic interest attaching to the various final revelations and dispensations remains at a further remove from life than the kind attaching to those earlier scenes in which Angelo confronts Isabella, or Isabella Claudio. It is no accident, I think, that the greatest poetry of the play is concentrated in the first half, while conflict reigns and before planning has taken over. The play's enormous concern with the nature of justice, the probing of motive, and the clash between surface and depths perhaps sustain the transition to allegory and the various *coups de théâtre* of the ritualistic finale; but in the transition, passionate individuality gives way before the iron march of pattern, and human beings in whose dilemmas we have been invited to sink our consciousness suddenly become presented to us from the outside, like figures (as indeed they now are) in a comedy.

Ritual triumphs, but its triumph is a symptom of something that has happened to the play.

Probably no scene in any of Shakespeare's mature tragedies is more overtly ritualistic in construction and in language than the holding of court that opens *King Lear;* all the force of Dryden's comment on rime in drama—that it will sound as though the speakers in a dialogue had got together and composed it in advance—would seem to apply to this gathering. First Lear speaks, announcing fully and formally what is about to happen; then come the questioning of the daughters in order of age, the breakdown of the four-part liturgy (challenge, response, comment, award) on its third performance, the ceremonial quarrel with Cordelia, followed by formal disinheritance, the ceremonial quarrel with Kent, followed by formal banishment, Kent's elaborate farewells, the public rejection of Cordelia by Burgundy, her ritual wooing by France, and a cluster of antiphonal farewells as the court breaks up. Except for Cordelia's sudden "Nothing"—a violent momentary break in the proceedings—the scene, even at its most passionate moments, is conducted in blank verse of a Byzantine stateliness, if not, indeed, in rime:

> Thy dow'rless daughter, King, thrown to my chance
> Is queen of us, of ours, and our fair France.
> Not all the dukes in wat'rish Burgundy
> Can buy this unpriz'd precious maid of me.

It used to be fashionable to call couplets not unlike those of France—at least when produced a century or so later by Pope or Dryden—frigid and lifeless; and indeed as recently as 1927 Professor Allardyce Nicoll has written that "One could have wished it were possible to prove that these lines were not by Shakespeare or that they were remnants of an earlier *Lear* of his callow youth, but we may accept them, I think, as his own, manifesting in their stiffness and mental rigidity the dramatist's recognition of his own failure to make his scene live and his obvious desire to push on to more congenial subject-matter." For Nicoll, as a matter of fact, the whole first scene of *Lear* is "a failure" and "easily the most uninteresting long scene of the drama." Here, surely, by contrast to the point of view of some more recent critics, we find modern uneasiness with ritual, and opposition to it, stated in the most uncompromising terms.

What can be said in defense of the scene?

In the first place, if it must be viewed as allegory, then as allegory, at least, it holds together extremely well. Its basic constituents are simply two contests of affection, the first among Goneril, Regan, and Cordelia; the second between France and Burgundy. That the second is a neat and ironic commentary on the first comes out in France's courteous lines to the reluctant Burgundy:

> My Lord of Burgundy,
> What say you to the lady? Love's not love
> When it is mingled with regards that stand
> Aloof from th' entire point. Will you have her?
> She is herself a dowry.

The aphorism about the nature of love, though not so intended by France, who was absent from the earlier contest, sums up the moral issue involved in that contest, and prepares for the appropriately religious formality of France's ensuing proposal:

> Fairest Cordelia, that art most rich, being poor;
> Most choice, forsaken; and most lov'd, despis'd. . . .

To the level of the preceding action no other style of declaration could possibly be adequate. It is no wonder that Granville-Barker finds "an actor of authority and distinction" requisite for this briefest, but not least important, of roles in the scene.[4]

In the second place, the balanced ceremony of the scene accords well with the mythic, the folkloristic nature of the story as it came down from the old chronicles to Shakespeare: the story of an ancient king of Britain who had three daughters, of whom two were evil and one was good. Such fairy-tale materials, of course, underlie more than one of Shakespeare's plots, and he has various ways of handling them; here, his method is the simplest and boldest possible: all questions of motivation are bypassed at the outset, and we start with the naked myth. For given such a myth, to raise the question of motive would be to undermine dramatic effect in advance. As the earlier play *King Leir* surely demonstrates sufficiently, any conceivable rationalization is bound to be weak and inadequate.

In the third place, the machine-like quality of ritual produces, in the first part of the scene, precisely the effect of nightmarish inevitability most useful, I think, for certain sorts

---

[4] *Prefaces to Shakespeare* (1947), I, 321 n.

tragedy. The driver is fully and terrifyingly in control of the car; every piston functions smoothly; and the road ends in a precipice just around the next corner. Any suggestion of deliberation, hesitation, or wavering between alternatives would but confuse and perplex the appalling spectacle.

I have so far mentioned only elements *within* the scene. There is also the question of its relation to the play as a whole, a relation mainly one of several sorts of contrast. In the first place there is the contrast, well commented on by S. L. Bethell, among other critics, between the rituals and their framework, those brief prose interchanges between Kent and Gloucester before the ceremonies start and between Goneril and Regan after they conclude. The prose dialogues are casual, colloquial, and the reverse of mythic in atmosphere. Because they allude to the motivation of the central figure in the rites without really attempting to explain it, they give the effect of going backstage and hearing the actors comment on the play. By this means the gap between ritual and more naturalistic drama is bridged at the same time that ritual itself is thrown into high relief.

Second, there is the contrast between Lear's courtroom and Goneril's household, where we get our second look at the King. In the household, action and imagery alike are trivial, domestic, and haphazard; again the effect is of going backstage, where fancy dress is partly thrown off, make-up smudged, and wigs awry. This effect is only temporary, however, for tension rises throughout the scene till, at its close, in curses and quarrel, Lear is evidently remounting an imaginary throne—how pathetically and ironically imaginary Goneril's reassurances of Albany remind us. The Lear who had disinherited Cordelia and banished Kent retains a power of banishment, but only over himself.

The third contrast is with the storm-and-madness scenes at the center of the play. In these, Lear, now unable to distinguish imaginary thrones from real ones, pardons Gloucester for adultery and pronounces a death sentence on Kent for treason:

> KENT [*speaking of Edgar*]. He hath no daughters, sir.
> LEAR. Death, traitor! nothing could have subdu'd nature
> To such a lowness but his unkind daughters.

In these scenes are embodied one enormous parody after another of the ritualistic opening of the play. Of the trial scene in the farmhouse Granville-Barker remarks: "Where Lear, such a short while since, sat in his majesty, there sit the Fool and the outcast, with Kent whom he banished beside them; and he, witless, musters his failing strength to beg justice upon a joint stool. Was better justice done, the picture ironically asks, when he presided in majesty and sanity and power?"[5] The trial scene in the farmhouse, moreover, is followed immediately by a yet more monstrous parody, the justice done on Gloucester by Regan and Cornwall.

Disorder of various sorts is basic to these central scenes. It is no longer as though we had passed backstage to observe the actors in their dressing gowns, but as though the theatre itself had suddenly been shaken by an earthquake, and the actors were improvising amid falling masonry. They seem continually to grasp for some shred of ceremony as the boards tremble beneath them and the footlights flicker uncertainly. "Come, sit thou here, most learned justicer," Lear beseeches the blanketed Edgar in the farmhouse. "Though well we may not pass upon his life/Without the form of justice," begins Cornwall at the trial of Gloucester, towards the end of which two stagehands, panic-stricken, suddenly refuse to cooperate longer, and one of them hastily murders the chief actor. On the cliffs of Dover, even scenery has to be openly improvised out of nothing.

The final contrast is between the opening and the conclusion of the play. At this conclusion, both in the reunion with Cordelia and in the final spectacle, ritual has lost all relevance to the King. His "I am a very foolish fond old man,/Fourscore and upward" is like Cleopatra's "No more but e'en a woman, and commanded/By such poor passion as the maid that milks/ And does the meanest chares"; but it is more final than Cleopatra's self-regarding momentary dethronement. We are now in the presence, not of the ceremonies by which human beings encompass their condition, the *rites de passage* of the anthropologists, but of the barest facts of that condition itself. King and daughter, no longer figures in myth or allegory, come before us fragile, irreplaceable, and particular, a pair of jailbirds and losers.

Meanwhile, however, the earthquake is subsiding and the stage getting swept up so that orderly drama can go forward. Act V is emphatically not without ritual, the chief rite being,

5 *Ibid.*, p. 294.

of course, the trial by combat which restores Edgar to status and inheritance, eliminates Edmund, and leaves the political field clear for Albany at last. Many commentators have analysed the double plot structure of *King Lear*, mostly in regard to its universalizing effect on the conflict of the generations; another important result of the subplot is that it keeps everybody so busy, especially at the end of the play. Wars have to be fought, traitors unmasked, and a final contest of affection adjudicated between Regan and Goneril, whose love rivalry for Edmund ironically parallels that of France and Burgundy for Cordelia earlier, just as Edgar's restoration restores some semblance of order to the judicial processes of primitive Britain. So much has been happening, in fact, that Kent creates a sensation by showing up on the stage and asking for his master. "Great thing of us forgot!" cries Albany, stupefied, "Speak Edmund, where's the King? And where's Cordelia?"

This moment in the play, which some have criticised as fortuitous, melodramatic, and contrived, needs to be regarded in the light of the ritual which started the whole chain of events in motion. In that opening scene, everything depended on Lear and Cordelia; around the conflict of their wills the fates of nations, literally, revolved. Now, they are of no importance; no role is left to them; what happens to them scarcely matters; it is as though they had been dropped from the play. Contrast the death of Hamlet, in the instant of Claudius's exposure; or the death of Cleopatra, foiling the purposes of Caesar. Left without function in the mechanism of society, Lear will not be, like Hamlet, carried to a stage and exhibited to the tune of a military dead march. He will not be given a few last words, like Othello, about the service he has done the state. Nor can Cordelia be arrayed like Cleopatra in the robes and crown of a princess and made to embrace her death as a bride embraces a bridegroom. So "formal and megalithic"[6] at the beginning, these two personages have passed beyond ritual altogether at the close. They cannot be expressed or comprehended by any of its forms—this fact is their greatness and their tragedy.

[6] *Ibid.*, p. 271. ("[The opening scene] has a proper formality, and . . . a certain megalithic grandeur. . . .")

XV

WILLIAM ROSEN

Antony and Cleopatra

The language of *Antony and Cleopatra* is a miracle of the imagination. It can sound the complete range of emotions and impart boldness and strength to the turmoil of passion as well as to the profound mysteries of love. But the rich texture of the poetry opposes the dramatic structure; Shakespeare lavishes his imaginative splendors not upon military values and the ideals which Antony must attain, but upon Cleopatra, love, and the Egyptian attractions he is called upon to renounce. Consequently, those who are dazzled by the incomparable language often celebrate its paean of love and minimize or disregard the unfolding events that chronicle a man's fall.

Cleopatra is repeatedly described in the language of magical wonder; she excels, Enobarbus tells us, even the delights of art, "O'er-picturing that Venus where we see/The fancy outwork nature" (II. ii. 205). So it is that the exciting drama inherent in the poetry surrounding Cleopatra competes with the more mundane drama of the play's action: when Cleopatra demonstrates most forcefully the power of her attraction, Antony is at his weakest, he is a woman's man, stripped of the judgment he must have to be his heroic self. While acknowledging the imposing beauty of the language associated with love, we should remember the consequences of the play's action. Antony sees his world demolished; he suffers the betrayal of faith and love; he perceives, however dimly, that he has dishonored Octavia, his loyal soldiers, himself. His fortunes have "corrupted honest men," and his own revulsion is as important to the play's central meaning as the alternative judgment, Dryden's version of a world well lost for love.

Reprinted by permission of the publishers from William Rosen, *Shakespeare and the Craft of Tragedy* (Cambridge, Mass.: Harvard University Press). Copyright 1960 by The President and Fellows of Harvard College.

Antony and Cleopatra is a puzzle to many because Shakespeare sustains things in perilous balance, so much so that critics have recurringly used the terms "paradox," "duality," and "ambiguity" to describe the complexity of emotions and events. Shakespeare's play world is not unlike the real world. It is a tangled skein; white and black merge; good grows up together with evil almost inseparably. What people do is not always what they know they should do, and there is neither the illusion that the traditional currency of virtue will find conventional reward nor the delusion that evil will of necessity meet with retributive punishment. Opposing values and beliefs are very often held in tenuous balance because they are presented as having equally compelling merit. Shakespeare's unparalleled strength comes not only from the marvels of language but also from his penetration into the bewildering incongruities and possibilities of human experience. Enobarbus, for example, is a cynic who rules his imagination with a soldier's firm logic and practicality, yet he is the one who garbs Cleopatra in the imaginative and lavish language of hyperbole. To serve a master who has lost his wits is folly, Enobarbus argues with himself; but to leave him in such straits is knavery. Enobarbus forsakes his lord because folly is indeed against all reason; unlike Antony, he dutifully follows the path of reason— but his heart bursts. The foolish man of passion proves worthier than the practical man of reason; Antony "continues still a Jove" (IV. vi. 28); he is magnanimous.

Contradictions are to be found everywhere in this drama of world power and love; opposites play against one another to form a monumental life-resembling work of art. There is the seeming contradiction of loving one's nemesis, of hating and loving the same person at the same time. There are strange occurrences to be reckoned with: that spiritual grandeur rises out of destruction, that life at its greatest moment is not a thing of joy but of sorrow, that happiness is the state of being well-deceived. And then there is the volatile Cleopatra who is both childish shrew and dignified queen.

"If Cleopatra kindles, she also quenches." This observation by W. B. C. Watkins[1] helps explain, with disarming clarity, why so many people disagree in their estimation of the play's

[1] *Shakespeare and Spenser* (Princeton, N.J.: Princeton University Press, 1950), p. 34.

lovers. Pursuing Cleopatra, Antony rushes towards his destruction; yet only in Cleopatra can he find fulfilment. There is the maddening paradox of running for a joy which, being found, torments. And in Sonnet 129 Shakespeare depicts an experience that might serve as an epigraph, for the same feelings are made to jostle each other—the sense of passion's enormous vitality and, cutting through this, the savage indignation at its destructive fury:

> Enjoy'd no sooner but despised straight,
> Past reason hunted, and no sooner had
> Past reason hated, as a swallow'd bait
> On purpose laid to make the taker mad;
> Mad in pursuit and in possession so;
> Had, having, and in quest to have, extreme;
> A bliss in proof, and prov'd, a very woe;
> Before, a joy propos'd; behind, a dream.

Shakespeare dramatizes; he does not unknot inextricable strands of experience and separate them to provide a moral lesson that will serve as a practical guide for living. His sonnet ends with the reminder, "All this the world well knows; yet none knows well/To shun the heaven that leads men to this hell."

The Egyptian queen rouses in Antony a passion that consumes him in frenzy. Like Eve, she embodies the temptation that imperils human destiny. Torn between two contraries—by Cleopatra who paradoxically threatens his manhood, and by military achievement which affords the only means of regaining honor and integrity—Antony recognizes the possibility of a tragic fall: "If I lose mine honour,/I lose myself" (III. iv. 22). But he is powerless before Cleopatra; he has neither the strength to dominate her nor the wisdom to understand her nature. She is, he acknowledges, "cunning past man's thought" (I. ii. 150), and audiences agree. Few women in literature have called forth so intense and personal a response. Cleopatra is either adored or vilified. No one treats her with indifference.

Cleopatra generates enormous excitement, and this accounts for her great appeal. Never passive, her energy is as boundless in grief as in love. Mistress of infinite variety, she commands a tremendous repertoire of emotions and moods to suit all occasions. At one moment her sincerity can be overwhelmingly poignant—as when she faces the inevitability of Antony's departure from Egypt. Trying to find words that will make her

tangled emotions felt and understood, she begins with facts—
parting and loving—but facts are hopelessly inadequate:

> Sir, you and I must part, but that's not it;
> Sir, you and I have lov'd, but there's not it;
> That you know well. Something it is I would . . .
>
> (I. iii. 87)

she breaks off; and groping for that which would explain all,
she reaches truth that is both poetry and illumination: "O,
my oblivion is a very Antony,/And I am all forgotten." Her
"oblivion" is the loss of Antony as well as of speech; without
him life is a senseless void.

But there are other moments when her sincerity is feigned,
when calculation leads her into enacting every kind of pose.
Again and again she becomes the incomparable actress, pro-
ficient in emotional acrobatics. Shakespeare calls attention to
her dominant characteristic in the repetition of "play-acting"
images and allusions. Her predilection for dazzling show is
made quite explicit at the play's beginning when Antony decides to return to Rome. Enobarbus anticipates the poses that
can be expected from Cleopatra, who "catching but the least
noise of this, dies instantly; I have seen her die twenty times
upon far poorer moment" (I. ii. 144). Nor does her appearance
upset his prediction, for we see her direct Charmian to seek
Antony and act out a role appropriate to the occasion:

> If you find him sad,
> Say I am dancing; if in mirth, report
> That I am sudden sick. Quick, and return.
>
> (I. iii. 3)

As soon as Antony enters, Cleopatra begins her performance:
"I am sick and sullen" (I. iii. 13); and she continues to dramatize herself and her emotions, passing from despair to joy, or
balancing the two extremes ("I am quickly ill and well,/So
Antony loves"), always with enormous presence, always with
poetry that presents the exact curve of feeling.

Sometimes it is difficult to determine whether Cleopatra is
merely playing a superb role, or whether she is completely
truthful; and perhaps one should not make the distinction, for
her personality is such that she always gives the impression of
playing at life, of being intensely aware of every stance, as if

she cannot help but live and die before a mirror. Acting is so much a part of her that at a time of great crisis, when after the Alexandrian defeat Antony seeks her, raging, "The witch shall die," she still attends to the staging of dramatic effects. Accepting Charmian's advice to feign death, she instructs her servant in the precise manner of speaking her lines:

> To th' monument!
> Mardian, go tell him I have slain myself;
> Say that the last I spoke was "Antony,"
> And word it, prithee, piteously.
>
> (IV. xiii. 6)

Finally, her act of suicide is at once the consummate escape from the world and her most accomplished self-dramatization. She carries off her last performance with perfect artistry, robing and crowning for death, speaking magnificent poetry in her farewell address.

In Act II, scene v, the repeated allusion to "playing" illuminates Cleopatra's character as well as her relationship to Antony. While Antony plays at world politics in Rome, Cleopatra whiles away her time in Egypt. At first she thinks of playing at billiards, but Charmian is tired; then she would play with the eunuch Mardian, but foregoes this to play, in reverie, at catching Antony again:

> Give me mine angle, we'll to th' river; there
> My music playing far off, I will betray
> Tawny-finn'd fishes; my bended hook shall pierce
> Their shiny jaws; and, as I draw them up,
> I'll think them every one an Antony,
> And say, "Ah, ha! you're caught."
>
> (II. v. 10)

The joy of knowing her own attraction is like no other joy that life can give; and this explains why, in remembering her past, she always sees herself captivating men.

When Cleopatra recalls how she playfully exchanged her tires and mantles for Antony's sword (II. v. 22), she makes an oblique commentary on the drama's central action. The "playing" incident points to the reversal of sexual roles. In the past, Antony fulfilled himself by dominating other lands and people; now, a woman's man, he surrenders himself completely to another. It is the woman who feels the masculine desire to take possession, and Cleopatra employs all sorts of stratagems and violence to impose her will on people and events. While Charmian advises her to give in to Antony, "cross him in nothing" (I. iii. 9), Cleopatra has her own device, "Thou teachest like a fool: the way to lose him." She knows how to keep Antony bound to her; she knows the effects a woman can produce with the skilful maneuver of attraction, followed by sudden disdain. This is made most apparent after the battle of Actium, when Antony loses the respect of his men and his own self-esteem. His shame turns to gall at the sight of the Queen's subservient behavior toward his enemy's messenger; and yet, no matter how low Cleopatra brings him, he cannot dismiss her. Inevitably the torments of dishonor fall away and rage dissolves into the fearful apprehension, "Cold-hearted toward me?" (III. xiii. 158). The thought of losing Cleopatra makes him sweat for her.

However great Cleopatra's appeal, we must question the popular view that Shakespeare advocates the romantic notion of passion's nobility and its power to absolve man from all duty. If we were to concentrate only on the imagery of love, neglecting dramatic context, there would be the danger of extracting Cleopatra's heightened vision of love, so magnificently phrased, to argue that the playwright presents it as life's highest value, more real than society or morality. Shakespeare's dramatic technique in portraying Cleopatra provides substantial evidence that this is not so. The general conclusions about the point of view established towards Antony have equal relevance for Cleopatra, whose actions are also framed by choric commentary: she too is subjected to prefiguring and to analysis by intermediaries. This mode of characterization is designed to make vivid and understandable Cleopatra's tremendous power to influence Antony's decisions. It explains why Enobarbus analyzes Cleopatra's charms and prefigures her wiles. It also explains why Cleopatra indulges in self-exposure, openly revealing to an audience that she will act out a pose to keep Antony bound to her. Because Shakespeare is primarily interested in having an audience understand the conflicting demands upon Antony, we do not become emotionally involved with the protagonists. Cleopatra, we know, is acting, rising, it is true, to magnificent heights, but we become more involved with the effect she has and will have upon Antony.

So dazzlingly impressive are Cleopatra's final moments in the play that they have always brought forth excited bravos from spectators and panegyrics from critics. Indeed, many commentators have been so overwhelmed by the ending that they read the play backwards, attempting to reconstruct a consistent characterization so that the final glory of Cleopatra may prevail. Such a reading would maintain that Cleopatra recovers full innocence at her death, that she and Antony are transfigured; therefore, Shakespeare's play is not about corruption and human weakness but the exaltation of love and its final triumph over death and the world. To interpret the ending this way, however, is to distort what we have seen to be the developing action of the play, Antony's attempt to regain his heroic past. It is to reconcile the irreconcilable, for we cannot gloss over Cleopatra's role as temptress, nor minimize the consequences of her preventing Antony from regaining his virtue to become again the wonder of the world, ideal man. Nor can we expunge the treachery she contemplated, her resolve to forsake Antony and yield to the triumphant Caesar (III. xiii. 60). Furthermore, even her conduct at the time of Antony's death is hardly exemplary. Indeed, the events approach the point of being ludicrous. Antony bungles his suicide. He is carried to the Queen, who looks down at him from the height of her monument. While she laments the misfortune and calls on the sun to burn itself out and cast the world in darkness, she refuses to come down to her lover, lest she be captured. Hoisted up to her, the dying Antony tries to speak a few words of comfort and advice: "I am dying, Egypt, dying./Give me some wine, and let me speak a little" (IV. xv. 41). But Cleopatra breaks in forcefully, "No, let me speak"; and what she says is merely the empty and shrill sounding of Senecan hyperbole:

> and let me rail so high,
> That the false housewife Fortune break her wheel,
> Provok'd by my offence.

> (IV. xv. 43)

In having Cleopatra enact this stock pose of tearing a passion to shreds, Shakespeare is certainly not intent on glorifying her. He makes the Queen appear even more vain and self-determined in the final exchange with her lover. In great pain, gasping his dying words, Antony tries to give advice:

> *Antony.*   One word, sweet queen:
>   Of Caesar seek your honour, with your safety. O!
> *Cleopatra.* They do not go together.
> *Antony.*   Gentle, hear me:
>   None about Caesar trust but Proculeius.
> *Cleopatra.* My resolution and my hands I'll trust;
>   None about Caesar.
>
>   (IV. xv. 45)

Each time Cleopatra sharply contradicts Antony, a departure from Plutarch's *Life*, for there she is persuaded by his speech: "When he had drunk, he earnestly prayed her, and persuaded her, that she would seek to save her life, if she could possible, without reproach and dishonour: and that chiefly she should trust Proculeius above any man else about Caesar."[2]

When Antony dies, Cleopatra is overcome with genuine grief. Because the language of her lament is so beautiful, no one could possibly be insensitive to her despair:

>   Young boys and girls
>   Are level now with men; the odds is gone,
>   And there is nothing left remarkable
>   Beneath the visiting moon.
>
>   (IV. xv. 65)

She even decides to join Antony in suicide "after the high Roman fashion" (IV. xv. 87). But in the next act she is still importuning death in beautifully shaped language, falling rather awkwardly from tragic heights when her treasurer reveals to Caesar her deceit in holding back her wealth. Clearly she entertains the possibility of living on, though Antony is dead.

Cleopatra's shifting moods and emotional acrobatics may testify to her infinite variety, but they do not lend great support to the view that her last moment, magnificent as it is, transfigures her and provides the key to the entire play: the assumption that Shakespeare's final vision is of a love which glorifies man and woman and ultimately redeems them. This judgment is based on a consideration of the play's structure and events. While a change seems to come over the protag-

---

[2] *Shakespeare's Plutarch*, ed. C. F. Tucker Brooke (London, 1909), II, 123.

onists towards the drama's end,[3] does this result from inner transformation, or is it to be explained by the sudden shift in character presentation and an attendant shift in point of view?

When Antony approaches his death, for the first time in the play all *raisonneurs* fall away; there is neither derogatory framing of his deed nor critical analysis. We see Antony directly, not though intermediaries who would alienate an audience by exposing discrepancies between what he says and what he does or should do. The irony, which has continually been directed at Antony's affirmations and aspirations, fades away; judgment, therefore, is held in abeyance. What Antony now says, we accept at face value. Furthermore, there is no ignominy to tarnish his end. He confronts death with stoic honor and dignity, and those who chorus on his imminent death invest it with solemnity and awe. "The star is fallen," the Second Guard intones. "And time is at his period," mourns the First Guard. "Alas and woe!" is the communal lament. Until this scene, choral commentary, whether individual or communal, provided a common-sense norm to measure Antony's actions. Now the chorus grieves the loss of a great public figure and elevates his stature.

There is a significant change in the way an audience sees Antony; there is no transfiguration. Antony's death does not glorify his love nor make of it the play's transcendent value. His final thoughts do not in any way extenuate his decline and fall; nor do they celebrate his love for Cleopatra. He tells her:

[3] Levin L. Schücking (*Character Problems in Shakespeare's Plays* [New York, 1922], p. 134) finds a sharp contradiction between the wanton Cleopatra of the early scenes and the tragic queen of the last two acts and explains this in terms of his theory that Shakespeare "composed according to the 'single-scene' method." E. M. W. Tillyard (*Shakespeare's Last Plays* [London, 1951], p. 22) also finds a radical change in the last two acts: "The vacillations of Antony and his neglect of duty, the cunning and cruelty of Cleopatra, find no part in the creatures who are transfigured in death; they remain unassimilated, held in tension against the pair's expiring nobilities. The reason why *Antony and Cleopatra* is so baffling a play (and why the rhapsodies it provokes tend to be hysterical) is that the effort to see the two main characters simultaneously in two different guises taxes our strength beyond our capacities. And yet that effort has to be made. Those who see Antony as the erring hero merely, and his final exaltation as ironic infatuation, are as partial in their judgment as those who think that his final heroics wash out his previous frailties. Both sets are part right, but each needs the other's truth to support it."

> The miserable change now at my end
> Lament nor sorrow at; but please your thoughts
> In feeding them with those my former fortunes
> Wherein I liv'd, the greatest prince o' th' world,
> The noblest; and do now not basely die,
> Not cowardly put off my helmet to
> My countryman,—a Roman by a Roman
> Valiantly vanquish'd. Now my spirit is going;
> I can no more.
>
> (IV. xv. 51)

To have an honorable reputation—this is what matters most. Antony dies with a vision of his best self before him. At the end of his life he does not invoke remembrances of a life with Cleopatra, but a time before, when he was the greatest of men. And he dies with the comforting thought that in taking his own life he shows himself strong and valiant, worthy of the virtue and nobility associated with his former fortunes.

It cannot be said, therefore, that Antony changes. He does not confront an experience that brings about a resettlement of his being. In drawing comfort and dignity from memory, he only repeats what he has previously done on many occasions. What Antony is at his death, he was before. There is this important difference, however: for the first time in the play we are not called upon to judge him; and we are asked to remember his public greatness—but this greatness, we should keep in mind, was of an Antony who flourished before the play began.

Cleopatra also faces death with royal dignity. The fear of a Roman triumph prevails over her fear of death and convinces her to escape the world's great snare. "Know, sir," she tells Proculeius,

> that I
> Will not wait pinion'd at your master's court;
> Nor once be chastis'd with the sober eye
> Of dull Octavia. Shall they hoist me up
> And show me to the shouting varletry
> Of censuring Rome? Rather a ditch in Egypt
> Be gentle grave unto me!
>
> (V. ii. 52)

Dolabella confirms her misgivings: Caesar will indeed lead her in triumph, make of her a public spectacle. She thinks of the degrading horror, of mechanic slaves with greasy aprons uplifting her to common view, of being enclouded in the stinking breath of the multitude. And she tells Iras:

> Saucy lictors
> Will catch at us like strumpets, and scald rhymers
> Ballad us out o' tune. The quick comedians
> Extemporally will stage us, and present
> Our Alexandrian revels; Antony
> Shall be brought drunken forth, and I shall see
> Some squeaking Cleopatra boy my greatness
> I' th' posture of a whore.
>
> (V. ii. 214)

The words describe what we have already witnessed in the play; we have heard Cleopatra called whore, we have seen Alexandrian revels and a drunken Antony. Her words even describe the present moment, for they are being delivered to Shakespeare's audience by a squeaking boy. The Egyptian queen creates a wonderful illusion: all the play, she would persuade us, has been fictional and cheap; what we are witnessing at this heightened occasion is more real than the play world. In embracing her own illusions, Cleopatra would have us imagine that she transcends the unreality of fiction, just as she would have Dolabella accept her dream of Antony as fact. "I dream'd there was an Emperor Antony," she tells him: "His face was as the heavens," "His legs bestrid the ocean," "In his livery walk'd crowns and crownets." "Think you there was or might be such a man?" she asks him; and he replies, "Gentle madam, no" (V. ii. 94).

For Cleopatra illusions are real and the real enactments of the play are but shadows. Dolabella's gentle rebuke has little effect upon her. Nor does it have too great an effect upon an audience because in these final scenes we become one with Cleopatra, seeing events through her eyes. There is no sharp discontinuity between the Cleopatra of the early scenes and the Cleopatra of the play's finale; she has not undergone any great change in vision or personality. But now there are no caustic commentators who stand about her to prefigure action, guide judgment, or tear aside illusions to uncover hypocrisy or self-deception. It is the radical shift in the point of view established towards Cleopatra that brings about audience rapport with her and helps explain why so many critics have insisted that an entirely new Cleopatra emerges in these last scenes.

Cleopatra's speeches before her death are incomparable self-dramatizations. In commenting on the self-dramatization of Shakespeare's heroes at moments of tragic intensity, T. S. Eliot has suggested that the death speeches of Othello, Coriolanus, and Antony are instances where "*bovarysme*, the human will to see things as they are not,"[4] clearly prevails. I would offer a slightly different interpretation: that in general when Shakespeare's tragic heroes face death, they render their final and best estimate of themselves; they embrace what is most meaningful in their lives. To lose one's meaning, one's status in life, is to be reduced to nothingness—this is the anguish felt by Richard II who, losing his crown, calls for a mirror to see how changed is a face that is bankrupt of majesty. He dashes the glass to pieces because, in losing his status, his face has lost its meaning.

At the moment before death, Antony seeks what is most noble in his life; once again he is in love with his honor, and he finally achieves integrity not through private love but the remembrance of his public worth. Antony's final commitment is to his reputation and his honor. At her end, Cleopatra strives for a comparable vision. She sees herself as wife. Robing and crowning for death, she embraces, with complete sincerity, a self-created dream and is overpowered by it. "Methinks I hear/ Antony call," she exclaims; and immediately she translates vision into fact: "I see him rouse himself/To praise my noble act." With self-conscious awareness, as if acting before Antony, seeking his approbation, she terms her deed "noble." "Husband, I come!" Cleopatra calls to him, and then, as if realizing the significance of her utterance, she would consciously elevate herself to noble thought and deed that she might be worthy of the name she has just taken: "Now to that name my courage prove my title." Whereupon she proceeds to verbalize her determined ascent: "I am fire and air; my other elements/I give to baser life."

An audience, awed by spectacle and superb language, can imagine a Cleopatra suddenly changed in personality, though her own words reveal that step by step she is convincing herself of the role she must enact before Antony. But unlike Antony, she cannot sustain the vision; hers is inspired by a dream;

[4] "Shakespeare and the Stoicism of Seneca," in *Selected Essays* (London, 1951), p. 131.

Antony's is the recall of an actual past. When Cleopatra forgets that Antony is watching, she breaks her own tragic spell. Seeing that Iras has died, she hastens to apply another asp, lest Antony "spend that kiss/Which is my heaven to have." The spell broken momentarily, she descends even further from tragic heights as she gloats that her action will thwart the great Caesar:

> Poor venomous fool,
> Be angry, and dispatch. O couldst thou speak,
> That I might hear thee call great Caesar ass
> Unpolicied!
>
> (V. ii. 308)

Her instinct to dominate and rule prevails to the end. She made a fool of the first Caesar; she will do the same to the second.

The energy of Cleopatra's thoughts and actions, her infinite variety, compel admiration, "since things in motion sooner catch the eye/Than what not stirs" (*Troilus* III. iii. 183). It is not too surprising that many people have ambivalent feelings towards characters like Dante's Paolo and Francesca, Ulysses, or Milton's Satan. Even when these are condemned, their intensity of desire, of mind and will is often admired. There is, further-more, the feeling in most men that a life of energy, even the satanic, partakes of nobility. Keats, in one of his letters, affirms this: "Though a quarrel in the Streets is a thing to be hated, the energies displayed in it are fine. . . ."[5] Consequently, there is the danger of confusing energy with moral stature and of so mis-taking admiration for approval that Cleopatra's final moments are wrongly interpreted as a redemption and a transfiguration which make all previous conduct of no account. Such a view distorts character and action in this play. Certainly Antony and Cleopatra achieve great nobility in death; but the play, after all, is a chronicle of their lives and an exposure of the illusions they would live. Neither Antony nor Cleopatra changes identity. Even in death Cleopatra looks "As she would catch another Antony/In her strong toil of grace." Caesar makes this observation at the close of the play; and he says further:

> their story is
> No less in pity than his glory which
> Brought them to be lamented.

[5] Letter 123, "To George and Georgiana Keats," *The Letters of John Keats*, ed. M. B. Forman (4th ed.; Oxford, 1952), p. 316.

XVI

ROBERT ORNSTEIN

Shakespeare's Moral Vision

Othello and *Macbeth*

Looking back upon the three decades of tragedy that ended with Ford, one sees an apparently eccentric pattern of creativity. Partly because many Jacobeans served their apprenticeship in comedy, there is no "curve" of artistic development in their tragedies—no fumbling ascent to Olympus. Their tragic genius flames into view at its apogee and consumes itself like a meteor falling in the earth's atmosphere. Their first tragedies are, generally speaking, their most brilliant; their later works have less artistic vigor but greater moral security or balance. In almost every instance the Jacobean tragic inspiration is short-lived. As the first white heat of scorn and indignation fades, the Jacobean tragic sense of life fades too, if it is not actually extinguished by philosophical or religious convictions.

We cannot expect that Shakespeare's drama will conform to a pattern derived from a study of his lesser contemporaries. They abide our scholarly questions because they were absorbed in topical and peripheral issues and because they used the stage for extraliterary purposes—to confute the politician or the naturalist. Shakespeare escapes the tyranny of scholarly exegesis because he grasped always the permanent significance of contemporary problems and because his vision of life was so comprehensive that his art has never lost its relevance to the human situation. Although we must familiarize ourselves with the Petrarchan codes of the Renaissance to grasp the witty conceits of *The Maid's Tragedy* and *The Changeling*, we need only see the world feelingly to understand Troilus' narcissistic hunger for an absolute romantic dedication.

Because he sees the world feelingly, Shakespeare performs the immemorial service of the artist to society: he humanizes the categorical imperatives which the stern didacticist offers as the sum of ethical truth. If all marriages were made in heaven, then it would be just to complain that Shakespeare romanticizes adulterous love in *Antony and Cleopatra*. But since marriages among the great have been, since the beginning of civilization, political and military alliances, there is a place in Shakespeare's sympathies and in ours for Antony and Cleopatra. Although he lived in an age which frequently confused the moral and the moralistic in art, he did not preach. He must have known there was really little danger that his nut-cracking listeners would go the way of his tragic heroes; they were not Hamlets, Lears, or Macbeths, nor were they likely to murder their wives over the loss of a handkerchief. A realist even in his fairy tales, he did not make a cautionary example of Autolycus; he knew all too well that a mere fiction was not going to eradicate the purse-snatching that continued in the very shadow of Tyburn.

As we might expect, Shakespeare's relation to his Jacobean contemporaries was one-sided. His tragedies preceded most of theirs; he was quite literally their master, not their colleague. It is difficult in fact to imagine what seventeenth-century tragedy would have been like had not Shakespeare developed the tragic art of Kyd and Marlowe to a miraculous perfection. His poetry, his characterizations, and his dramatic situations are an integral part of the creative experience of the men we have studied and are assimilated in their plays. Perhaps the richness and variety of his achievement overwhelmed minor talents and inspired immature writers to self-destructive pursuits of "originality." For the major talents, however, he was a creative and liberating force, a dramatist who expanded the horizons of artistic possibility. Because he did not have a clearly defined theory of tragedy and because his view of life was deceptively neutral, his influence did not channel tragedy into as restricted a mode as that which Jonson established for seventeenth-century comedy.

It was easier, in fact, for the Jacobeans to write under the shadow of Shakespeare's genius than it is for us to place him among his contemporaries. The richness and variety of his art only accentuate the singleness of mood and subject matter and the narrowness of vision in their tragedies. How earnest and

unnecessary seem Chapman's attempts to reconstruct philosophical values when the truth and beauty of moral ideals
appear in Shakespeare as the bedrock reality of human experience. How superficial seem the terrors of Tourneur and Webster compared to that intuition of the horror and absurdity of
life which is given to Macbeth. The compassionate ironies of
Measure for Measure were beyond the scope of other Jacobeans, who could see only the mockery of man's fumbling attempts at justice, who could portray the twisted dedication to
the "cause" of honor which dooms Othello but not the sublime
charity of Cordelia's "No cause, no cause" which redeems
Lear's sufferings. Because Shakespeare's was the most comprehensive mind, we cannot treat his plays as another fraction of
the totality of Jacobean tragedy. His vision of life is the whole
that includes and exceeds the sum of the other dramatists' partial perceptions. There is hardly a tragic theme or mood of the
first decade which does not find expression in his plays, particularly those between *Hamlet* and *Macbeth*. Even in the dark
comedies, we can trace Shakespeare's progress towards the all-
embracing spiritual and moral drama of *Lear*, the only Jacobean play large enough to confront and resolve the challenge
which evil presents to man's belief in himself and his universe.

Some readers will protest that Shakespeare's "solution" to the
problem of evil lies not in the great tragedies but in the plays
that followed. Just as Dr. Johnson found the last scenes of *Lear*
too painful to contemplate, so critics refuse to accept its vision
as Shakespeare's most profound dramatic intuition. *Lear* is to
them a part of a spiritual journey that ended only on the mystical heights of the late romances. They look beyond the anguish
of the tragic period to the autumnal grace of *The Winter's
Tale* and *The Tempest*, in which innocence is rediscovered
and reborn, and evil is only an appearance. It seems a pity,
however, to burden such lovely and fragile plays with a stag-
gering weight of philosophical, allegorical, and symbolic significances. Their charm is melancholy; their wisdom lies in a bit-
tersweet acceptance of the maturity and sophistication that inevitably replaces the innocence of youth and that makes possible
the corrupted "artistic" sensibility of Leontes. There is no certainty, moreover, that Miranda's brave new world will not end
in the sorrows that Prospero vividly remembers or that the
romantic illusions of youth will not be shattered by a society

that breeds Antonios and Sebastians. The vision of *Lear* is not transmuted by *The Tempest;* in different moods and modes both plays express the ineffable goodness of life and the transcendent experience of love in a world where brother turns on brother and age suffers painfully and long.

If Shakespeare's art were more like Chapman's, we might seek in it the kind of intellectual and moral pilgrimage that led from *Bussy D'Ambois* to *Caesar and Pompey*. Indeed, because Chapman's ideals evolved throughout his artistic career, his tragedies must be studied as a continuum. But because Shakespeare's values never altered, each of his plays bears separate witness to the quality of his mind and art; they are unique entities informed by common ideals and standards of judgment. By statistical measurements, the satiric mood of *Troilus and Cressida* is uncharacteristic of Shakespeare, but so too, by the same standard, is the apotheosis of sensual love in *Antony and Cleopatra* and the vision of depravity in *Lear*. The "essential" Shakespeare is in each of the plays and in all of them, not in any particular group or dramatic mode. At different times he was absorbed in different aspects of life—in the gaiety and innocence of youthful courtship or in the animality of sexual vice, in the intrinsic decorums of political authority or in the anarchic ambition that destroys social order. Particularly at a time when traditional values were being questioned, his imagination dwelt upon the brutality of evil that in all ages challenges man's ideals. But though we can say that Shakespeare's understanding of man and society broadened and deepened throughout his career, we cannot say that in any play he lost faith in humanity and in its ideals, or that in the late romances he rediscovered the belief in universal harmony shattered in *Lear*. It is a reckless critic indeed who undertakes to describe what personal metaphysical assumptions (if any) underlie the plays.

The art of Shakespeare's early plays may be imperfect and immature; but the characterizations and values are never jejune. He offers no unexamined enthusiasms, no facile or naïve optimisms. The darker side of heroic aspiration, the sacrifice of humane values in the arena of public action, and the egotism that breathes in a lover's sigh—all are as manifest in his Elizabethan as in his Jacobean plays. There is as acute a perception of political realities in *Richard III* as in *Coriolanus*, as clear-sighted a view of honor in the "Henriad" as in *Troilus and Cressida*. We must assume also that Shakespeare's capabilities as a dramatist determined, particularly in his early years, the subjects that he chose and the manner in which he treated them. Although he constantly explored the possibilities of his art and in play after play enlarged the frontiers of poetic drama, he maintained a just correspondence between aspiration and achievement; his artistic reach lengthened only as his grasp of the medium became more certain. We can if we wish condemn *Richard III* as crude and immature tragedy, but it would be more accurate to describe it as one of the most successful melodramas ever written. At each stage of his development, Shakespeare brought to their highest perfection the various genres of the Elizabethan and Jacobean stage. And because his genius was bounteous, he did not feel the necessity of repeating an earlier triumph at a later date. Had Shakespeare's genius been less fecund, the pattern of his drama might have been quite different. Hence we must be extremely wary of those critics who read his plays as a form of spiritual autobiography.

We find nothing in *Antony and Cleopatra* or *Coriolanus* which suggests that Shakespeare's view of the struggle for power changed after *Macbeth;* and despite its questionable shape *Timon of Athens* bears witness to Shakespeare's capacity for tragic emotion at the very time that he was about to embark on the late romances. I omit these later tragedies from discussion only because they seem to me quite removed from the "Jacobean" issues which link the earlier tragedies and dark comedies to the works of Shakespeare's contemporaries. They add to our knowledge of Shakespeare's mind and art, but they shed little light on the epistemological questions which lie at the heart of Jacobean tragedy. If we approach Shakespeare primarily by way of plot, we may conclude that *Othello* and *Macbeth* are the most "Jacobean" of his tragedies, because, like many of the plays of Tourneur, Webster, Middleton, and Ford, they portray the disintegration of moral will and purpose. Great soldiers who become cowardly assassins, Othello and Macbeth are infinitely closer to such hero-villains as Byron, Vindice, Brachiano, De Flores, and Giovanni than are Hamlet and Lear. But any broader view makes it apparent that *Hamlet* and *Lear* represent Shakespeare's deepest involvement in the tragic issues of the first Jacobean decade. Their larger, more philosophical actions and choric commentaries define the problem of moral decision and belief in an evil world and dramatize the tragic need of the idealizing mind to discover, accept, and relate itself to the realities of the universe. In one way or other, of course, all of Shakespeare's great tragedies are discoveries of moral and spiritual reality; all are concerned with what man knows and what he needs, with his capacity to conceive and adhere to ideals. And, not surprisingly, these tragic themes can be found in the other plays written during the same period. It has often been noted that *Troilus and Cressida* and *Measure for Measure* deal with the disparity between appearance and reality. More importantly, it seems to me, they are concerned with man's hunger for ideal values and dedications—for honor or justice, for ideal passion or purity. I discuss these plays in detail because their questionings of values and their analyses of justice, legality, and charitable love guide us to the central moral and intellectual drama of *Lear*. They are also interesting in that they anticipate the concern with societal morality which we find in Middleton and Ford. Because they present moral situations as ambiguous as those in *The Broken Heart*, they too divide the critics and demand the kind of liberal ethical response for which Donne pleads in *Biathanatos*.

The dark comedies fall in a line of artistic thought that runs from *Hamlet* to *Lear*. *Othello* is not so much outside that line as a tangent leading from it. More specifically, it restates the universal questions of *Hamlet* and *Lear* in the personal terms of a single intimate relationship. Although recent critics have found weighty intellectual significances in the imagery of *Othello*, it seems to me that less is at stake in its action than in the other tragedies because of the intense particularity of its characterizations. What other Shakespearean hero has Othello's carefully defined exotic past and racial background? What other villain manifests his evil as Iago does, not in the unscrupulous ambitions or acts of a Claudius or Edmund but in every utterance of a meticulously detailed and highly individualized personality: the vulgar, lewd, money-hungry, chiseling, envious, disappointed Ancient? When we ignore this particularity and attempt to make universal or symbolic figures of the characters in *Othello* we only distort them. That is to say, the jealous Moor would seem to us as fatuous as Roderigo were it not for the unique circumstances of his personality, his race, his innocence of Venetian society, and his belated discovery of a love so rare and miraculous as to be outside the ordinary realm of belief. From *Othello* as from all Shakespearean tragedy we can abstract certain profound and general truths about the world in which we live. Man's vileness, Iago demonstrates, we know; his purity of heart we only think we know. His guilt we can prove; his innocence we must believe in because it cannot be "proved." But Othello's own tragic recognition is of a much more limited sort. While sentimental critics would have us believe that all of Shakespeare's tragic heroes are "improved" or ennobled by their suffering, it is not clear that Othello gains a new or greater wisdom from murdering Desdemona. Though he recovers enough of his former stature to admit that he is an "honourable murderer," he learns only the simple truth which was obvious to the coarse Emilia, to Cassio, and even at last to the foolish Roderigo—that Desdemona was chaste. His discovery of the "truth" about marriage was itself an illusion, his moment of truth simply a reversal of the maddened and obscene judgment passed on his wife.

Like *Hamlet, Othello* traces the deceptive appearances of life, but its plot inverts the tragic situation of Denmark. In Cyprus the faithless woman is true to her husband and the disillusioned idealist false; the revenger's desire for "ocular proof" is an unmitigated horror and his revenge a travesty of justice. In Cyprus Iago is a debased and pathological Hamlet, an aggrieved malcontent plotting his vengeance, hypersensitive to any show of falseness, witty and theatrical in his temperament, expert in staging impromptu dramas. Where *Hamlet* celebrates the capacity of the philosophical mind to penetrate beneath illusion, *Othello* reveals the capacity and will for self-deception which the ego nourishes. It reveals too the cunning irrationality of human reason and the subtlety with which man can prove to his satisfaction a truth which has no connection to fact. To be sure, Iago speaks always of fact, but he is the least empirical of Shakespeare's villains. His philosophy rests upon a continuing denial of the reality he daily perceives: the reality of Othello's "constant, loving, noble nature" and of Desdemona's "goodness" and "virtue." His specious logic, which descends syllogistically from lewd and twisted postulates, is more ancient than modern, more a perversion of Scholastic reasoning than an adumbration of a scientific or positivistic rationalism.

Middleton, one imagines, would have made *Othello* into an ironic tragedy of "honor" similar to *Women Beware Women*. There is no tinge of mockery, however, in Shakespeare's portrait of Othello, though the Moor's anguish, like Troilus', reveals the involvement of masculine ego in ideals of sexual fidelity. Shakespeare would have us pity the vulnerability of his greathearted soldier, who, used to absolute trust in himself and in those about him (his treasured Michael Cassio), requires certainty in love when there can be no certainty but the intuition of the heart. A stranger in Venetian society, instinctively feared by those who need and applaud his generalship, he has no other support than his sense of personal worth. The overwhelming sadness of his fate is that he could love Desdemona selflessly only when he had lost all sense of self, only when he had nothing left to wager on her faith.

Though the poison which Iago pours into Othello's ear has violent and at last fatal results, it is quickly purged by the antidote of Emilia's scorn and insistence upon the truth. As Othello returns to soldierly dignity, the heart aches for the innocence (his as well as Desdemona's) that has been destroyed, for the nobility that has been laid waste, and for the rare love that cankered in first blossom. With the characters on the stage we wonder at the senselessness of Iago's malice, but we are not touched by his cynicism, for its vulgar errors and distortions of life are manifest in Desdemona's radiant spirit and in Emilia's and Cassio's capacity for devotion. We cannot be intellectually persuaded by the casuistry of his "divinity of hell" because it makes no appeal to the intellect. It has finally only a reptilian logic; it seeks to hypnotize the mind by the sinuous weaving of obscene suggestion and image. *Macbeth* is a more disturbing play than *Othello* because it is embraced by the darkness which is focused in Iago's mind and because its hero falls into so deep a spiritual abyss that Othello's position is by comparison angelic. Where Othello struggles against the poison of Iago's lies, Macbeth struggles dreadfully against his own nature and wins the terrible victory of his damnation. There is nothing mean in his envy of others or in his nihilism. Crime is to him a mystical experience: he sees visions and hears voices. He knows what it is to surrender to the darkness of the soul.

It is interesting that J. W. Allen should refer to *Macbeth* when he discusses the moral fallacies of *The Prince*. Machiavelli, Mr. Allen remarks, "would have his Prince commit murder and feel like Lady Macbeth: 'A little water clears us of this deed.' He has no glimpse of the possibility that, later, the murderer may in despair be asking: 'Will these hands ne'er be clean?' The sense of the mysterious in good and evil, the sense of the poisonous nature of evil that Shakespeare felt so strongly, had no existence for his mind."[1] No less than Machiavelli is Lady Macbeth blind to the relation between acts and consequences, between what men do and what they become. Her speeches breathe contempt for those who have the "natural" will to power but not the nerve or the candor to accomplish what they will. Her exaltation of treachery—this "great business" of murder—translates into dramatic terms that admiration of heroic evil which is a recurrent aspect of Machiavelli's thought. To be sure, Lady Macbeth and her husband are fumbling politicians. The one is too weak, the other too cruel to enjoy sovereignty. They do not know how to reap the benefits of peace, order, and stability which Machiavelli thought could come from the vilest of deeds. But then who could have succeeded where they failed? Although Machiavelli could imagine that a murderer might successfully pretend to virtue, he had only the barest realization of the central moral truth of *Macbeth*—that only a murderer can play a murderer's role successfully. Those who might rule well—those who have the milk of human kindness—must shrink from the vicious act which sovereignty requires or, having committed it, must become the deed's creature.

Far more greatly than Webster in *The Duchess of Malfi* Shakespeare explores in *Macbeth* the mystery of man's will to self-destruction—his capacity to commit the acts which violate his essential being. If Macbeth did not covet the throne, he would have no "reason" to kill Duncan; yet Shakespeare does not make us feel that he thirsts for the sweet fruition of an earthly crown in the way that Richard III and Claudius do. The most that Lady Macbeth can say in her astute analysis of her husband's nature is that he is "not without ambition." When Macbeth weighs the act before it is committed, he lame-

---

[1] *A History of Political Thought in the Sixteenth Century* (3d ed.; London, 1957), p. 478.

ly concludes that he has "only ambition" to spur him on. If Shakespeare wished us to feel that Macbeth was driven by an insatiable lust for power, he failed miserably to achieve his purpose. But why need we demand that a tragic hero be more logical in his motives than a hero of a novel? If we applaud Dostoevski's understanding of the psychopathology of crime, must we not also applaud Shakespeare's portrait of Macbeth, who, like Raskolnikov, commits a crime that revolts him; who, like Raskolnikov, rehearses it first in hallucination; who, like Raskolnikov, walks towards the deed as in a trance, scarce believing that he can commit the act which fortune has cast in his way? Macbeth no more murders for ambition than Raskolnikov murders for money. Like Raskolnikov he kills for self, for "peace"—to end the restless torment of his imagination. He must prove to himself under the goading of his wife that he is a "man," even as Raskolnikov must prove to himself that he is not a louse or a bedbug like the people around him. Macbeth kills because his wife makes him admit that he wishes to kill; and because he condemns himself before he kills Duncan, the act of murder is fraught with a hatred of self which eventually and inevitably becomes a hatred of all of life.

If the murder of Duncan seems to us unmotivated, what shall we say of Macbeth's later and more gratuitous villainies? Before he kills Duncan Macbeth is harrowed by the fear of "consequences," of the chain of retribution which will return the poisoned chalice to his lips. His fears are mistaken; the great business succeeds beyond imagining. Duncan's sons flee and are accused of the crime; Macbeth is accepted as King, and Banquo, the one man who suspects his guilt, is willing to keep silent and be his chief counselor. There need be no fearful consequences for Macbeth except that the "peace" of murder has not descended; on the contrary, his self-loathing has been intensified by the need to hide his true self from the eyes of others. He tells himself that his fears in Banquo stick deep, yet quite obviously his true need is to murder Fleance. How much more "logical" would be his desire to extinguish Banquo's line if we felt that Macbeth had strong dynastic ambitions. But he has no children, only envy of all those who live at peace with themselves and with the world. For Macbeth, hell is other people.

A more conventional dramatist would have suggested that Macbeth piles murder on murder because his first act of blood brutalizes his nature. Shakespeare gives us a more terrible Macbeth who is driven to kill again and again because he cannot live with the memory of his first crime. Though the crime was perfect, neither he nor his wife was perfect in the crime. After the intoxicating rapture of murder wears off, she sinks into madness. Her diseased mind seeks to erase the horror of what she and Macbeth have done by rehearsing the murder scene over and over again in her dreams until the memory no longer tortures. Macbeth, more accustomed to killing and more capable of enduring in blood, seeks to erase horror with horror. He will re-enact the crime again and again until his nature and his role are one, until he is "perfect" in his part, and a full feast of slaughter has blunted all moral sensitivity. As the recurrent imagery of drunkenness intimates, Macbeth's craving for blood is like a drunkard's thirst for oblivion, one that can bring no release because each satisfaction merely intensifies the original need, and the only oblivion can be in bestiality itself.

No other passage in Jacobean tragedy touches the nihilism of Macbeth's final soliloquy. Only Webster could conceive of a similar horror at the lunacy of existence and a similar weariness and hopelessness of spirit. Having wasted time in the attempt to seize its promise and its offered opportunities, Macbeth is at last haunted by the deserts of vast eternity that inclose man's minuscule existence in time. If the anguish of the damned sounds musically on the ears of the saved, then there is comfort here for some; otherwise *Macbeth* is the most unpleasant of the tragedies. Though order is restored at its close, though evil is purged and Macbeth receives the gift of oblivion, there is no sense of repose or reconciliation in its final scenes. Macbeth is the only hero of mature Shakespearean tragedy who goes to his doom struggling wildly against it, clinging to the life that torments him because he cannot bear the thought that it is the be-all and end-all of sentience. His death becomes him better than the hired slaughter of Macduff's wife and children, but it is of a piece with the sequence of vile and bloody deeds which make up his life within the play. Fear, horror, blood, darkness, hallucination, are merely a part of the special world of *Macbeth*, a world which breeds neither a Desdemona nor a Horatio. The dry-eyed sons of Duncan flee after his murder lest they be suspected of the crime. Banquo is equivocal in his virtue; Macduff allows his defenseless family to be slaughtered and displays a curious worldliness in his interview with Malcolm. Of course he finally passes the test which Malcolm offers, he is finally revolted by Malcolm's self-portrait of vice; yet how much, how very much of vice will Macduff accept in a sovereign before his stomach turns.

The darkness to which Macbeth surrenders is not, like the filthiness of Iago's thoughts, engendered wholly in the mind. It is as much a part of the "order" of nature as is the light of the spirit. When one part of nature sleeps, another preys. Only the codes of civilized society allow the weak and aged to lie safely beside the fierce and practiced warrior. Only because Macbeth is strong in Duncan's right, is Duncan king. Actually Macbeth casts himself out of the community of men by committing the crime that occurs to many men—to Banquo as well as Cawdor. He fails to restrain those cursed thoughts which nature gives way to in repose and which trouble the sleep of many innocents. The difference between Macbeth and Banquo is that the one would murder for the throne while the other "wouldst not play false,/And yet wouldst wrongly win": that is to say, Banquo is content to repress his suspicions of Macbeth and to collaborate in his regime because his son will profit from Macbeth's crime.

Unable to admit that he has made the world a hell, Macbeth attempts to project the horror of his life as the pattern of all existence. For if consciousness is nothing more than a cosmic joke, then the senseless fury of his acts is no worse than the peaceful lives of those who are led quietly to oblivion. Do we feel that Macbeth's hatred of life is as diseased as Iago's vision of reality? Or do we feel that within the imaginative confines of the play the values which give meaning to life—honor, obedience, love, "troops of friends"—are dwarfed by the vastness of Macbeth's intuition, that these values are final only to those who do not look into the darkness, who stay within the finite circle of light which the candle of society casts upon the infinite darkness of time and space? I do not mean that Shakespeare uses Macbeth to express a personal sense of the absurdity of existence. I mean only that we must turn to the other tragedies to feel the infinite worth of those human qualities which outshine the darkness.

XVII

A. P. ROSSITER

Coriolanus

Shakespeare may have felt some disappointment with *Corio-lanus*. He would not be the last, for I think that few see or read it without feeling that they "don't get as much out of it as they hoped to" or that it "somehow doesn't seem to *pay*" or is "less profitable than others I could think of" or something like that. But whatever he thought he meant by the play is likely to be very different from what *we* make of it, unless we keep our attention fixed on what was going on inside Shakespeare's head in 1607—and what was going on in the year 1607, too. I do not mean that unless we know the barley markets for 1606–8 and the state of malt investments, we cannot understand *Corio-lanus*. I suggest only this: that there are many ways of inter-preting this play, and the one that begins nearest to Jacobean times is one that is necessarily a long way from our own. More-over, so far as I can judge, the interpretations that arise spon-taneously in our own times are so violently opposed to one another, and lead so inevitably into passionate political side-tracks, that almost any line of thinking that gets us away from them gives the play a better chance: a chance as a tragic play.

"Political"—there, I said it. *Coriolanus* is about power: about State, or *the* State; about order in society and the forces of dis-order which threaten "that integrity which should become 't" (III. i. 159); about conflict, not in personal but in political life; and—the aspect which catches our minds first?—about the con-flict of classes. I put that last deliberately, for two related but separable reasons. First, if we begin at that end, the play's tragic qualities are endangered at once: it tends to be seen as political, i.e., to be filled with imported feelings which are too partisan

From *Angel with Horns*, by A. P. Rossiter (London, 1961), pp. 235–52. Reprinted by permission of the editor, Mr. Graham Storey, Longmans, Green & Co., and of Theatre Arts Books, New York. Copyright 1961 by Longmans, Green & Co.

for the kind of contemplation which is tragedy. It also readily becomes polemical and seems to be giving *answers*, solutions to human conflicts, which tragedy does *not*. Secondly, it suffices here to summarize a few conclusions, merely as examples of "passionate political sidetracks."

1. Hazlitt: "The whole dramatic moral . . . is that those who have little shall have less, and that those who have much shall take all that others have left. The people are poor; therefore they ought to be starved. They are slaves; therefore they ought to be beaten. They work hard; therefore they ought to be treated like beasts of burden."[1] And so on. It is only necessary to read the text to say that Hazlitt's Jacobinical comments are false and nonsensical. No question of politics arises: it is simply one of reading.

2. In December, 1933, *Coriolanus* was played at the Comédie française. Every performance turned into a demonstration by right-wing groups (it was the time of the Stavisky affair, and parliamentary government itself seemed to be quite likely to come to an end); and the Royalists cheered every outburst against the "common cry of curs," the populace, and the bald tribunes whose power should be thrown in the dust. The play was withdrawn; M. Daladier dismissed the director, put the Chief of the Sûreté in his place; and events went forward to the great riots of February 6, 1934.[2] While one can admire the French enthusiasm for making Shakespeare really about something that matters here and now, this is still something other than Shakespeare criticism. For the view that Caius Marcius should be—or ever could be—the good and great dictator, the integrator of a shaking state, is one that the play cannot support for a moment. Shakespeare's source, Plutarch, had indeed said precisely the opposite; and Shakespeare has put enough into the mouth of Aufidius alone (IV. vii. 35 f.) to make further reference superfluous.

3. I have been told that the Russian view is (or was) that this is an entirely acceptable play, on the class-war, but showing how the Revolution is betrayed by self-seeking demagogues who mislead the workers for their own private ends. So Brutus and Sicinius are wicked persons (with their modern counter-

[1] *Characters of Shakespeare's Plays* (1817).
[2] See "Class War by the Avon," *Manchester Guardian*, March 21, 1952.

parts in the Labour party, I suppose), since the deviationist is worse than the despot. This is only what I have been told.

4. But Mr. Donald Douglas, in the *Daily Worker* (March, 1952), saluted the Stratford production with the interpretation that *Coriolanus* is a revolutionary play, but one gone wrong, and patched up at the end to appease the censorship. The crack can be seen in Act IV, Scene vi, when the First Citizen leads the rest astray by saying:

> For mine own part,
> When I said banish him, 1 said 'twas pity.
>
> SECOND CITIZEN. And so did I.
> THIRD CITIZEN. And so did I; and, to say the truth, so did very
>   many of us.

—and it is not the Party Line at all. For the rest, let Mr. Douglas speak for himself: "In the citizens' revolt against the Roman profiteers who are hoarding corn against a rise in prices . . . we have the fact of the people's power. In the banished Coriolanus, vowing destruction on his native city . . . we have the counterpart of the modern capitalist determined to ruin his country if only he can destroy the people."

Those four views will do. I shall not argue with any of them, beyond saying that, given similar latitudes of interpretation (not to say perversion) of Shakespeare's words, I will demonstrate that Coriolanus is an allegory of more than one political idealist of our time, who followed his own inner counsels, despised common humanity, betrayed his trust, to become a lonely dragon in a fen; and then felt some new promptings of human nature and threw away the game he had given away—to end in ruin and the mystery of the darkness of a mind that has set itself to stand

> As if a man were author of himself
> And knew no other kin.

Is that so far-fetched? In a sense, the three tragedies which belong to this stage of Shakespeare's writing are all about traitors and treachery. But treacheries of a particular kind. I remember Donne in *Twicknam Garden:*

> But O, selfe traytor, I do bring
> That spider love, which transubstantiates all,
> And can convert Manna to gall.

Coriolanus, Antony, Timon of Athens—all could be called self-traitors, and their spider loves examined as Bradleyan "tragic flaws." But that is no line of mine; it will only lead round to moral advice, moral answers: and though moral are worth more than political answers, they cannot be the tragic heart of a tragedy. The "tragic flaw" analysis is far too simple. It will never do to say that Coriolanus's calamity is "caused" by his being too proud and unyielding and just that, for one of the play's central paradoxes is that though Caius Marcius appears as a "character" almost unvaryingly the same, yet, for all his rigidity, he is pliant, unstable, trustless—traitor to Rome, false to the Volsces, then true to Rome and to home again, and twice traitor to himself. It is this "self-traitor" element which makes one feel reservations over applying those words of Charlotte Brontë's in *Shirley*. Caroline Helstone recommends the play to Robert Moore, the factory-owner, whom Caroline wants to see that he cannot haughtily pass over the feelings of common men. He asks: "Is it to operate like a sermon?" She replies: "It is to stir you; to give you new sensations. It is to make you feel life strongly." Taken by themselves, those words suggest a stirring experience, the romance of power, the stimulating contact with great characters or great events, a glory in history. It is assumed that to "feel life strongly" has the opposite of a depressant effect. Yet the conclusion of *Coriolanus* is not one bit like that. It is flat, hurried, twisted off and depressing. One traitor steps off the other traitor's dead body: "My rage is gone," and turns sentimental traitor to his own successful treachery, "And I am struck with sorrow."

Look at it one way and you can say, "That is exactly the way in which the unstable and trustless emotions of politics always *do* switch and swivel." And sardonically wait for Aufidius to turn on the stock rhetoric, as he does, capitalizing the occasion as glibly as Antony over the dead Brutus. How well we look, assuring our dead foes of "a noble memory," a grand funeral! And it is only a Gilbertian candour that adds "and fireworks in the evening. You won't be there to see them, but they'll be there all the same." Look at it a little more deeply, and that is how *history* goes. Is it perhaps only Shakespeare's sense of fitness that makes his end so inconclusive, so unsatisfying? Because history does not end conclusively? Look at it like that, and the play not only takes on more meaning, but ends in utter blackness. To say that that was the outcome of "feeling life strongly" would stamp me as a pessimist. Yet is it not the outcome of feeling history strongly, of a strong feeling for *political* life, epitomized in a Roman example? That is the approach I make to the play. It is a History, and about the historic process. It is political. And, being both these things, it makes intellectual demands which cause people to find it (in T. S. Eliot's phrase) "not as 'interesting' as *Hamlet*."[3]

By "political" I do not mean the class-war, or even narrowly the Tudor system of God-ordained order. I mean *Coriolanus* plays on political feeling: the capacity to be not only intellectually, but emotionally and purposively, engaged by the management of public affairs; the businesses of groups of men in (ordered) communities; the contrivance or maintenance of agreement; the establishment of a will-in-common; and all the exercises of suasion, pressure, concession, and compromise which achieve that *will* (a mind to *do*) in place of a chaos of confused appetencies. I have the impression that many who believe they feel strongly about politics (in the sense of this party or that) have but little of this "political feeling" I am trying to suggest to you. They find it easy to back a "side" (as if at a Cup Final), but not to feel about what makes a "side" an entity —as the result or resultant of the forces of many separate wills. In the extreme case, such people are "partisans" with no sense of State whatever. No, more than that: they lack all sense of party as an organic thing; for they desire the "victory" of their party, and desire it so childishly, that, if they had the power, they would destroy the very principle by which party exists: the recognition of conflict and uncertainty in human minds, confronted with the complexities and uncertainties of human events. The partisan would destroy all opposed groups. That is, he would see complex human situations and eventualities only in his own terms.[4] That is, see them only simplified to his one-eyed creed. And that is, not see them at all. His assumption is that, given the power, right action is *easy*. All history refutes

[3] He says this in the context of the comment that *Coriolanus* is, "with *Antony and Cleopatra*, Shakespeare's most assured artistic success" (*Hamlet: Selected Essays*, p. 144).

[4] Like Brutus and Sicinius with the slave who brings the bad news from Antium: they want him whipped until he shares their desire to deny the inconvenient facts.

that. As W. Macneile Dixon said (on tragedy), "In this incalculable world, to act and to blunder are not two, but one."[5]

The political feeling of *Coriolanus* is different—utterly so. It concerns you (if at all) with the workings of men's wills in the practical management of affairs; with the making (by some), the manipulation (by others) of "scenes," emotional eruptions of individual or group will; with all that unstable, shifting, trustless, feckless, foolish-shrewd, canny, short-sighted, self-seeking, high-minded, confused, confusing *matter* which makes up a State's state of mind; with all that can be made—but only through feeling—its determined will. Lack of feeling about such things means that much of the play seems frozen. For there lies its excitement. If you cannot be excited about what happens to the Roman State (a branch or *exemplum* of what happens in States), then you cannot feel the play. For it is a kind of excitement very different from that generated by "What happens to George?"

The advantage of such an approach—"political" in the sense of the word in Aristotle's *Politics*—is that it leads you out of any academic or antiquarian restrictions, without landing you in the troubles which arise from prejudices about democracy imported from the nineteenth century or later. The terms in which the mob is described need not worry you. "The mutable rank-scented many," "the beast with many heads": those are Elizabethan commonplaces. The root phrase was Horace's (*belua multorum capitum*), and that was not original; a Stoic, Ariston of Chios, called the people πολυκέφαλον θηρίον; and versions and variants can be found in Bacon, Chapman, Dekker, Marston, Massinger, Middleton, Ford, and (as we should expect) Beaumont and Fletcher. To get indignant with Shakespeare for such expressions is quixotic absurdity. He did not insult his audience, for the simple reasons that they knew nothing of voters' vanity, and *did* know, quite certainly, that they were *not* a mob. Yet, when I say that, do not imagine that a man does not *mean* a "commonplace," merely because it is a commonplace. The many-headedness of those expressions is, surely, a measure of Shakespeare's fear: his fear of disorder, civil commotion, the disintegrated State. I shall return to that point.

The other advantage of responding to political feeling in the

5 *Tragedy* (1924), p. 136.

play is that we need not freeze it to a rigid Tudor-myth pattern of order. That is, we need not narrow it to what it doubtless showed to many *circa* 1607–8: an exposition of the evils which arise in the God-ordained microcosmic State when degree is neglected; when pride and Luciferian ambition make a great soldier into a "limb diseased" of the body-politic; and when subjects attempt to judge what rulers are good for them —which is (as the Thirty-third Homily said, in a very convenient phrase too) "as though the foot must judge of the head: an enterprise very heinous, and must needs breed rebellion." That is by far the easiest way to systematize or pattern the play. Make the Fable of the Belly the key; turn all to Tudor political-moral allegory; throw in all the images of the body, disease, physic; and it all comes out pat. But you will have lodged the play back in Tudor distances, stopped all live political feeling, and set yourself the task of imaginatively thinking about the State solely in terms which can mean nothing whatever to your political self—unless you are highly eccentric and an anachronism in the twentieth century.

None the less, some imaginative attempt of that kind must be made; for the explicit political principles in the play are mainly put into the mouth of Coriolanus; and particularly in Act III, scene i, where he makes what is in effect a single political utterance, though in several parts. He says that the power of the people has increased, and must be diminished; the senators have nourished the cockle of rebellion by the corn-dole: made themselves no better than plebeians to let these tribunes play the senator with their "absolute shall"; the people think that concessions have been made through fear; no stable or ordered policy can come from direction by ignorant numbers through "voices" (votes); and the State is ruined and disintegrated unless this power of disordering policy and vetoing wise decisions is taken away from them. No statement of policy could be more sincere: none less well-timed. It is Marcius's "tragic blunder" (the Aristotelian ἁμαρτία) to state these convictions when he does. Yet so far as Shakespeare tells us what is right for the State in the play, there we have it. We may dislike it: we can say it belongs to a past age (and that Charles Stuart lost his head because he did not see that that age was past); we can say that we dislike the man who speaks (and there is no reason that I can see to like Coriolanus at any stage of the play). But the personality of Caius Marcius is one thing, and the convictions of Coriolanus are quite another. The rightness of a man's ideas or convictions is not affected by his unpleasantness *or* by his popularity, his "popular shall." Indeed, being right is rarely too conducive to popularity. What is amiss with demagogy, but that it confuses popularity (what people like hearing) with rightness (expediency)? What do Brutus and Sicinius display, but just that?

In considering what Shakespeare gave Coriolanus to think right, we cannot overlook the fact that in May, 1607, there was an insurrection which began in Northamptonshire and soon spread to other counties. It was a peasant insurrection; and partly about corn—anyway, about food. It was mainly against enclosures, but the engrossing of corn was a simultaneous grievance—an endemic economic evil of the day. The insurrection of the *Romans,* as told by Plutarch, was about *usurers* (they get a line at Act I, scene i, line 79, but nobody would see it unless told to look for it). I wish no emphasis on Shakespeare's role as investor in malt. I only say: There were these risings; they kept happening in Elizabethan times; and if you ask what is his fear of the mob and disorder, it is answered at once in Marcius's mouth:

> my soul aches
> To know, when two authorities are up,
> Neither supreme, how soon confusion
> May enter 'twixt the gap of both and take
> The one by th' other.
>
> (III. i. 108 f.)

Taking that with what we find elsewhere, in this and other plays, I cannot doubt that those lines are heart-felt. They are (for once) what William Shakespeare also thought—in 1607. It follows that we must swallow our democracy, and, if we would grasp the play, accept it that the political convictions of Marcius are *right.*

The personality of Caius Marcius, his attempts to manage men everywhere but on the battlefield, are, you may say, wrong throughout. But his convictions about the State are good and right, however impolitically he may phrase or time them. There you have a tragic clash: the basis of a political tragedy, not a Tudor morality. And to achieve that, Shakespeare had to twist his source, for he and Plutarch are entirely at odds.

Plutarch has a real sense of democracy, and his Coriolanus is an ill-educated man, suffering from being brought up by a widow (and "spoilt"), till by natural arrogance and wilfulness he is made quite incapable of any right ideas in communal life. He suffers from what Plato called "solitariness"—whereby, from self-opinion and an obstinate mind, men "remaine without companie, and forsaken of all men" (North's *Plutarch* ii. 160). The charge that Marcius planned "to take the soveraine authoritie out of the peoples handes" means nothing in the Shakespearian scheme of things. Shakespeare cannot conceive of sovereign power in the hands of the people. Thus the fact that they go on strike, so that the senate cannot raise armies; and that the Roman way of life gives them a right to the exercise of their own wills through their elected representatives: all that is suppressed or missed by Shakespeare. In simplifying and Elizabethanizing his source, Plutarch's *Life*, he misses the point. But he gives it another, and quite different one, of his own: about history, and the valuations of men in the ceaseless Heraclitean flux of the drama of power.

Let me take but a single example of the peculiar clashes we can feel in the person of Caius Marcius. Mainly, Shakespeare views him with detachment. And yet he has achieved an amazing imaginative triumph in the affair of the consulship: in his penetration to the very feel and surge of patrician hauteur, in all its passionate wilfulness, its physical loathing of the rubs and smarms of the "democratic" bowling-green, where every Jack is there to be kissed by his would-be master. Do not jump to wild conclusions about my politics. Surely any man of any dignity must feel something base in the pranks that men (apparently) must employ to get the good opinion—and the vote —of other men? If so, there is a comical rightness in old Volumnia's image for the way he is to behave:

> Now humble as the ripest mulberry
> That will not hold the handling.[6]

(III. ii. 79)

It is a derogatory image, worthy of Ben Jonson; and in its context, a satiric comment on all political candidates. Is there not ethical rightness, too, in Marcius's sudden revulsion against

[6] Stratford, 1952, cut these lines. Is even Shakespeare's mulberry tree forgotten there?

playing the male harlot to catch votes, piping like a eunuch, smiling like a knave, and whining for a handout like a beggar?

> I will not do't,
> Lest I surcease to honour mine own truth,
> And by my body's action teach my mind
> A most inherent baseness.

(III. ii. 120)

He is excessive, no doubt. But if there is some truth and honourable rightness there, then so much the greater the conflict: the conflict proper to a political tragedy.

I shall not analyse his character, but these few comments seem worth offering. Marcius's pride and arrogance need no examples. But the comic touch that that kind of self-greatness invites is by no means absent from the play. It is nonsense to call it a satire—as O. J. Campbell[7] did—yet throughout there are deft touches of ironical suggestion that strike the iron demigod between the joints of the harness. The sadistic ways of Marcius junior with unamenable butterflies are neatly pointed home by his mother's "One on's father's moods" (I. iii. 66). Shakespeare is keenly interested in this terrifying man, and certainly not standing aloof to condemn his sinful pride; yet he is aware of a potential absurdity. Or, put another way, he is aware of the *precariousness* of this self-greatness. Marcius's rages totter on the edge of a line which Jonson would have pushed them over—into ridicule. And when Menenius is putting the fear of the demigod into the Tribune Sicinius for the last time, this Jonsonian topple does occur, revealing a grotesquely comic aspect of the bogeyman which had been kept under till then:

> The tartness of his face sours ripe grapes; when he walks, he moves like an engine and the ground shrinks before his treading. He is able to pierce a corslet with his eye, talks like a knell, and his hum is a battery.

(V. iv. 17 f.)

We laugh—at the scared Tribunes, or at Menenius's *Schadenfreude;* but the comment still rebounds on Marcius. It is a queer preparation for the death of the tragic hero.

This comic irony is paralleled by the ironies of the major political scenes, where we watch great events being deter-

---

7 *Shakespeare's Satire* (1943).

mined; yet watch them with some infiltration of an awareness that there is a preposterous unreasonableness about the ways in which the destinies of peoples are settled: much rather by the shortcomings and littlenesses of men than by anything great about them. It is an awareness of potential absurdity (as in the galley scene in *Antony and Cleopatra*). Our reaction may be only *discomfort:* it depends on one's ironic capacity. Pursue that irony—present all through Act III—and another aspect of Marcius is found: one near the heart of his tragedy. It is an irony of frustration; and when I hit on that phrase, I almost find it all prefigured in the little incident in Act I, scene ix, lines 79 f. when, after the battle, he asks for the life of the poor man who was his host at Corioli. Cominius, as general, gives him it at once; but what happens?

> LARTIUS. Marcius, his name?
> CORIOLANUS.   By Jupiter, forgot!

No such forgetting in Plutarch. It is Shakespeare's invention. "New-made honour doth forget men's names," he wrote in *King John.* The man's self-greatness frustrates himself, his own good aims, endangering not merely life but honour. As here.[8]

Now look at Marcius as a political force. He has had, from Volumnia's upbringing and from active life, the profoundest concern for the Roman State: not merely as conqueror, but from his feelings for law and order (*"Tu regere imperio populos Romane memento"*). But his very nature, passionate and willful, makes it impossible for him to contrive to carry out those things which will maintain the unity of the State, that very unity he values so highly, "that integrity which should become't": the source of any man's (or any group's) power to make the State do good.

All this gives Menenius his place in the pattern: Menenius whom Shakespeare *made* from two lines in North's *Plutarch:* "certain of the pleasantest old men, and the most acceptable to the people. Of those Menenius Agrippa was he, who was sent for chief man." And that, with the Fable of the Belly, is all. Shakespeare did the rest: to give his play a humorous, ironical, experienced, sensible, critical commentator; and simultaneously, in the Roman political world, an "anti-type" and counterpoise to everything that is Marcius.

[8] Stratford, 1952, cut this incident!

Menenius is much more than a comedian. He is "humorous" (both in the Elizabethan and our senses), but a "humorous *patrician*"; a mocker, but one who can "spend my malice in my breath"; and he spends or vents it largely in irony, covering it with an air of sorely tried moderation and good nature; so that even in rebuke, he implies that it is all really the other man's fault, for being so unreasonable (e.g., IV. vi. 115 f.). He is a conciliator, aims at political compromise, but is not a weak old man. He handles the rebellious mob skilfully, and is apt with hecklers:

FIRST CITIZEN. What could the belly answer?
MENENIUS.   I will tell you;
    If you'll bestow a small—of what you have little—
    Patience awhile, you'st hear the belly's answer.

                               (I. i. 122–24)

The rhythm that Shakespeare gives those lines *is* Menenius (or one side of him). So is it earlier, when at Act I, scene i, line 106 Shakespeare gives him the only belch in English blank verse: the

                    kind of smile,
Which ne'er came from the lungs, but even thus—. . . .

These touches show the politician as well as the "humorous" man. As politician Menenius is able to move with the dialectic of events. He is pliable, but like the reed in the fable; Caius Marcius is the oak. All through the central Act III he is saying things like "Be calm, be calm"; "Well, well, no more of that" (III. i. 115, on Coriolanus's corn speech); "Come, enough." But his "mildly . . . calmly . . . temperately" is not the positive side of him. That comes out in his bulletin-phrase after the riot in Act III, scene i: "This must be patch'd/With cloth of any colour." There speaks a mind which is able to keep before itself the "political feeling," or emotion of political life, which I tried to outline to you—a mind which does not lose the great aim of integrity in the State, whatever immediate personal provocation it may encounter. Menenius is, therefore, a direct contrast to Caius Marcius, the hypersensitive battleship, so strangely constructed that though no weapon can harm it seriously, there is an open way to the magazine for the word "*traitor*," which blows the whole fighting-machine to ruins. Say that to Coriolanus (and the Tribunes know this), and his private honour makes him lose every thought of the integrity of the State. He becomes like Achilles in *Troilus and Cressida:*

> Imagin'd worth
> Holds in his blood such swol'n and hot discourse
> That 'twixt his mental and his active parts
> Kingdom'd Achilles in commotion rages,
> And batters down himself.

(II. iii. 167–71)

Indeed, the Marcius-Menenius pattern repeats—in a very different tone—much of the Achilles-Ulysses pattern in that earlier play; as it also repeats the themes of power, honour, and war. But Menenius is not lacking in feeling (as Ulysses is, perhaps). He is quite sincere in saying that he too would put his armour on, before Coriolanus should thus stoop to the herd. But in between comes the all-important proviso:

> but that
> The violent fit o' th' time craves it as physic
> For the whole state.

(III. ii. 32)

That is: he would *not* put his armour on to fight the plebs. He accepts the necessity of "stooping," for an aim beyond self: beyond himself or Marcius's self.

With those few passages I have examined, you have the central significance of Menenius. His love of Marcius, his breathless tumble of words in welcoming his warrior back from victory, his pathos, his comically cruel treatment by the sentries—all those have their importance. But they do not give his main significance in the tragic pattern. To develop that further I should have to examine the other counterpart-*cum*-contrast to Menenius—Volumnia. Throughout, Caius Marcius hangs between the influence of the two. They are opposites, and the irony is that they both desire the same victory for him. Only it never could be the same: for in political life, means determine ends, and the "identical" end, won by opposite means, is quite another end.

Menenius's significance is one thread to take told of the tragic pattern by: he is (what Marcius is not) a political mind which moves with the dialectic of events. As he can *think* (and will) *dialectically*, he remains true to the major loyalties: Rome and himself. Marcius, the man of "principle," does not. In this play, Bradley's generalization is entirely true: "To meet these circumstances something is required which a smaller man might have given, but which the hero cannot give."[9] Thus Marcius's "greatness" is fatal to him. But *is* it great? I do not propose to answer that: only to insist that the comic ironies of the action (and phrasing) push the question at us; and that reflection offers the paradox that Menenius is "greater" in mind than Marcius.

The valuation of Marcius is, however, offered by Shakespeare himself: in Aufidius's speech at the end of Act IV (IV. vii. 35 f.), a speech which perplexed Coleridge utterly.[10] It is, as he rightly says, "out of character"; but in it Shakespeare sums up Marcius. He was first "a noble servant" to Rome; but whether from pride, or defect of judgement, or unadaptable rigidity of nature (which made him attempt to manage peace as he did war)—and he had "spices" of all these—he came to be feared, hated, and banished. That he epitomizes any of these faults is explicitly denied. But two of them particularly concern what I used Menenius to focus: the qualities of a political mind, able to remain effective in a changing world of events. Whatever pride may be, rigidity (however high-principled) and "defect of judgement" are the opposites of those qualities. But Aufidius (and Shakespeare) adds:

> So our virtues
> Lie in th' interpretation of the time.

Now that, in one and a half lines, gives the essence of the play. Run over the whole action, act by act, and each is seen as an "estimate" or valuation of Marcius: enemy of the people— demigod of war—popular hero home in triumph—consul-elect —and then (through his assertion of what he always *had* asserted) public enemy and banished man, "a lonely dragon" (IV. i. 30). Throughout all this, he himself is almost an absolute *constant*. Then, on his way to Aufidius at Antium, we have his one soliloquy:

[9] *Shakespearean Tragedy*, p. 21.

[10] *Lectures on Shakespeare* (1818). Coleridge cherished the hope that he would become wiser, and discover some profound excellence in what he could only see as an imperfection; but I think he could never see it except as "out of character."

O world, thy slippery turns! Friends now fast sworn,
Whose double bosoms seems to wear one heart,
Whose hours, whose bed, whose meal and exercise
Are still together, who twin, as 'twere, in love
Unseparable, shall within this hour,
On a dissension of a doit, break out
To bitterest enmity.

(IV. iv. 12 f.)

It is strangely reminiscent of the sad midnight reflections of
Henry IV, looking back over Richard's time; yes, and thinking
about history. But what is Marcius's speech about, if not that
same world of history, where all is change, nothing absolute;
where all "virtues" lie in the interpretation of the time, and all
times lie about the virtues they have lost the use for?

This is very near to what Ulysses tells Achilles about Time's
wallet and the "one touch of nature" that "makes the whole
world kin." The "touch" is an incessant writing-off of past
values, an interminable revaluation-series. This is what happens
in the historical process: history always *goes on;* goes on, if
you like, to the sad and cynical tune of *Frankie and Johnnie:*

This story has no moral,
This story has no end,
This story only goes to show
That there ain't no good in men. . . .

Or shall we say, "There is not enough good of an effective
kind, in men as they appear in the historical process"? Be that
as it may, this is what happens in that process. History always
goes on, and in this play even Bradley could not say that re-
established order and rightness are left to console us. There
is no Albany; not even a Fortinbras or a Malcolm; the survivor
is Tullus Aufidius.

Coriolanus is the last and greatest of the Histories. It is
Shakespeare's only great political play; and it is slightly depressing, and hard to come to terms with, because it is *political*
tragedy. The idea of the State runs through it:

the Roman state; whose course will on
The way it takes, cracking ten thousand curbs. . . .

(I. i. 67)

And ten thousand men. Yet it is *not* the ideal or cosmic state
of the other plays: rather, an abstraction from an organism,

or a real state. Real states are dynamic; hence the constan‌
irony in the play, especially of Marcius and Aufidius saying
what they *will* do, and then not doing it or doing it in a way
that neither had foreseen.[11] Hence too the changing valuations
of the same Marcius by Aufidius, or by the comic servants in
Antium, who snub him muffled and then say they knew all
along he was "somebody." This re-estimation of Marcius goes
on to the bitter end: to Aufidius's stepping off his stabbed
body—"My rage is gone"—and calling for a hero's funeral. "O
world, thy slippery turns!"

But, in a sense, Caius Marcius *Coriolanus* was dead already.
That fine speech which Shakespeare made by transforming
North:

> My name is Caius Marcius, who hath done
> To thee particularly, and to all the Volsces,
> Great hurt and mischief. . . .
>
> (IV. v. 65 f.)

What is it but the equivalent of a *dying* speech, a summary of
expiring greatness? "Only that name remains" is no more than
truth: he is no more *Coriolanus*—as Aufidius will tell him, before he stabs him.

The final depressing paradox is that Marcius's unyieldingness
and would-be self-sufficiency make him so pliant to force of

---

[11] Examples are Marcius's statements about what he will do to Aufidius:

> Were half to half the world by th' ears, and he
> Upon my party, I'd revolt, to make
> Only my wars with him;
>
> (I. i. 231–33)

and

> At Antium lives he? . . .
>
> I wish I had a cause to seek him there,
> To oppose his hatred fully.
>
> (III. i. 18–20)

Others are: Aufidius's early threat to murder Marcius "were it/At home
. . . even there,/Against the hospitable canon" (I. x. 24–26); and Marcius's assurance to his mother, as he leaves Rome in exile, that he "Will
or exceed the common or be caught/With cautelous baits and practice"
(IV. i. 32–33). Here the irony is double: both things happen, but in no
foreseeable sense.

circumstance. All told, he is as unstable and trustless as those whom he abused with:

> You are no surer, no,
> Than is the coal of fire upon the ice
> Or hailstone in the sun . . .
> and your affections are
> A sick man's appetite. . . .
>
> (I. i. 170 f.)

Shakespeare spares him that last twist of bitter reflection: the words were spoken to the mob. But the reflection is there, in the play. And on my view, it ends—as J. W. N. Sullivan says that Beethoven's *Coriolan* ends—"in utter darkness": the darkness of history, from which Shakespeare finally absconded—with *Cymbeline*. I cannot accept Bradley's hint to make this the bridgehead towards the Romances: but I rejoice to concur with Mr. Eliot: *one* of Shakespeare's most assured artistic successes—as perfect in control as Part I of *Henry IV*.

XVIII

NICHOLAS BROOKE

The Tragic Spectacle in
Titus Andronicus and *Romeo and Juliet*

The differences between Shakespeare's earliest tragedies are so striking as to suggest a deliberate, formal distinction between different modes of tragedy: the historical-political in *Richard III*, the Roman (Senecan and Ovidian) in *Titus Andronicus*, and the romance in *Romeo and Juliet*. This deliberation extends, I think, to the obvious stylistic differences between the plays, and a clue to its character may be found in their different relationships to Shakespeare's non-dramatic poems. *Titus* abounds in parallels with his Ovidian narratives, *Venus and Adonis* and *The Rape of Lucrece*, whereas *Romeo* echoes the sonnets, and actually employs sonnet form both for the chorus and for the climax of Act I. The implication is that these plays are conscious experiments in poetic drama, conceived in the highly sophisticated tradition of Elizabethan poetic,[1] the formal ordering of figures, emblems, and language which governs the variety and range of *The Faerie Queene;* and thus, in one aspect, they may be seen as dramatic explorations of the poetic forms on which they draw.

Such a deliberate formality is obvious enough in the non-dramatic poems, and directly affects our response to them: *Lucrece* deals with melodramatic material, and is frequently very perceptive about emotional experience; but notoriously its sustained tone of cool detachment precludes any simple emotional involvement between reader and heroine, or villain. The result is that we shall never lose our hearts to either, or for a moment cease to sit in judgment on the moral spectacle

This essay has been written at the editor's invitation, for inclusion in the present volume.

[1] See M. C. Bradbrook: *Shakespeare and Elizabethan Poetry* (1951), esp. chap. vii.

with which we are confronted; if our feelings were seriously engaged we could hardly bear the poem's conclusion, that Lucrece must bear the guilt for an experience in which she had no responsibility. These are the qualities involved in the most striking parallel between the poem and *Titus*, Marcus' long speech to the deflowered, lopped, and hewed Lavinia at the end of Act II:

> Alas, a crimson river of warm blood,
> Like to a bubbling fountain stirr'd with wind,
> Doth rise and fall between thy rosed lips. . . .
>
> But, sure, some Tereus hath deflow'red thee. . . .
>
> And, notwithstanding all this loss of blood,
> As from a conduit with three issuing spouts,
> Yet do thy cheeks look red as Titan's face
> Blushing to be encount'red with a cloud.
>
> (II. iv. 22–32;[2]
cf. Lucrece 1730–43)

The baroque development of bloody mutilation is not pleasant; but the formal elaboration of fountain and conduit distances the actuality of the wounds, and almost literally turns Lavinia to stone. Yet she is there, on the stage, and the verse does not quite allow us to forget that she is alive: the "crimson river" is of "warm blood," and the secondary sense of "encount'red," the accosting of a prostitute, has a sharp application to Lavinia (as to Lucrece).

Such writing may be static, undramatic; but it is not the frigid blundering of a hack; nor is it funny, as Dover Wilson thought. Its weakness, compared with *Lucrece*, seems to me to derive from an unsatisfactory fusion of the cold, detached tone of the poem with a stage situation, uncle addressing deflowered niece. The *Lucrece* passage, like the poem at large, makes an emblem out of the situation, rather than a narrative description of it. In these terms, the function of Marcus' speech becomes clear: it emblemizes Lavinia's mutilated trunk and moral state at the end of Act II, which has contained the major criminal action against her (and her brothers). If it were

---

[2] Quotations from *Titus Andronicus* are from the Arden edition, ed. J. C. Maxwell (1953); those from *Romeo and Juliet* are from the New Shakespeare edition, ed. J. Dover Wilson and G. I. Duthie (Cambridge, 1955).

labeled "chorus," and the speaker thus allowed a divine knowledge of events, no problem would arise. As it is, Marcus' "knowledge" has to be clumsily disguised as guesswork—"Shall I say 'tis so?"—and the choric commentary is simultaneously felt as dialogue, so that words like "thee" and "thy" have a personal force scarcely felt in *Lucrece*. Finally, for such formalized writing, rhymed stanzas have an advantage over the diffusion of blank verse.

The experiment in using non-dramatic techniques on the stage is not wholly successful at this point. It would, in fact, be less embarrassing as a soliloquy; but Lavinia is on stage as a visible emblem, much as woodcuts accompany interpretative verses in the emblem books, and this is as characteristic of one aspect of the play's use of the stage as the formal verse is of its use of language. Titus groveling on the floor while the state of Rome passes by in Act III, scene i, and exiting to Revenge's cave with the heads of his dead sons, his own hand in Lavinia's teeth, or, in Act IV, scene iii, shooting arrows at the stars— these, and many more, are *visual* images of a kind we may rather expect to find described in a poem than enacted on the stage; but they are powerfully effective in establishing emblems of the play's significance. They lead naturally into the emblematic punishment allotted to Aaron, "Set him breast-deep in earth, and famish him" (V. iii. 179), and to the strange conclusion which the discovery of the First Quarto restored to the play:

> Her [Tamora's] life was beastly and devoid of pity;
> And being dead, let birds on her take pity.
>
> (199–200)

The final reference to pitiless birds is not fortuitous: it is the conclusion of a chain of references to Ovid's account of the rape of Philomel by Tereus, and her revolting revenge with his wife Progne, for which they were all metamorphosed into birds. This allusion first becomes explicit in Marcus' speech quoted above: the seemingly clumsy rhetorical questioning does serve a purpose in introducing the reference, "But, sure, some Tereus hath deflow'red thee," which is extended in the later lines of the speech. Ovid is used again in Act IV, scene i, to identify the criminals, and at the dénouement Titus explicitly states: "For worse than Philomel you us'd my daughter,/And

worse than Progne I will be reveng'd" (V. ii. 194–95). Eugene
M. Waith[3] has shown that Golding, and other Elizabethans, regarded Ovid's tale as moralizing the deterioration of men and
women, under the stress of passion, into beasts; and Ovid himself (Penguin translation) speaks of "a plan that was to con-
found the issues of right and wrong" when the victim outdoes
her assailant in bestiality.

This identifies the central idea on which Shakespeare con-
structs his play. The "translation" (Ben Jonson's word for
metaphor) of the Roman story into these terms is achieved in
Acts I and II, to which Marcus' speech provides the final
clarification. The play opens with a ritual display of the splen-
dor of Rome. The election of a new emperor and Titus' triumphant return from the wars are presented in formal group-
ings and processions, with drums and trumpets, and a verse of
rather self-conscious pomp and elaborate heroic simile. The
Roman-ness of it is given additional interest in the conflict between primogeniture and popular election; and this spectacle
of political sophistication and personal nobility is contrasted
with the assumed barbarity of the Goths. But in Act I, scene
i, lines 96 ff. an ironic tone emerges which insinuates the suggestion of barbarity within the Romans themselves:

> LUCIUS. Give us the proudest prisoner of the Goths,
>   That we may hew his limbs, and on a pile
>   *Ad manes fratrum* sacrifice his flesh. . . .

The heroic tone is sustained, inflated with Latin, but the colloquial "hew his limbs" implies a coarse brutality, more marked
after Titus has rejected Tamora's plea for mercy (because his
dead sons "Religiously . . . ask a sacrifice"), when Lucius repeats his words, "Let's hew his limbs till they be clean con-
sum'd" (129). This provokes from the Goths the fair comment: "Was never Scythia half so barbarous!" The sequence
is completed on Lucius' return from sacrifice:

> See, lord and father, how we have perform'd
> Our Roman rites: Alarbus' limbs are lopp'd. . . .
>
>   (142–43)

3 "The Metamorphosis of Violence in *Titus Andronicus*," *Shakespeare Survey*, X (1957), 39–49.

Barbarous Roman rites set the chain of revenge in motion, and "lopp'd" joins "hew" to mark the brutality which Marcus sees returned on Lavinia in Act II, scene iv:

> Speak, gentle niece, what stern ungentle hands
> Hath *lopp'd* and *hew'd* and made thy body bare.
>
> (16–17)

The first act establishes the grounds of tragedy in a succession of revelations of this kind: Titus' obsession with family leads to his blind support of the boorish Saturninus; Saturninus, betrothed to Lavinia, addresses a courtly couplet to Tamora which anticipates the lust he shortly after displays; and when Titus' sons rescue Lavinia, he betrays the violence in himself: "What, villain boy,/Barr'st me my way in Rome? [*He kills him.*]" (290–91.) The barbarity in the Roman is fully revealed, as Marcus observes: "Thou art a Roman; be not barbarous" (378).

Act I is crowded and involved; but it cannot be called confused: each discovery follows anticipation with striking if slightly too deliberate skill. The conclusion is a false cordiality, itself anticipating the disasters of Act II in the suggestive choice of beasts:

> TITUS. To-morrow, and it please your majesty
> To hunt the panther and the hart with me. . . .
>
> (492–93)

The hunt, which lasts throughout Act II, governs an apparently complete change of tone. This is not a matter of changing authorship, but of decorum, much like the shift from heroic to pastoral in canto vi of Spenser's *Mutabilitie*. The theme of nobility-barbarity is translated into terms of the natural world, "seen" by the characters in a succession of emblematic descriptions which cannot take effect if painted scenery is used (or separate "localities" described in scene-headings). Titus opens Act II, scene ii, with the pastoral charm of a hunting song: "The fields are fragrant and the woods are green," contrasting with Aaron's plans for villainy in scene i: "The woods are ruthless, dreadful, deaf, and dull" (128). To Tamora it is an erotic landscape:

> The birds chant melody on every bush,
> The snake lies rolled in the cheerful sun. . . .

> We may, each wreathed in the other's arms,
> Our pastimes done, possess a golden slumber. . . .
>
> (II. iii. 12–13, 25–26)

But to Aaron the sense is opposite:

> . . . an adder when she doth unroll
> To do some fatal execution?
> No, madam, these are no venereal signs:
> Vengeance is in my heart, death in my hand. . . .
>
> (35–38)

And Tamora herself, rashly baited by Lavinia and Bassianus, gives yet another version later:

> A barren detested vale you see it is;
> The trees, though summer, yet forlorn and lean. . . .
>
> (93–94)

—the haunt of owl and raven and a thousand hissing snakes.

Nature that is at once a paradise garden and a barren detested vale has the same duality as man, who may be noble or bestial, or more disturbingly, both at once. The emblematic development interprets what, if this is ignored, is simply a sequence of bloody absurdities; and here delivery of the verse on the stage enhances the vividness of the visual effect. Once Marcus' speech in Act II, scene iv, has associated this with Ovid, we are prepared to understand the climax of Act III, scene i, the metamorphosis of Titus from noble and suffering man to irrational revenging beast:

> MARCUS. Now is a time to storm: why art thou still?
> TITUS. Ha, ha, ha!
> MARCUS. Why dost thou laugh? it fits not with this hour.
> TITUS. Why, I have not another tear to shed. . . .
>
> Then which way shall I find Revenge's cave?
>
> (262–70)

This eruption of laughter is the play's supreme dramatic irony. It has been characteristically anticipated by a more obscure one, Lavinia kissing Titus before line 250, which Marcus misinterprets as gentle, but which in fact seals the turn to vindictiveness. A similar irony occurs in Act IV, scene i, when the boy offers to stab Tamora's sons, and Titus replies: "No, boy, not so: I'll teach thee another course" (119). The course, that is, of Progne's cannibal banquet, though Marcus misinterprets "But yet so just that he will not revenge" (128), and so invites the heavens to "compassion" Titus. This is the clue to an aspect of the last two acts which has puzzled critics: we are not invited to any final compassion for Titus, or Lavinia either. The metamorphosis involves a total alienation, extending from noble and gentle nature to barren detested vale. The dramatic anticipations of Acts I and II have been echoed in the emblems of nature. It follows that, contrary to our expectations of tragedy formed by Shakespeare's later plays, the end here is a spectacle of human degeneration by which we are appalled, but from which our pity is largely excluded. Alienation from Titus' right mind involves insanity, but there is little pathos. The collapse of human dignity, viewed externally, becomes a farcical spectacle, an effect which develops from the horrid trick in Act III, scene i, by which Aaron persuades Titus to cut off his hand. Reduced to wrangling as to whose hand should go, the Andronici merit Aaron's gleeful snub: "Nay, come, agree whose hand shall go along" (174). That farcical edge erupts in Titus' laughter ninety lines later, and is sustained through the arrow-shooting into the final scene with Tamora and her sons.

Sympathy is not a usual ingredient of earlier tragedy, whether academic like *Gorboduc*, or popular like *Cambises;* and the alienation of the hero deteriorating into farce is hinted in *The Spanish Tragedy*,[4] or in a very different way in *The Jew of Malta*. From Marlowe, Shakespeare derived the figure of Aaron, emerging as master of the ceremonies of Titus' decline. It is part of the play's structural symmetry that as Titus increasingly reveals his bestiality, the beastly Aaron discovers a startling human feeling in defense of his black baby. His splendid vitality grows from the vaunting soliloquy of ambition in Act II, scene i, through his triumph in Act III, to a dominant role in the last act. The issues of right and wrong are thus indeed confused. It is at least a satisfaction that nobody can pretend to find in this play suffering portrayed as an ennobling experience.

---

[4] Especially after the "Vindicta mihi" speech (III. xiii. 1–44). Philip Edwards in his Introduction to the Revels Plays edition (1959), pp. lviii-lx, argues that Hieronimo does not forfeit our sympathy here; there is probably some degree of ambivalence in the rest of the play.

There is not space here to do justice to Aaron, nor to the political concerns that begin and end the play. As tragedy, it is as ambitiously inclusive as, in the opposite genre, *The Comedy of Errors.* By concentrating on the central theme of metamorphosis I have hoped to suggest the remarkable degree of unity in the play, its dramatic and linguistic vitality, and its dependence on the achieved traditions of Elizabethan poetry. The alienation of sympathy inherent in such a theme requires of the audience just such a judicial detachment as we experience in *Lucrece;* but at the same time, to grasp its significance, we must be exposed to the shock of extreme physical horror. The matching of these opposite reactions in formal verse or brutal farce is not uniformly successful in the whole, any more than it is locally in Marcus' choric speech. But the play is governed by the same imaginative intelligence which later found the blinding of Gloucester necessary to the tragedy of *Lear. Titus* is very obviously an experimental play; and the experiments ultimately proved fertile indeed.

Unlike *Titus, Romeo and Juliet* has retained its popularity on the stage, though frequently given, until quite recently, in "improved" versions. This popularity rests firmly enough on the romantic idealism of the lovers and the earthy comedy of the Nurse and old Capulet. Seen thus, the play has an apparently simple outline, and it may seem perverse to suggest that it is too simple to be true; yet it is obvious that the romance can be accepted at a magazine level that is not really superior to the horror-film aspect of *Titus.* Recognition of human bestiality was unpopular for two and a half centuries before the revelations of Belsen and Auschwitz; sentimental romance, however, flourished throughout that period. To put the point in a different way, one can say that either *Romeo and Juliet* is concerned with a more complex view of experience, or that a great deal of the play is at best unnecessary, at worst irrelevant.

Symmetry of structure is as evident here as in *Titus* (or, of course, *Richard III*). The opening and closing acts are governed by a very marked formality, suspending the play between the ceremonial of the sonnet encounter at the dance and the ritualized ceremony of death in the tomb. This ceremonial stress tends to give the play the over-all quality of a stately dance, a secular erotic ritual appropriately inclined to formal rhyme-patterns in its verse; and the ending is commonly felt,

I think, to be effective rather in the way of spectacular ballet than of tragic drama. By contrast, the central climaxes of the play round which these ceremonies are balanced are very markedly unceremonial: the marriage is off-stage and unimportant, the consummation clandestine, and Mercutio's death scene is not allowed the dignity of verse. Structural formality is again echoed in the staging, most obviously in the dance of Act I, scene v, and probably in the placing of Juliet's table-tomb in the same discovery-space which had earlier held her bed—a visual juxtaposition which points the fulfilment of the Prologue's anticipation of a death-marked love.

The Prologue, and periodic echoes of it in the first two acts, are an insistent part of the formal structure, and they can seem uncomfortably blatant in anticipation of tragic themes— the family feud, the star-crossed lovers, and so on. Their insistence, however, has to be set against the fact that without them we should certainly feel a predominant tone of comedy, and be ill-prepared for the change of key in Act III. From the trivial prose of Samson and Gregory, through the mock-devotion of Romeo for Rosaline and the earthy humor of the Nurse, to the skeptical laughter of Mercutio and the diminutive malice of Queen Mab, there is little to suggest that the end will be in tears rather than laughter. Without the direct statements we could almost believe ourselves watching a sequel to *The Two Gentlemen of Verona*. Almost, though not quite, for there are serious suggestions in the lightest passages, and in the first scene these emerge through a rapid development not only of stage action but also of rhythm and seriousness in the mode of utterance. Bawdy prose yields to Benvolio's first introduction of blank verse: "Put up your swords; you know not what you do" (64); and that in turn gives way to the fully heroic tone of the Prince's rebuke to the assembled cast. This is not necessarily a tragic pitch, but it is certainly serious; and its seriousness emerging from the seemingly comic intensifies the thematic relevance of even the bawdiest punning about death and love:

GREGORY. Draw thy tool; here comes two of the house of Montagues.
SAMPSON. My naked weapon is out: quarrel; I will back thee.

(31–34)

Pun and paradox, light or ominous, govern an exceptional proportion of this play; they derive from the tradition of comedy, and of Elizabethan love poetry such as Chapman's *Shadow of Night*, and the sonnet sequences. This play is as much an exploration of that tradition as *Titus* was of the Ovidian narrative. Love may be cruel-kind, absurd-beautiful, trivial-serious, earthy-divine, life-death, and so on; and these possibilities are pursued through a multiplicity of detail focusing on the central paradox of "death-marked love," through the structural interaction of comic and tragic tones, as well as the contrast of the casual, clandestine, accidental with the purposive implications of the formal and ceremonial. The insistence on wit and wordplay continually reminds us of the non-dramatic tradition, and has again the consequence of formal detachment, of reminding us that we are critical spectators, not participants. Critics used to be as offended that Juliet should play with names, or pun on "I" at an emotional crisis, as they still are by Marcus' speech; but the adjustment is more successful in *Romeo*, for Freudian reasons that Professor Mahood[5] has demonstrated.

The decisive shift from comedy to tragedy is achieved in Mercutio's death, which is simultaneously the extreme demonstration of the serious emerging from the trivial. Act III, scene i, develops a lightness of touch which has already been conspicuous through most of Act II; the scuffle of Tybalt and Mercutio appears casual and unimportant, and its devastating result is scarcely apparent to the actors themselves:

ROMEO. Courage, man; the hurt cannot be much.

MERCUTIO. No, 'tis not so deep as a well, nor so wide as a church door, but 'tis enough, 'twill serve. Ask for me tomorrow and you shall find me a grave man.

(94–97)

The justly celebrated pun marks the play's most directly moving moment as a transition to gravity; and at the same time uses the plainness of prose to expose Romeo's unperceptiveness and the shocking inadequacy of his later "I thought all for the best" (103). The fanciful and poetic world of love is, with Romeo, reproved by the prosaic event of death, as poetry is apt to be reproved by reality (as Keats repeatedly affirmed).

5 M. M. Mahood: *Shakespeare's Wordplay* (1957), chap. ii.

The effect of this scene is very like the intrusion of death in the last act of *Love's Labour's Lost* and, placed centrally, it challenges the whole direction of the play. The poetic romance must ultimately be fulfilled in a poetic death, but the "beauty" of that will have to be established against not only the earthiness of the Nurse or old Capulet but also the sharper sense of cold reality here as Mercutio dies the way men do die—prosaically, accidentally, irrelevantly, absurdly.

In short, either the poetic structure must prove capable of sustaining this shock, or be exposed as trivial prettiness. One may feel that neither is quite the final situation, but the best of the play is to make us recognize both. This is not, of course, the first time that Romeo is reproved. When their joint sonnet has celebrated the first moment of mutual recognition, his attempt to extend the tone beyond the completion of the form is met by Juliet's "You kiss by th' book"; and more disturbingly, in Act II, scene ii, he never matches Juliet's frankness, so his efforts to substitute vows for confidence are repeatedly criticized in lines 107–31. Against this kind of thing, the bawdy incredulity of Mercutio is most welcome. But the critical interaction is two-way: Mercutio points the absurdity of sonneteers, but he has no perception of the values they can really represent. In Act II, scene iv, his mockery assumes that Romeo has been to bed with Rosaline, and the double mistake—that it was not Rosaline, and not to bed—emphasizes the ignorance that limits Mercutio's vision.

On the likeness and difference of comic and serious values Shakespeare provides a commentary in set-speeches which reinterpret emblems in a mode directly comparable with that of *Titus Andronicus*. The comic view of love personified in Mercutio is epitomized in his speech in Act I, scene iv, about Queen Mab, the diminutive wagoner who whips her steeds through the night to feed men's dreams of sex, wealth, and power, cheating them with fear, blisters, and unwanted pregnancy. The same emblems of night figure in the radically contrasting speech with which Juliet opens Act III, scene ii:

> Gallop apace, you fiery-footed steeds,
> Towards Phoebus' lodging! Such a waggoner
> As Phaëton would whip you to the west
> And bring in cloudy night immediately.

Juliet's night, as vast and momentous as Mercutio's was minute and trivial, is no less a setting where love and lust are at their climax indistinguishable: "civil night" is again the madam of a brothel hooding the virgin's unmanned blood

> With thy black mantle till strange love, grown bold,
> Think true love acted simple modesty.
>
> (15–16)

The speech echoes Queen Mab in more than Juliet's discovery that she must be a prostitute in order to be a wife; the emblems of night include the predatory and destructive raven:

> Come, Night! Come, Romeo! Come, thou day in night;
> For thou wilt lie upon the wings of night
> Whiter than snow upon a raven's back.
> Come, gentle Night; come, loving, black-browed Night:
> Give me my Romeo; and, when he shall die,
> Take him and cut him out in little stars. . . .
>
> (17–22)

The familiar pun on death as orgasm is used to focus an association in "Night" between love and actual death, and so suggest a rendering of "death-marked love," which is, as I take it, the play's profoundest paradox. This is the particular concern of Act III, where the sequence of scenes is very clearly established to bring death and love to an intertwined climax. The initial projection of a new tone is provided by the shock of Mercutio's death; Juliet's soliloquy follows that, but is not a consequence because she is not yet aware of what has happened. The contrast between her speech and "Queen Mab" depends first on the experience of the love scenes in Act II, of which Mercutio remained for ever unaware; but our attention is sharpened by the sense of death, and though Juliet's desire is not here stimulated by it, the consummation in Act III, scene v, is achieved in the knowledge of its immanence. This sequence therefore associates their love with death without any confusing suggestion of necrophilia (which we may feel later). Nevertheless, the association is so strong that it seems only a slight variation on her earlier longings when Juliet says:

> Come, cords; come, Nurse: I'll to my wedding bed,
> And death, not Romeo, take my maidenhead!
>
> (III. ii. 136–37)

She later displays impatient desire for her mock death at the Friar's hands in charnel-house images (IV. i. 77–88), and finally in

> Give me, give me! O tell not me of fear!
>
> (121)

she grasps the poison that leads her into the tomb, where the mock death gives place to the ceremonial suicides in Act V, as the mock love and official coming-of-age in Act I had yielded to the ceremony of actual passion.

The significant point in this is that the desire of Juliet and Romeo moves without interval from love to death; and we are not allowed to think it could be otherwise, since its core is found in the emblems of night which exclude the ordinary and productive light of day. Remarkable as the love poetry of the play is, especially Juliet's "Gallop apace," it is as remarkable for what it is not. It contains no suggestion at all of continuity in life, no equivalent even of the fertile mud of the Nile; and though Juliet is compared to a flower occasionally, it is to be nipped by frost, not to fructify. Their love is, in fact, contrasted with much that is most vital in the play: the Nurse, Mercutio, the old Capulets. In all of these the stuff of life is earthy, bawdy, comic, certainly thoughtless, and impatient; in many respects it seems only a cheapened version of what the lovers can show, but it has a continuing warmth and resilience that is reassuring and utterly in contrast to the glory of Romeo and Juliet. This very vitality, in Capulet's impatience, precipitates disaster. It is the play's characteristically paradoxical suggestion that this sense of life is entirely alien to the romantic vision of love, and that each criticizes the other. The ecstatic love-death experience becomes unreal fantasy against this other; this becomes tawdry set against Beauty's ensign and Death's pale flag. As much as Mercutio can mock the absurdities of sonnet love, Juliet in turn can denounce her Nurse's exposed shallowness, "Ancient damnation" (III. v. 235 ff.). The formal poetry of the play enshrines, as no other form of utterance could, the profoundest imaginative values in the play; but it forces us to see that a shrine is a place of death. In so far as love has this absoluteness, it is absolute for death. Hemingway's admirers often compare his novels with *Romeo and Juliet;* and it is true of *A Farewell to Arms* or *For Whom the Bell Tolls* that one feels that the necessity for death as the end derives, not from the narrative circumstances, but from the fragile romanticism of the love itself. Shakespeare, unlike Hemingway, establishes this limitation as part of the substance of the play. However early in his output, this is a play *about* immaturity rather than an immature play.

Romeo and Juliet is, as I have said, completely unlike *Titus Andronicus;* the latter is political, brutal, hysterical, farcical, while the former is domestic, lyrical, comic (not farcical), and has no interest in insanity. These differences are consistent at every level of action, staging, speech, and verse. Yet one can see considerable likeness in the techniques employed for presenting these unlike themes. Both plays employ the formal achievements of Elizabethan verse to expound a spectacle of human experience from which we are in a measure detached by the formality of staging and utterance. Both contrast this with an emergent vitality of an alien kind: Aaron, or the Nurse. It is obvious that the range of utterance and perception is wider in *Romeo,* and that we may respond more easily to a play where our sympathy can be continued to the end. Yet the last act of *Romeo* often baffles that sympathy—for good reason— and the effort that is sometimes made to view the tragedy in straightforwardly personal terms, moralizing on the lovers' juvenile impatience, can never be more than partially convincing because the play is composed, like *Titus,* as much as a spectacle of human experience as a plea for individual pathos. The tragic conception implied is that the finest of human experiences have inherent limitations, regardless of who embodies them. Romantic love is a lightning before death; the dignity of Roman nobility is founded on barbarous bestiality. A sense of individual personality is present, of course, in both plays; but the generic condition dominates. Both plays are immensely ambitious, overcrowded, experimental; when they were written it was not just in poetry that they surpassed their predecessors (if they did in that—this popular comment on *Romeo* seems to forget Marlowe): in range and control of dramatic idea and language they are both achievements far beyond any other dramatist of the time.

DATE DUE